ANIMAL RIGHTS & HUMAN MORALITY

REVISED EDITION

ANIMAL RIGHTS

& HUMAN MORALITY

REVISED EDITION

BERNARD E. ROLLIN

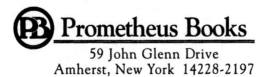

Prometheus Books

59 John Glenn Drive
Amherst, New York 14228-2197

To Linda and Michael, to Yetta,
and to
the
memory of
Dr. Bernard Schoenberg

Published 1992 by Prometheus Books

Inquiries should be addressed to
Prometheus Books
59 John Glenn Drive
Amherst, New York 14228–2197
VOICE: 716–691–0133, ext. 207
FAX: 716–564–2711
WWW.PROMETHEUSBOOKS.COM

06 05 04 03 02   7 6 5 4 3

Library of Congress Cataloging-in-Publication Data

Rollin, Bernard E.
    Animal rights and human morality / by Bernard E. Rollin.—Rev. ed.
        p. cm.
    Includes bibliographical references.
    ISBN 0–87975–789–2 (pbk. : alk. paper)
    1. Animal experimentation—Moral and ethical aspects. 2. Animal rights. [1. Animal experimentation—Moral and ethical aspects. 2. Animals—Treatment—Moral and ethical aspects. 3. Animal rights.] I. Title.

HV4708.R655   1992
179'.3—dc20
                                                            92–21979
                                                            CIP

Contents

2. ANIMAL RIGHTS AND LEGAL RIGHTS

3. THE USE AND ABUSE OF ANIMALS IN RESEARCH

Preface to the Revised Edition

Ten years have elapsed since the publication of the first edition of this book. Much of what I have argued in the book has come to pass. In particular, my philosophical strategy of extracting a new ethic for animals from our consensus, common sense, social ethic for humans seems to be indeed what is taking place in society. Second, and most gratifying, significant changes are taking place in the scientific community in response to this emerging ethic. The proposed legislation I described in the first edition has recently become federal law, and entrenched scientific attitudes about the ethics of animal research and about animal consciousness and animal pain are beginning to change.

At the same time, during those ten years, I have enjoyed remarkable opportunities to explain the new ethic and help put it into effect all over the world. I have spoken to lay audiences and experts over three hundred times in fields I would initially never have imagined possible. I have consulted for the governments of the United States, Canada, Australia, the Netherlands, and South Africa on the issue of animals in research; lectured to scores of veterinary schools on four continents on animal ethics; and helped these schools to develop new courses dealing with the moral status and treatment of animals. I have spoken to business people, medical researchers, psychologists, rodeo managers, ranchers, farmers, circus promoters, wildlife managers, librarians, genetic engineers, cowboys, animal scientists, humane societies, activist groups, veterinarians, church groups, elementary schools, toxicologists, and corporate executives; and I have found them almost universally open to and intrigued by the issues of animals and morality. I have been fortunate enough to see people put my philosophical ideas to use in reforming traditional practices involving animals in teaching, research laboratories, rodeos, and government offices that set policy for wildlife. At the same time, I have learned incalculable amounts from the people I talked to, and have been forced to learn more when they demand of me not only philosophical arguments, but practical solutions as well. Thus, for example, I have been compelled to learn a good deal about laboratory animal care, husbandry, and analgesia so that I can help change odious practices, and about such things as alternatives to castration in cattle raised for beef. Contrary to my training, I have come to learn that a philosopher working in applied ethics cannot be content with midwifery of ideas, conceptual clarification, and helping people to articulate their own ethic; one must also be prepared to help them put the ethic into practice, or else one is throwing away priceless opportunities for effecting morally positive reform.

All this has been exciting and gratifying and has forced me to sharpen, refine, and apply my earlier ideas. This new edition contains some of these refinements, as well as extensive revision of the chapter on animal research in the light of what has occurred during the past decade. I have continued to emphasize reform in animal research not only because it is an excellent exemplar for reform in all areas of animal use, but also because it is the area I know best, not only theoretically, but in virtue of daily interactions with researchers for almost fifteen years. There is a great deal more to be said about animal consciousness and animal pain than I have been able to include in this book. Readers interested in this question should read my recent book, *The Unheeded Cry: Animal Consciousness, Animal Pain, and Science* (Oxford University Press, 1989).

The main problem, which continues to concern me the most, and which I discussed in the introduction to the 1980 edition, is polarization and irrationality on the animal ethics issues by both sides. There is hardly any more rational dialogue between the two camps in 1990 than there was in 1980—very likely there is less. The American Medical Association's recent paper on animal rights labels all animal advocates as "terrorists," and scientific and medical researchers continue to equate animal rights supporters with lab trashers, Luddites, misanthropes, and opponents of science and civilization. Animal rights activists continue to label all scientists as sadists and psychopaths. Thus an unhealthy *pas de deux* is created that blocks rather than accelerates the discovery of rational solutions to animal ethics issues.

Not surprisingly, I have been assaulted by extremists from both sides. In one notable week, in reviews of the first edition of this book I was called an "apologist for the lab trashers" and one who "exonerates the Nazis" by the *New England Journal of Medicine,* and a sell-out for "accepting the reality of science" by an extreme animal rights person. So incredibly virulent have been some of the reviews, in fact, that the reviews themselves, rather than the book, have been the subject of an article by a philosopher who marvelled that such a straightforward, clear work could elicit such extreme reactions.

Nor did I fare any better when giving speeches. Some years ago, I was asked to give the keynote address to the twenty-fifth annual general meeting of a major national humane organization. I was specifically asked to avoid my usual tendency to raise hackles and blood pressures. I agreed and prepared what I thought was a rather innocuous talk arguing for the need for more rationality in the humane movement, especially for greater attention to moral reasoning and greater command of scientific knowledge relevant to animal issues. In any event, my speech was well received and I was given a standing ovation, but I noticed that the chairman of the board of the organization, a prominent lawyer who shared the podium with me, was less than happy; in fact, he was turning purple. As soon as the applause ended he strode toward me in a rage. "I knew we shouldn't have invited you. We don't need your kind of people. We don't need reason, logic, science, or philosophy in the humane movement—all we need are emotion and Christian ethics!" I pointed out that emotion had not carried the humane movement very far—that it simply evoked counter-emotion— and that Christian ethics, to my knowledge, had traditionally very little to say about our obligations to animals. At this, he grew even angrier and told me, in front of hundreds of people, "You're lucky I didn't get up there during your speech and pull you off the stage physically." Later, after I had gone, he admonished the audience not to listen to "Jew logic."

A remarkably parallel response from the other side occurred when I was invited to give the banquet speech to the international annual meeting of a group of researchers who study circulatory shock in humans and animals and do some significantly invasive things to animals in research, including inflicting trauma, septic and burn shock, and so on. The night of the banquet, I sat at the head table, where I was introduced to the president of the organization. I extended my hand to shake his. In full view of all, he pointedly refused it and snapped "How long is your speech?" "Forty-five minutes," I replied. "That's what the program chairman told me to prepare a year ago." "Cut it to ten minutes," he snapped. "No one wants to listen to you for any longer than that." "Tick me off," I replied, "and I'll talk for two hours."

It is to the great credit of the rank-and-file members of both these audiences that they turned on their leaders and supported my speeches wholeheartedly—in the case of the shock researchers, our discussions went on for almost four hours. But the point to bear in mind is that the leaders felt no compulsion to be rational or even polite.

Thus, I conclude that there is perhaps no set of social issues on which otherwise sane people on either side of the question allow themselves to be so overwhelmingly irrational as in matters pertaining to the treatment of animals, and our moral obligations to them. Certainly these issues generate a great deal of emotion, but so, too, do women's issues or homosexuals' rights issues. But there is a great difference between these cases: whereas gays and women are powerful and vocal constituencies, animals are voiceless and powerless, so we are not forced in issues pertaining to their welfare to be rational even in public forums, let alone in private. Thus, however much the male rednecks in the United States might wish in their heart of hearts to have all women barefoot, pregnant, and chained to the microwave, if not the pot-bellied stove, they resist the urge to say this in public. But, as the above anecdotes illustrate, there is no such pressure regarding animals.

This is a truly tragic situation. Anyone with any historical perspective on the United States knows full well not only that we have never had a social and moral revolution that was not incremental, but also that one cannot hold back these revolutions. In a democracy, such incremental change should surely proceed by rational dialogue and consensus, not through hysteria, bullying, and crisis management. The animal issues are in principle no different from any other issues except, perhaps, that we have no track record in dealing with them. It is all the more exigent, then, that we be guided by the light of reason and not be drawn toward the seductive songs played on the pipes of expediency and emotion.

In preparing the revised edition, I have received valuable assistance from Grace Bell, Marguerite Forest, and Linda Rollin.

Introduction

This book concerns itself with the theoretical and practical issues related to animals and morality. The origins of the book were themselves both theoretical and practical. In the first place, my research in philosophy of language had led me to believe that one could not draw a neat line between human beings and animals on the basis of language and reason. Denial of this gap in turn led me to question the moral status of animals, since it is on the basis of the absence of reason that animals are usually excluded from moral concern or, at least, from moral concern on a par with that granted to humans.

My interest in these questions, which was initially abstract and academic, became very practical and immediate when I began to teach veterinary medical ethics at the Colorado State University College of Veterinary Medicine, the first such course ever taught anywhere. To teach this course properly, I was forced to become acquainted with a number of very specific problems related to the use and abuse of animals in our society. At the same time, I was asked to help draft legislation for the State of Colorado aimed at improving the condition of laboratory animals. My activities in these areas led to my working almost daily with both scientists and animal welfare workers on such varied problems as the use of animals in teaching surgery, the problem of the unwanted pet, and the legal status of animals. These activities in turn led to numerous speaking engagements all over the United States, where I found myself addressing very diverse audiences ranging from veterinarians to research scientists to those who would stop research on animals altogether.

In the course of these lectures, I became aware of some disturbing facts. First, I discovered that there was very little dialogue or open communication between the opposing parties on most of these issues. Many scientists tended to dismiss those concerned with animal welfare as "bleeding-heart humaniacs." Many people concerned with animal welfare tended to view research scientists as ravening sadists who enjoy torturing puppies and kittens. These stereotypes, which I knew from my own experience to be in the main false, were perpetuated by profound ignorance on both sides of the opposing position and a failure to seek common ground. The net result had been a sort of trench warfare, with each side firing salvos at the unseen enemy. Yet from my own perspective, I knew that there was much room for compromise and common interest between the two extremes, and I said as much in my lectures to all parties.

Second, I saw that a major stumbling block to dialogue was posed by the extraordinarily emotional nature of the issues involved. Both scientists and animal welfare workers tended to shoot from the heart. Fortunately, many of these people recognized this when it was called to their attention. I found myself being asked to present a rational argument for the moral status of animals to both sides. Such an argument, people suggested, might provide a basis for dialogue, both within the opposing groups and across them. Why, I was asked, didn't I write a book that was philosophically argued, yet accessible to nonphilosophers, and that discussed the question of animals as objects of moral concern? Furthermore, I was told, such a book should also use these philosophical ideas to provide rational suggestions for solving actual concrete, practical problems.

The present book is my response to this challenge. It is an essay in applied philosophy, attempting to stimulate dialogue and provide a rational framework for solving specific moral problems. And the requests for the book have determined the shape it has taken. Most importantly, it is written in such a way as to be rigorous and detailed yet accessible to people with no background in philosophy. Unlike most books in philosophy, it is anecdotal and personal—nonphilosophers enjoy the relief this provides from abstract argument. Both the problems discussed and the solutions offered result for the most part from firsthand experience of the issues involved, and I will often cite these experiences. I have focused upon the problems of research animals and pet animals. First of all, these are the areas in which I have worked most closely with the problems. Second, along with the subject of food animals, these are the areas of greatest concern to people actually working with animal welfare. I have not dealt with food animals because there already exist admirable and detailed surveys of the problem, notably James Mason and Peter Singer's *Animal Factories,* and Michael Fox's book, *Farm Animal Husbandry and Ethology: Ethics, Productivity, and Welfare.*

The discussions in chapters 1 and 2 are meant to provide a moral ideal, a yardstick against which to measure current practice, a target to aim at, and a basis for dialogue. These chapters present the philosophical basis for the moral status of animals, and for their moral and legal rights. In chapters 1 and 2, I have held practical considerations in abeyance. What, I have asked, would the moral and legal status of animals be in the best of all possible worlds? In chapter 3, the discussion of research animals, I have tried to find the best approximation of these ideas that one could reasonably hope to achieve for these animals in our current sociocultural context. In chapter 4, recognizing the importance of empathy in changing people's moral gestalt, I have applied the moral ideas to a practical problem with which, unlike the question of research animals, most people have direct and immediate existential involvement: the pet problem. These chapters, taken together, I hope will provide the reader with a philosophical and factual basis for rational—and passionate—thought and action in some important areas where the lot of animals needs significant improvement and will provide as well the tools for dealing with other problem areas.

If scientists, animal welfare workers and advocates, veterinary students, and other nonphilosophers cannot read and enjoy this book, I will have failed in my mission. And if I have not illuminated very specific problem areas regarding research animals and pet animals and have not offered workable solutions for ameliorating the suffering of these animals, I shall also have failed. In order to ensure as far as possible that the book does what I would like it to do, I have tested it upon both volunteers and captive audiences. Earlier versions of the manuscript served as required texts in my freshman honors biology courses and in my course for veterinary students. I am grateful to these students for their lively responses and for showing me what areas needed reworking. The manuscript was also read and criticized by veterinarians, including laboratory animal veterinarians, private practitioners, and academics; animal welfare advocates and workers; humane society officials and members; animal shelter managers and workers; biomedical research scientists; lawyers; philosophers; government officials; and interested laypersons. The value of their criticisms has been considerable. In addition, the entire book grew out of constant dialogue with persons in all of the above categories, as well as university administrators, physicians, and leaders of organizations opposed to animal welfare legislation.

Among all of these people, I am most indebted to Dr. David H. Neil, laboratory animal veterinarian by vocation, philosopher by predilection, and the man from whom I learned the most about the practical issues discussed in this book. We engaged in almost daily dialogue for four years and worked together on innumerable specific problems. There are others to whom I owe a similar debt: the late Dr. Harry Gorman, past president of the American Veterinarian Medical Association, renowned surgeon, and my fellow teacher of veterinary ethics; Mr. Robert Welborn, attorney and longtime Humane Society leader, and the motive force behind the Amendment to the Animal Welfare Act described in the book; Dr. Michael Fox, director of the Institute for the Study of Animal Problems, veterinarian, ethologist, and author; Dr. Andrew Rowan, associate director of the Institute for the Study of Animal Problems, biochemist and authority on research animals; Dr. Robert Phemister, dean of the College of Veterinary Medicine at Colorado State University, the force behind my work in veterinary ethics, and the man who gave me the chance to put philosophy into practice; Dr. M. Lynne Kesel, artist and veterinarian, who is equally comfortable in science and the arts and who gave me repeated insights into science education; and most of all, my wife, Dr. Linda M. Rollin, a humanist and mathematician, with whom I have discussed every idea I have ever put on paper and who refined and sharpened them all.

Among veterinarians, I am grateful to the late Dr. Harold Breen, who first directed my attention to veterinary medical ethics; Dr. Dale Brooks; Dr. Bill Hancock; Dr. Wally Morrison; Dr. William J. Tietz, former dean of the CSU Veterinary College; Dr. R. F. Van Gelder; Dr. James Voss; Dr. James Wilson, veterinarian and attorney; and Dr. Stephen Withrow.

Among research scientists, I have benefited from dialogue with Dr. Bill Banks, anatomist; Dr. Jay Best, physiologist; Dr. Dale Grant, microbiologist; Dr. John Patrick Jordan, biochemist; Dr. William Marquardt, zoologist; Dr. Murray Nabors, botanist, with whom I teach biology; Dr. David Robertshaw, physiologist; Dr. Robert Tengerdy, microbiologist; Dr. Frank Vattano, psychologist; and Dr. Wayne Viney, psychologist.

Among philosophers, I have received cogent criticisms, suggestions, and dialectical interchange first and foremost from Professors David Crocker, Donald Crosby, and Daniel Lyons, and also from Professors Jann Benson, Arthur Danto, Kenneth Freeman, Kevin Keane, Richard Kitchener, Holmes Rolston, and Ron Williams.

In dealing with the law, I benefited from discussions with Darryl Farrington.

People in the humane movement from whom I learned much in dialogue are Marie Carosello, Pat Curtis, Jeff Diner, Ilse de Hoff, John Hoyt, Neil Jotham, Barbara Orlans, Martin Passaglia, Victoria Ward, and Linda Wildman. I am especially grateful to John Hoyt, president of the Humane Society of the United States, for his commitment to this book, and for his willingness to provide the support of the Humane Society of the United States to ensure its publication in its first edition.

I am grateful to Eva Wallace, Clarice Rutherford, and Irene Lewus for typing the manuscript, no mean feat considering my handwriting.

Finally, I wish to thank all those people who have attended my lectures across the country and abroad and whose questions, suggestions, and enthusiasm were ultimately responsible for my undertaking this project.

1

Moral Theory and Animals

INTRODUCTION

Ever since human beings have begun to think in a systematic, ordered fashion, they have been fascinated by moral questions, for it is upon morality that the possibility of all cultural advances depends. Few of us confronting the *Dialogues* of Plato, the *Nicomachean Ethics* of Aristotle, the Bible, or the Talmud fail to experience a sense of awe at the breadth and depth of moral theorizing initiated in Athens and Jerusalem, and at the timeless nature of the questions addressed. If, as Thomas Hobbes remarked, leisure is the mother of philosophy, it is surely natural philosophy of which this is most true, for civilization itself is the mother of moral philosophy. At all stages of the development of human thought, mirrored in the development of each human child, questions of right and wrong, good and bad, emerge and cannot be avoided. With the origin of medicine in Greece, for example, came questions of medical ethics, not as a separate area of study, but as part and parcel of the thought of the school of the physician, now known as Hippocrates, whose oath eloquently bespeaks the unity of medicine and morality. And so it has been with morality and law, morality and politics, morality and art, and so forth. In our post-industrial age of specialization and analysis, we have often tried to bury these questions as "unanswerable" or to shunt them off to be dealt with by "experts" or, worse, by theologians, but they always reemerge, for they are as inseparable from culture as life itself.

Yet despite the perennial presence of ethical questions, and the perennial writings of those individuals who articulate these questions for their own age, Western thought has been characterized by a major omission, an omission so pervasive as to have become essentially invisible. Though the child's mind invariably frames this question, it is forgotten as we grow up, repressed by some strange mechanism that allows us to ignore what makes us uncomfortable. To be good philosophers, Thomas Reid reminded us in the eighteenth century, we must become again as children and allow ourselves to wonder. For the question is indeed childlike in its simplicity and profundity: Why do we restrict our moral theorizing and the practices that follow in its wake to human beings? What makes something an object of moral attention, worthy of being spoken of in the moral tone of voice? What brings a thing into the moral arena; what makes it an object of moral concern?

Is moral concern something owed by human beings only to human beings? Certainly two thousand five hundred years of moral philosophy have tended to suggest that this is the case, surprisingly enough, not by systematic argument, but simply by taking it for granted. Yet this answer is by no means obvious, and it crumbles when exposed to the most childlike question of all, "Why?" Few thinkers have come to grips with the question of what makes a thing a moral object, and again, one wonders why. Philosophers have, after all, devoted much attention to proving that motion is impossible, that time is unreal, that change is an illusion, that the mind exists in the brain, that the brain exists in the mind, that God must be one or three or a committee, that there are neither minds nor bodies, and so forth. Surely the question of the moral status of nonhuman beings, of whether animals are direct objects of moral concern, is at least as legitimate a subject for inquiry. Yet, as we shall see, few thinkers have addressed this issue, and those who have done so have done it in a way that will not stand up to rational scrutiny. What has prompted our ignoring of this question? Perhaps a cultural bias that sees animals as tools, in Martin Heidegger's phrase, "ready at hand" to be used by us. Or, perhaps, a sense of guilt, mixed with a fear of where the argument may lead. For if it turns out that reason requires that other animals are as much within the scope of moral concern as are humans, we must view our entire history as well as all aspects of our daily lives from a new perspective. When Nicholaus Copernicus moved the center of the universe, the core of our existence was untouched. Whether or not the earth is at the center of the universe, we eat, sleep, and work. But if animals must be brought under the umbrella of moral concern and deliberation, the comfortable sense of right and wrong, which securely governs our everyday existence, is no longer tenable, and we can no longer eat, sleep, and work in the same untroubled way.

MORAL INTUITIONS AND MORAL THEORY

How does one answer this question? As with most moral questions, we are inclined to start with our moral intuitions, our "gut feelings," about right and wrong and the scope of morality. Whether ethical intuitions are inborn or socially conditioned or parentally instilled, we all have such feelings. When such intuitions are virtually universal, ethical theorizing proceeds most easily, for at least all are tentatively agreed on the raw material. So, for example, virtually all of us share the intuition that it is wrong to boil babies for fun (our babies or anyone else's), though perhaps many of us could not provide a very articulate defense of that intuition. When it comes, however, to the moral status of animals, our intuitions are mixed and inchoate and inconsistent: for example, we may feel that our dog is an object of moral concern but not our neighbors', and they in turn feel just the opposite. Or we may feel that it is not immoral to chain a dog, provided the chain is not too short. Or we may feel it is fine to kill ten Siberian tigers as long as they are not the last ten Siberian tigers. Or we may feel that it is legitimate to kill an animal "for its own good," while also feeling that the ultimate value for any living thing is life. Historically, we find the Catholic Church denying that animals have souls, yet excommunicating them. (In the Middle Ages, a horde of locusts was excommunicated in France for destroying crops!) We find secular society denying that animals are free agents, yet putting them on trial. In his book, *The Criminal Prosecution and Capital Punishment of Animals,* M. P. Evans chronicles these extraordinary proceedings, which continued into the nineteenth century. As early as 1697, Pierre Bayle, the great skeptic, marveled at this absurdity in his *Dictionary.*

Fortunately for all ethical thought, intuitions are just a starting point. We begin with our intuitions; proceed to construct theories that explain, justify, and ground these intuitions; and most interestingly, we oftentimes change our intuitions on the basis of our theories. For example, many of my ethics students begin with the intuition that there is nothing immoral about telling a "little white lie." After reading Immanuel Kant on ethics, however, they often tend to modify that intuition on the basis of Kant's powerful theoretical argument that all lying, whatever the purpose, is immoral and irrational. Or, to take a more personal example, throughout much of my adult life I have had strong intuitions about abortion, namely, that abortion is essentially a matter of a woman's control over her own body, and thus I had no feelings that it was immoral. As I began to theorize about the moral status of animals, it was pointed out to me that many of my arguments extending the scope of moral concern to animals applied equally well to unborn children. In the face of these arguments, I was led to new intuitions more consonant with my general theory.

Thus, the relationship between intuitions and theory proceeds dialectically, each modifying the other. A strong analogy exists here between ethics and science. Just as intuitions lead to ethical theories that modify intuitions, so perceptions give rise to scientific theories that may in turn modify our perceptions. Consider primitive people who see, as do children, the sun and the moon as small objects, not far away. They develop theories about these objects, test them, find them wanting, and conclude that they are large objects, far away. With this new theory the perception changes, and the sun and moon are seen differently. Or think of how one's perception of other people's remarks changes after one first encounters the theoretical notion of "Freudian slip." One of my colleagues recounts the story of the nervous, male adolescent student who stands up in a literature class and quotes the line, "The best planned lays of mice and men gang oft aglay." Another of my colleagues recalls with amusement his response to a worried, buxom coed seeking solace about the final examination: "Don't worry, just do your breast."

When dealing with the question of the moral status of animals, our intuitions, both individual and societal, as we have seen, send mixed messages. So we must turn to theoretical accounts in the hope of finding some stable conceptual framework for tethering our intuitions or for cultivating new ones. Unfortunately, as we indicated, few moral theorists have directly addressed the question in any detail. Yet an examination of some of the standard grounds for excluding animals from the scope of moral concern may well give us the clue for arriving at a satisfactory account.

FINDING A FULCRUM—THE NEED FOR AN IDEAL

It is patent that both traditional moral theory and traditional moral practice have failed to deal adequately with the moral status of animals. In the face of such disregard, how can one make rational progress on both the theoretical and practical fronts pertaining to the treatment of animals we so depend upon in society? Wherein lies the fulcrum for levering change? One is, of course, free to approach the question *de novo* and to generate an ethical theory for animals *ex nihilo*. Such a strategy presents an almost irresistible temptation to creative philosophers, to soar unfettered in ethics as they have soared in metaphysics.

Yet to succumb to this temptation would be socially irresponsible. As Kant realized, ethical theory cannot soar unfettered, but must be tethered to common sense, common practice, and ordinary moral experience. If our ethical account of human moral obligation to animals cannot effect sympathetic resonance in the hearts and, even more so, in the minds, and ultimately in the practices of those in society to whom it is addressed, then it is of no value. Like a good motor, a good piece of moral philosophy should not only spin freely, it should also move something. Similarly, our ethical account must speak not only, or even primarily, to the converted, to those already convinced in their hearts that we owe more to animals than we have provided, but even more importantly, to those not so convinced. This was the dilemma I faced when I began to work in the area of animal ethics in the mid-1970s. On the one hand, I could get little help from extant social behavior and established moral theory because they essentially ignored animals. On the other hand, I could not merely generate my own ideal ethic for animals, for, however elegant I might find it, why should it be at all persuasive to others? Yet it seemed to me imperative that we in society have an articulated and shared ideal for the treatment of animals, as we do for the treatment of humans. To be sure, we do not always live up to our ideal for treating people, because of lack of resources, weakness of will, selfishness, and the like. We do not really treat people equally; all sorts of prejudices color that ideal. But we try, and we judge ourselves remiss when we fail. An ethic is a yardstick, a measure of where we are deficient, or a target to aim at that sharpens our skill. As Aristotle put it in stressing the need for an ideal:

> Will not the knowledge of it, then, have a great influence on life? Shall we not, like a hero who has a mark to aim at, be more likely to hit upon what is right?

Without an ideal, we confuse the way things are with the way things ought to be, and we are smug and complacent. Only by having an ideal to move toward can we progress beyond the status quo. It is by referring to the ideal of equality that we were able to achieve progress for blacks, women, and other minorities in the past few decades. It is by appeal to the ideal of fairness that we redistribute income, or share our wealth.

Similarly, we stand in desperate need of an ethical ideal for the treatment of animals in society. As we shall see later in our discussion, the closest we have come to an ideal for the treatment of animals is the notion embodied in what I have called the Presley Principle—"Don't be cruel"—which essentially enjoins us not to maliciously, willfully, or sadistically hurt animals for no purpose. Such an approach is basically flawed. For one thing, it describes our obligations to animals solely in terms of what is prohibited but is silent on our positive obligations to them. Second, it assumes that animal abuse is a matter of intentional cruelty, something patently not the case. Most animal agriculturalists, animal researchers, hunters, trappers, circus people, rodeo cowboys, zoo managers, and others who use animals are not cruel. They are decent people trying to make a living, advance human welfare, or pursue some other natural human goal; or else they are trapped by habit, tradition, training, lack of thought, and improper education. Yet, in pursuit of these goals, they cause incalculable amounts of animal suffering. The overwhelming majority of animal suffering is not the result of cruelty, and therefore the injunction to avoid cruelty is largely irrelevant to the treatment of animals in society. At the same time, restricting one's moral vocabulary to "cruelty" in assessing the treatment of animals leads to a situation where those who are concerned about animals tar all those who cause animal suffering with the same brush, be they dog fighters or medical researchers; if they cause animal suffering, they are *ipso facto* "cruel."

By the same token, the paired exhortations to "be kind to animals" or to "love animals" are equally misdirected. Kindness suggests that the proper treatment of animals represents an overflowing of benevolence on the part of human beings rather than a duty or moral obligation binding on them. (Imagine someone suggesting that women should have equal access to educational opportunities only because we should "be kind to women"!)

In the absence of a rationally based, shared ethical ideal for the treatment of animals, the categories of kindness and cruelty are asked to bear far more weight than they are structurally capable of doing, and a social vacuum is created that is filled by emotion, sentiment, and much debate with little social awareness. Polarization inevitably occurs, with animal advocates stereotyping animal users as sadists, and with animal users seeing animal advocates as sentimental, misanthropic "bunny huggers." Social policy resulting from such polarization is inevitably irrational as well. Thus, when the Animal Welfare Act, allegedly designed to protect laboratory animals, was passed in 1966, it covered only cute and cuddly animals. For purposes of the act, as we shall discuss in detail later, a dead dog is an animal while a live mouse or rat is not.

CONSTRUCTING AN IDEAL FOR ANIMALS

But our earlier question still remains: How does one arrive at a shared ideal for the treatment of animals? After a considerable number of years spent pondering this question, I finally realized that the answer lay in the teachings of Plato. (It is not for nothing that Alfred North Whitehead remarked that all subsequent philosophy may be viewed as a series of footnotes to Plato!) Throughout his writings, Plato stresses that a philosopher (especially a moral philosopher, which was his main concern) cannot teach others; he or she can only *remind*. In other words, while I can certainly teach you the state capitals, the names of the Moguls of India, or some other body of facts, I can't simply impart to you the facts of right and wrong. In morality, as in geometry, the issue is not communication of data; it is leading you to extract, by reason, conclusions from assumptions you see to be true. Thus the philosopher can help you to reason out these conclusions; in Plato's beautiful metaphor, the philosopher helps you to *recollect,* to draw from inside of you in a clear way what you don't realize is there.

Being of a combative nature and often asked to explain the ideal for animals to hostile groups of animal users, I tend to augment Plato's characterization of this enterprise with one of my own. One can conceive of the task of attempting to hammer out an ideal ethic for animals as analogous to physical combat. Physical combat can be approached either as sumo or as judo. In sumo, two large, well-nourished opponents attempt to remove each other from an eight-foot ring. If one combatant weighs two hundred pounds and the other weighs five hundred pounds, chances are that the smaller chap will quickly exit the circle. Such is my own situation in addressing, say, members of a scientific society with vested interests in seeing animals as tools. If we clash head-on, I will get nowhere.

Fortunately, there is another form of combat where size is not the key factor. This, of course, is judo, where the ninety-eight-pound weakling can happily send a sand-kicking bully packing by turning the opponent's force back against him. If you throw a ferocious punch at me with all your might, I simply side-step and give you a slight encouraging push in the direction of your punch. You are off balance and are defeated by your own force.

This is precisely the strategy one must adopt to create an ethical ideal for animals in society. I cannot force my ideal, however polished and articulate, on you. I can, however, attempt to show you that you are already committed to that ideal by virtue of certain assumptions you already hold, and thereby show you that the ideal I am pressing upon you is in fact a consequence of beliefs you yourself entertain.

Not surprisingly, this judo strategy is far more effective than direct confrontation. It is, in fact, a standard approach that has been successfully utilized in advancing our ethic for human beings. One can argue that the success of the civil rights movement, or of the movement to provide equal opportunity for women, lies to a large extent in the fact that what was being proposed was not a revolutionary, new ethical principle, but rather that it was already implicit in moral beliefs that opponents of equal opportunity themselves shared. In other words, segregationists, or those opposed to equality for women, typically did share with other Americans the belief that all humans should have equal opportunity. They simply failed, because of powerful habit and tradition, to combine that belief with the premise that blacks and women were human and thereby, by simple reasoning, to extract the conclusion that blacks and women should enjoy such opportunity. If something along these lines had not occurred, these social movements would have been as ineffective as Prohibition!

One of the most dramatic and moving examples of the efficacy of this judo approach to a hostile audience occurred when I was invited to lecture to a group of ranchers in Kiowa, Colorado, on animal rights. One of my ex-students, an agricultural extension agent, had invited me to address the Stockman's Seminar, an educational series for ranchers run by the extension service. When the day of the talk came, I had some trepidations, significantly magnified as I drove into Kiowa, which looks very much like a set for a cowboy western movie (dirt streets, elevated sidewalks, tumble-weed). I was scheduled to speak at the high school, so I flagged down the sheriff's car and asked for directions. He lowered his mirrored sunglasses and looked at me through Clint Eastwood eyes: "You the speaker?"

I didn't feel a great deal better when I was introduced to the group of eighty or so ranchers who responded to the introduction by booing, whistling, and stamping their feet for well over a minute as I stood at the podium. This, I realized, would not do. So I said, "Wait a minute. I've just driven two and a half hours to get here. You aren't paying me. And you haven't heard what I have to say yet. I'm also pretty sure you haven't read my material, and you're not familiar with my ideas. Yet you're booing me. So, I have to conclude that you are booing me personally. You are probably looking up here and seeing a sissy, a commie, a damn wimp, a do-gooder, right?" "Damn right," they roared. "That's what I thought," I said. "And I'm taking it personally. So I'd be happy to take you outside one at a time and kick your butts!"

Silence suddenly reigned, silence one could have sliced and sold at a roadside stand. I had gotten their attention because I was not as their stereotype dictated. I then said, "Okay, now that I have your attention, let me ask you two questions in hope of clearing the air. If your answers turn out as I hope, we will have a profitable evening! If not, I'll go back home, and you guys can spend the evening lynching somebody or whatever you do for recreation." "Fine," they said. "Ask your questions."

"First question: Do you guys believe in right and wrong?" "Hell yes, this is Kiowa, not New York." "Good. Second question: Would you guys do anything at all to an animal to increase profit and productivity? What I mean is, suppose you could increase weight gain or milk production by torturing a cow's eyes with hot needles, would you do it?" "Hell no," they replied. "Good," I said. "Then we're just haggling about price!" The hostility vanished like smoke. We went on for over four hours and they came up to me afterward and apologized, and later invited me to speak at the annual Farm Bureau banquet.

In the course of our discussion, we made excellent progress on a variety of issues. For example, during the question period, they asked me to indicate what aspects of the cattle business were morally problematic from an animal-ethical perspective. "Why ask me?" I replied. "What do I know? I am merely a college teacher, whereas you people are experts." They proceeded to detail far more examples of animal abuse than I could have done! When they later argued that ranching was a business and that the only values that enter into judging the situation were economic, I was able to get them to realize that this was not the case. Few of them were willing to endorse the corporatization of agriculture even if it was in fact more "economically efficient"; even fewer would choose to become dress manufacturers for the sake of tripling their incomes.

Indeed, when I was criticizing the standard ranching practice of castrating cattle without anesthesia, I suggested that perhaps they believed, as some scientists had suggested, that animals didn't feel pain, a Cartesian position that became widespread in twentieth-century science, as we shall discuss shortly. Their reply was eloquent, brief, and very commonsensical. One rancher waved his pocket knife at me and asked, "How'd you like *yours* cut off with a rusty pocket knife?"

I have subsequently addressed well over fifteen hundred ranchers on the same issues and repeatedly found them quite open to the ethic I espouse, as long as I take the trouble to extract it from *them* and do not appear to be preaching at or attacking them.

So, at last, we can see the strategy whereby we can create a consensus ethical ideal for the treatment of animals in society, despite the traditional absence of such an ideal and despite the incoherences in our practices. The key to creating such an ethic lies in the existence of a consensus social ethical ideal for the treatment of humans in society. Although we tend to make much of ethical disagreements in society—these are the stuff of fiction, film, and theater—in actuality we have far more ethical agreement than disagreement. If we did not, we simply could not live together. We tend to focus on disagreement, which is much more attractive than agreement, but our agreements are legion and our major disagreements relatively rare. If, as I have actually done on hundreds of occasions, I ask my lecture audience for examples of major ethical disagreements in society, they invariably come up with abortion and capital punishment, and then hesitate. I, in turn, show them that for every such disagreement, we manifest literally hundreds of agreements: We don't take candy from a baby even if we're hungry and no one is watching; we don't approve of cheating on tests; we don't punch our conversation partners in the face when we can't refute their points, and so on.

The point is that we do have a consensus ethical ideal for the treatment of humans, a consensus we share in our society, one that is encoded in our theory, our practice, and, most significantly, in our legal and political system. We will discuss this in detail in chapter 2. Here we need only point out, as we have indicated earlier, that we have not always applied that ethic fairly and uniformly to humans. At various times, we have excluded humans from that ethic for reasons such as gender, place of national origin, race, color, and the like. By the same token, by rational examination of those reasons, we have seen that they are bad reasons, and so we have to transcend them.

So, our strategy is as follows: Given that we have a consensus ethical ideal for the treatment of humans, and an elaborate moral machinery associated with that ideal for judging and weighing our treatment of humans in society, the question before us is whether there are any good, defensible grounds for excluding animals from the scope of moral concern or the moral arena, that is, from having our treatment of them assessed *mutatis mutandis* by the same moral machinery we have developed and all share for the treatment of humans in society. Or, to put the question differently, are there any rationally defensible reasons for not protecting the core interests of animals in our moral system as we protect the core we have postulated as essential human interests? (Note that I talk of a "moral arena" because one can be treated as a moral object, yet not have one's interests prevail. If I ask all my students what sort of exam they wish and, out of fifty students, twenty-six vote for an in-class test and twenty-four vote for a take-home, and I go by majority rule, twenty-four students will not win, but they will still have been treated as objects of moral concern.)

Our first task, then, is to examine the standard grounds that have historically been offered by philosophers and others for excluding animals from the moral arena, or from being covered by the same sorts of protections we afford humans.

HAVING A SOUL

It is instructive to examine one of the most pervasive reasons usually offered for excluding animals from being direct objects of moral consideration—the claim that whereas humans possess an immortal soul, animals are not so blessed. Though such a claim is invariably met with raised eyebrows among intellectuals in our age of skepticism, it permeates the popular mind and has certainly dominated Catholic thought for centuries. (It is still, in fact, official Catholic dogma.) Laying aside positivistic doubts about the grounds for such a claim, let us explore its logic. Even if we suppose that animals do not have a soul while humans do, the key question is this: What does the possession of a soul have to do with being an object of moral concern? Why does the lack of a soul exclude animals from moral consideration? In fact, even some Catholic theologians who did deny souls to animals drew an opposite conclusion from that fact. Since, argued Cardinal Bellarmine, animals do not have immortal souls, wrongs perpetrated upon them will not be redressed in the afterlife in the way human wrongs will be rectified. For this reason, animals most certainly *ought* to be objects of moral concern for us and even ought to be treated better than we treat one another!

The point of this example is clear. For excluding animals from moral concern it is not sufficient simply to cite some alleged difference, metaphysical or practical, between humans and animals. The key point is that difference must also be shown to be *morally relevant*—to have rationally defensible bearing on being an object of moral attention. As we have just seen, the soul example, if anything, serves the opposite of its intended purpose—it does not exclude animals from moral concern, but rather gives us some grounds for including them and even giving them pride of place.

RELEVANT DIFFERENCES

The lesson to be learned, then, is this. It will not do simply to cite differences between humans and animals in order to provide a rational basis for excluding animals from the scope of our moral deliberations. Certainly man is the only creature who grates Parmesan cheese over his food, wears panty hose, pays taxes, and joins health clubs. There are innumerable differences that obtain between people and animals. The question is, do these differences serve to justify a *moral* difference? After all, there are innumerable differences among humans. I have curly hair; some men have no hair. But surely no one would accept my excluding bald men from the province of my moral deliberations simply on the grounds of baldness. Suppose I suddenly walk up to another man and punch him in the eye. When asked why, I reply, "Because he is bald, that's why." Obviously, this is unacceptable; baldness is not a morally relevant reason for striking someone or for suspending the usual moral strictures against striking someone. On the other hand, if I say that I struck him because I saw him molesting a child, that does seem to be morally relevant, i.e., to be a difference that makes a moral difference.

Some reincarnationist theories seem to have grasped this point about moral relevance and the soul when they have made life as an animal a punishment the soul must suffer for transgressions in previous lives as humans. Such a theory at least utilizes the notion of the soul in a morally relevant way, for to be an animal is in some sense to be *guilty*. But such a move is of course untenable for Christians for whom, ironically enough, being born a *human*, with an immortal soul, involves being born guilty, in virtue of the doctrine of original sin.

It is this notion of *morally relevant differences* between humans and animals that serves as the most powerful tool in the investigation of the moral status of animals. If we can find no morally relevant differences between humans and animals, and if we accept the idea that moral notions apply to humans, it follows that we must rationally extend the scope of moral concern to animals. Armed with this notion, let us examine some other alleged differences between people and animals that have traditionally served to exclude animals from the scope of moral concern.

HUMAN DOMINION

It is often argued that humans have been granted dominion over the rest of nature by God. This claim is also put non-theologically when it is asserted that humans stand at the apex of the evolutionary pyramid. Once again, holding theological skepticism in abeyance, we may unearth a profound philosophical point in discussing this claim. Even if humans have been placed by God at the peak of the Great Chain of Being, or even in command of it, it does not follow that the creatures beneath them may be treated by them in any way they see fit. (The Bible, in fact, as we shall see, clearly and explicitly counters this claim in the many passages devoted to kindness toward animals.) Correlatively, even if we can sensibly talk about an objective "top" of the evolutionary scale (which I doubt, since in evolutionary terms there is only survival, nonsurvival, reproductive success, and adaptation), the same point holds. Being at the top does not entail that one can treat the creatures beneath in any way one chooses. (Ironically, Darwinism has historically been used both to justify exclusion of animals from moral concern, because of human supremacy, and to justify inclusion of animals within the scope of moral concern, because of the evolutionary continuity between people and animals!)

To better understand our rejection of the moral relevance of human "supremacy," one must consider what sense can be made of the claim that humans are at the "top." Of course, since humans create the ratings, they can do as they choose, but what is the criterion of superiority? Surely it is not longevity, adaptability, and reproductive success, else turtles, cockroaches, and rats would be at the top. Is it intelligence? But why does intelligence score highest? Ultimately, perhaps, because intelligence allows us to control, vanquish, dominate, and destroy all other creatures. If this is the case, it is power that puts us on top of the pyramid. But if power provides grounds for including or excluding creatures from the scope of moral concern, we have essentially accepted the legitimacy of the thesis that "might makes right" and have, in a real sense, done away with all morality altogether. If we do accept this thesis, we cannot avoid extending it to people as well, and it thus becomes perfectly moral for Nazis to exterminate the Jews, muggers to prey on old people, the majority to oppress the minority, and the government to do as it sees fit to any of us. Furthermore, as has often been pointed out, it follows from this claim that if an extra-terrestrial alien civilization were intellectually, technologically, and militarily superior to us, it would be perfectly justified in enslaving or eating or experimenting on or exterminating human beings.

Some may be tempted to assert that might does, in a fundamental sense, make right. After all, those in power do call all the shots. But this is to ignore a very basic distinction. While those in power are indeed in a position to impose their will on others, and even to *call* what they decree "right," that does not of course mean that it is *in fact* right. I may, at the point of a gun, force you to call black "white" and white "black," but that would not make black into white and white into black. To accept the principle that might makes right is to vitiate all talk of justice and injustice, to render meaningless any claims about what ought to be the case. Even to assert that it is right that might makes right or it ought to be the case that might makes right is self-defeating, for the very possibility of making the assertion presupposes some notion of right above and beyond that created by superior force, since, presumably, the person who holds that position holds it even if *in fact* what is considered right happens to be determined at that time by something other than superior force, for example, religious tradition.

The superior position of humans does not serve as adequate grounds for excluding animals from moral concern. Once again, as we saw in the case of the immortality criterion, if it has any moral relevance at all, it is in the other direction altogether. From a moral standpoint, one can plausibly argue that humans are obligated to behave morally towards other creatures precisely because of their supreme position and superior power. Just as we morally expect fair and benevolent treatment at the hands of those capable of imposing their wills upon us, so ought we extend similar treatment to those vulnerable to us. To my knowledge, no one has put this point better than David Hartley, the great eighteenth-century psychologist. Speaking of animals, Hartley said:

We seem to be in the place of God to them, to be his Viceregents, and empowered to received homage from them in His name. And we are obliged by the same tenure to be their guardians and benefactors. (pp. 414–415)

DUTIES TOWARD ANIMALS AS DUTIES TOWARD HUMANS

One of the most pervasive claims about the moral status of other creatures—a claim that, as we shall see, permeates our laws concerning cruelty to animals—grows historically out of the positions we have discussed. This approach, epitomized in the writings of Saint Thomas Aquinas and Immanuel Kant, suggests that although animals are not themselves direct objects of moral concern, there are nonetheless certain things that are not morally justifiable when done to animals. On this view, unnecessary cruelty to animals is forbidden, not, however, because animals are intrinsically objects of moral attention, but rather because of the psychological fact that people who brutalize animals will or may tend to behave cruelly toward other people. Interestingly enough, similar arguments were used by early abolitionists against slavery. It was argued that although Negroes were not *really* human, they were sufficiently like humans to brutalize people who abused them, with subsequent danger to *real* humans. Clearly, on this view, people are the only objects of moral concern; animals are relevant only insofar as treatment of them might affect our treatment of people. If we had good psychological evidence that certain sadistic individuals could expunge their brutality by exercising it on animals, say by torturing kittens, and thereby become more moral toward people, this view would not only permit the torturing, but would seem to make it morally obligatory!

Thus this position, while seeming in some measure to allow animals within the scope of moral concern, in fact is totally irrelevant to our fundamental question. For this approach takes it for granted that the only morally relevant creature is the human, and treatment of animals is at best instrumental *vis-à-vis* human morality. To make the point more clearly, let us suppose that psychologists had established through research that beating rugs resulted in wife beatings, because the rug beater's bloodlust was aroused. The Aquinas-Kant position would presumably consider rug beating immoral, at least for those persons so affected, not because rugs were objects of moral concern, but rather because wives were.

REASON, LANGUAGE, AND MORAL CONCERN

We turn now to the most serious and important criterion of demarcation that has historically served to delineate the scope of moral concern. At least since Plato and Aristotle, and even in the Catholic tradition, the notion of the soul providing the basis for excluding animals from moral concern has been given philosophical content by equating the soul with the rational faculty or the ability to reason. Humans are rational, or at least have the capacity for rational thought, while animals do not, and for this reason, the scope of morality does not extend beyond humans. This claim that only humans are rational has traditionally been linked to another criterion used to distinguish people from animals, the claim that only humans possess language or the ability to use what are called "conventional signs." (This is often put in various other ways—humans use symbols, animals have only signs or signals; humans use artificial signs, animals are restricted to natural or instinctual signs; etc.) The great philosopher René Descartes saw the possession of language as the only real evidence we have that other beings have minds like ours and could think, feel, and reason. For Descartes, animals were just machines and were thus incapable of thinking or feeling. This Cartesian view was terribly important as a justification for the burgeoning science of physiology, since it provided a convenient rationale for ignoring the "apparent" suffering that experimentation engendered. Many Cartesians, such as the residents of the famous Port-Royal Abbey, were actively involved in research on animals, research that was shocking to contemporaries who had not accepted Cartesianism. The influence of Descartes, coupled with the development of ingenious machinery in the eighteenth century that could behave in lifelike ways, has left its mark on the Western mind, and to some extent current thought about animals is still very Cartesian, as we shall see in subsequent discussion.

The position linking rationality, language, and moral status may very briefly be schematized as follows:

1. Only humans are rational.
2. Only humans possess language.
3. Only humans are objects of moral concern.

Although a great number of thinkers have historically entertained this view and it is still quite prevalent today, remarkably little has been done to spell out or defend the connections between (1), (2), and (3). There are, after all, many questions to be asked here. We may ask, for example, what is rationality, and what grounds do we have for asserting that only humans possess it? We may further ask, what is the connection between rationality and language? Is language evidence for rationality, as Descartes suggests, or is language somehow the essence of rationality? And most important for our purposes, we are faced with the question of why the possession of rationality and language is morally relevant, i.e., makes a difference to morality.

It is easy to see, of course, why rationality would be important for a being to be considered a *moral agent,* that is, a being whose actions and intentions can be assessed as right and wrong, good and bad. We are certainly not inclined to hold anyone responsible for his actions, if he is incapable of reason—even our laws reflect this notion. We do not hold children, the insane, or idiots morally or legally responsible for their actions. But it is, of course, not obvious that one must be capable of being a moral agent before one can be considered an object of moral concern. In fact, we certainly consider children and the insane to fall within the scope of moral concern even though we do not hold them responsible or consider them to be moral agents. So our other questions still remain.

SOCIAL CONTRACT THEORIES

There is one theory, which dates back to the Sophists, that attempts to link being a moral agent with being a moral object. This theory has appeared in many forms in Western ethical and political thought and is quite popular today. According to this view, only creatures capable of acting morally, i.e., rational creatures, are themselves deserving of moral concern. Moral laws and principles are the product of convention, or of social contract, and only rational beings are capable of participating in a social contract or, indeed, in any agreement at all. The social contract is an agreement among rational individuals to treat others a certain way provided they are themselves treated the same way in return. For example, valuing my own possessions, I agree to respect your ownership of certain things in return for your agreeing not to encroach on mine. Since animals are incapable of entering into such agreements, lacking both reason and language and not being moral agents, they are not objects of moral concern either.

There are many questions that can be raised about this account. For one thing, when encountering this sort of theory for the first time, most people wonder how such theorists can know for certain where and when in prehistoric times such a contract took place. Even more important, if it did indeed take place, why are we today bound by it? After all, my children are not bound by my contracts. And I was never asked to agree to any such contract! In actual fact, this is not a problem for the contract theorist, for the contract is not alleged to be a single historical event that binds all humans for all time. Rather, the contract is an agreement in action rather than a verbal contract that rational beings implicitly agree to simply by living in society, and to which any rational being would agree, if asked, and be able to articulate. Thus, for example, I respect your property on the assumption that you respect mine and, as a rational being, would affirm this if asked to do so.

In a recent version of this view developed by John Rawls, the theory is sharpened by recourse to an imaginary device called the veil of ignorance. On Rawls's view, the parties to the social contract should be seen as looking at the contract, i.e., the principles of morality and justice that they set up, behind a "veil of ignorance," whereby no one knows his own strengths and weaknesses. No one knows if he is rich or poor, strong or weak, aristocrat or peasant. This ensures that the principles agreed on will be fair, for none of the parties can know with what advantages or disadvantages they may happen to be endowed. Once again, for Rawls animals are not moral objects because they are not party to the moral deliberations that are involved in setting up the contract.

Whatever merits this theory may have, it does not seem to provide us with legitimate grounds for excluding animals from the scope of moral concern. Most basically, it does not follow on either version of the theory that just because only rational agents can set up or be party to the rules, only such agents are protected by the rules. In a nutshell, there is no argument showing that only moral agents can be moral recipients. Why is agency morally relevant? Let us suppose moral concepts do indeed arise out of concerns that humans have relative to one another. And suppose, further, that humans intend to exclude animals. Given all this, it can still be that the logic of these moral concepts as they are set up requires that we, as rational beings, extend them to animals if it can be shown that animals cannot be clearly demarcated from individuals to whom we do wish the concepts to be applied. Basically, suppose we set up these rules because we want to live and because we don't want to be hurt, yet are vulnerable. These characteristics hold of animals as well. Would it be rational not to cover these creatures by the protective rules? On the contractualist view, it is also hard to see why animals differ in a morally relevant way from all sorts of humans who can't rationally enter into contracts—future generations of humans, infants, children (especially terminally ill children, who will not live long enough to actualize rationality), the retarded, the comatose, the senescent, the brain-damaged, the addicted, the compulsive, the sociopath, all of whom are also incapable of entering into or respecting contracts. If the contractualist wants to say that we have no obligations to these sorts of humans, the theory becomes wildly implausible in its failure to account for our basic, deep, and broad moral intuitions about such people. And if the contractualist wishes to include these humans as entities to whom we have obligations, then he must admit that entities become moral objects in virtue of characteristics other than the rational ability to enter into contracts—characteristics like the ability to suffer, or to have needs. But if that is the case, then animals must be covered by moral rules, since they, too, have these characteristics.

The point is that whatever the motivation behind moral principles or adherence to moral principles, these principles have, so to speak, a life of their own, and implications that the rational contractor must respect, even if he or she was not initially aware of or favorably disposed toward these implications. Euclid may well have objected to my using geometry to set out a football field; the ancient Shahs may spin in their graves at the thought of commoners playing chess—nonetheless, geometry, chess, and morality have lives of their own which transcend the intentions of those who first articulated them.

A related point must be made relative to the Rawls version of contractualism. Even if Rawls is correct that only rational beings can enter into the original contract position, it does not follow at all that such individuals would necessarily adopt moral rules that apply only to themselves, and that exclude animals from concern or protection. It is perfectly possible, and indeed plausible, that rational agents setting up moral rules would favor a society where these rules were applied to animals. It is also possible that such rational agents might choose to make animals party to the original position by proxy, where their interests are represented by rational agents. Rational agents might well want a society where nonrational beings are granted rights and protection just like those granted to rational beings. (The fact that many of us rational beings would like to see just such an ideal society if we were starting from scratch is good evidence of its possibility!) In short, nothing follows from Rawls's theory about excluding animals from the scope of moral concern.

Shortly we shall show that rationality is but one component in what can serve to make something an object of moral concern. But we shall also show that it is not clear that animals are not rational! Is it obvious that animals, lacking language, are incapable of entering into contracts or agreements of the sort posited by the contract theories, since animals cannot deliberate and cannot affirm if asked their acceptance of moral or other rules? Not at all. As David Hume pointed out in his *Treatise of Human Nature,* two men who must row a boat across a river may adopt one certain rhythm from among many possibilities without verbally articulating this agreement in action, or even being able to affirm their acceptance. The point is that even if these rowers refuse to affirm that what they are doing involves an implicit agreement, they would surely still have one. The ability to affirm linguistically what one is doing seems irrelevant to having an implicit agreement—the mutually adjusted actions are what is important. So obviously, language-using reason is not necessary for such agreements. And it is quite clear that animals also exhibit behaviors that qualify as agreements, both with humans and with each other. Anyone who has seen different species of animals taking turns at a water hole can hardly doubt that they have rules governing this activity—including not molesting one another. Given the variety of such rules and their flexibility in myriad situations, including new situations that could not plausibly have been evolutionarily programmed, it is hard to call these rules purely blind natural instinct. Even more interesting, it seems likely that the animals would affirm what they were doing if they suddenly were granted the power of speech. And it is also clear to anyone who has been around domestic animals that they are locked to us and to each other by an intricate series of agreements. When my Doberman pinscher does not bite the head off the kitten stealing her food, or snap at my baby when he is hanging from her ears, she is surely obeying rules that are very like human "conventional" rules. When a horse and rider interact, the same point holds. If someone objects that it is stretching the concept to call this a contract, I would suggest the same thing about the whole concept of "social contract." If someone else suggests that animals have been bred by artificial selection or natural selection to exhibit such apparent contractual behavior, I should suggest that the same thing is probably true of humans. (Humans who did not exhibit this sort of behavior are likely to have been selected out of the gene pool!) Furthermore, humans are capable of entering into social relations with nondomestic animals, as in the case of my friend, Michael Fox, who raised a wolf from cub to adult—and these relations go both ways.

In fact, some animals even seem to exhibit behavior that bespeaks something like moral agency or moral agreements. Canids, including the domesticated dog, do not attack another when the vanquished bares its throat, showing a sign of submission. Animals typically do not prey upon members of their own species. Pack carnivores share kills according to fair "rules." Elephants and porpoises will and do feed injured members of their species. Porpoises will help humans, even at risk to themselves. Some animals will adopt orphaned young of other species. (Such cross-species "morality" would certainly not be explainable by simple appeal to mechanical evolution, since there is no advantage whatever to one's own species.) Dogs will act "guilty" when they break a rule such as one against stealing food from a table and will, for the most part, learn not to take it. I had an attack dog once, a giant German shepherd, who had spent six years as a security dog. He was left at construction sites and gas stations, never had a master, and was trained to attack savagely anything—man, woman, child, animal—that set foot on the property. I was told by experts that such a dog could not be domesticated, that he was dangerous and unpredictable. Yet, after six weeks of close work, we were bonded—I could pick him up, tussle with him, even strike him. He returned good for good. To my amazement, he allowed puppies and kittens to share his food and a turkey to share his doghouse!

To such examples the stock reply is to say "Animals do it by nature; we do it by convention." Unfortunately, the distinction between nature and convention is not a clear-cut line. As I have shown in my book, *Natural and Conventional Meaning: An Examination of the Distinction,* it is impossible to give clear-cut criteria for distinguishing what is natural from what is conventional. (In fact, it was working on this question that got me interested in the question of the moral status of animals in the first place.) In my view, anything called a "social contract" will be an admixture of both "natural" and "conventional" elements. As we shall see, reason is traditionally equated with the use of conventional signs or meaning vehicles or language. But again, it does not seem possible to provide a clear-cut line between nature and convention. The result is that we should not expect a clear split between "rational" human moral action and certain aspects of animal behavior, though, for the most part, human behavior obviously exhibits infinitely more of what we would call moral agency than does animal behavior. In short, the split is fuzzy enough that we cannot say all that confidently that if there is a social contract and associated moral rules, animals cannot ever be said to be party to it. In fact, we shall be discussing pet animals later in the book, and we shall see that the notion of a social contract seems quite appropriate there, since the role of the dog, for example, in human society is essentially a complicated fabric of agreements in action between people and animals.

In general, then, contract theories do not seem to provide us with a good argument for cashing out the claim that rationality represents an adequate ground for distinguishing humans from animals as moral objects. We now turn to another attempt to develop such an argument.

KANT'S THEORY OF REASON

One major philosopher whose work explores the questions we have been raising is Immanuel Kant, the great German philosopher of the Enlightenment. In fact, Kant's moral theory can be seen as an attempt to extract all of morality, both being a moral agent and being a moral object, from a particular concept of rationality. In this attempt, Kant represents an articulation of a tradition begun in Greek moral thought (by which he was influenced), and an amplification of the position taken by Descartes. In his discussion, Kant argues that only rational beings can count as moral agents and, even more important for our purposes, that the scope of moral concern extends only to rational beings. Because of the crucial importance of this sort of argument for contemporary views of animals and moral concern, we shall carefully explicate and delineate Kant's position before criticizing it. We shall also attempt to show the alleged connection between reason, language, and morality.

The notion of reason is central to the philosophy of Kant, who was a major figure in the Age of Reason. For him, the bases of science and ethics needed to be logically proved, much as theorems in geometry are proved, not merely assumed or derived from experience. In his major work, *The Critique of Pure Reason,* Kant devotes a good deal of attention to explaining and justifying reason, and defining what it means to be a rational being. Kant was very much opposed to the British empiricist tradition, the tradition that based all knowledge on sense experience or perception, and that had culminated in the skeptical writings of David Hume. Hume, like an early Pavlov, had concluded that reason was merely habit, custom, and conditioning, and that if men could be said to reason, so, too, could animals. For Hume, the scientist who expects a given mixture to behave the way other such mixtures have behaved in the past is in exactly the same position as the chicken who expects to get fed when it hears the farmer come out in the morning. Just as the farmer may kill the chicken on the next morning, so the world may change for the scientist, and his or her predictions, carefully based on past experience, can be totally invalidated. The net effect of Hume's work was to call science and reason into question, and Kant's work is in essence a defense of reason. But in addition to saving science, Kant's work serves to preserve the unique place of humans in nature.

Kant proceeds by stressing the human ability to arrive at what philosophers call *a priori* knowledge, that is, knowledge that cannot be shown to be false by experience and can be known to be true simply by thought. A good example of *a priori* knowledge is "The sum of the angles of a Euclidean triangle is 180 degrees." As we all know from studying geometry, we can prove that by reason, and once we have proved it, we can know that it must always be true. Kant ingeniously shows that science rests upon certain items of knowledge that we can know *a priori,* and for this reason, a number of things in science *are* certain, contrary to Hume's claim. The important point for our purposes is Kant's claim that only human beings can possess *a priori* knowledge, and only the possession of *a priori* knowledge can allow a being to go beyond the particular instances one finds in sense experience of the world and assert judgments that claim universality, not tied to specific times and places. This for Kant is the essential meaning of rationality. Since only humans can entertain, understand, apprehend, and formulate statements that are universal in scope, only humans are rational. This is because, according to Kant, animals are tied to stimulus and response reactions. An animal may respond to this particular fire in a way that indicates its awareness that this fire is dangerous here and now, but only a human has the mental capacity to understand and formulate an assertion like "all fires, wherever and whenever they may occur, are potentially dangerous."

KANT'S ETHIC

Kant thus characterizes rationality in terms of the ability to understand and articulate universal claims or, as he calls them, *laws.* (In science and in social life, of course, laws are meant to be universal in scope.) But what does all this have to do with morality? Kant's reply, developed in his great works, the *Foundation of the Metaphysics of Morals* and the *Critique of Practical Reason,* is ingenious. If man is by nature a rational being, in fact, the only rational being we know of, then it is his function to be rational in all aspects of life, be it knowledge or action or in his dealings with others. In science he must seek universally true laws; in his daily actions he must intend, plan, and evaluate his activities according to whether they are rational, that is, whether they meet the test of rationality, namely, universality and generality. This in turn means that given any action or intended action, a person must ask himself if his own action can be expressed as a universal law, without generating an inconsistency or contradiction. This is Kant's moral theory in a nutshell and is expressed in his famous Categorical Imperative or basic moral law:

> Act only according to a principle which you can will would be a universal law. (p. 421)

To appreciate the ingenuity of Kant's ethical theory, let us take a forceful example. Suppose I have been out drinking with the boys, a practice my wife abhors. I come home three hours late, and she asks me where I have been. I am considering a "little white lie"; in order to avoid a battle, I propose to tell her that I have been working on my book. Suddenly Kant, like Jiminy Cricket, appears on my shoulder. He informs me that as a rational being, I cannot lie at all. I then ask why. He asks me to consider what happens if I universalize lying at will, that is, imagine it to be a law governing human behavior that anyone can lie whenever they choose to. If I universalize lying at will, I essentially destroy the concept of telling the truth, since no one could trust anyone else. But if I destroy the concept of telling the truth, I also destroy the concept of lying, since without truth telling there can be no lies. Thus I destroy the possibility of the very act I am considering doing! So it is irrational to universalize lying, and lying is therefore immoral. A similar argument works for stealing. If I try to universalize stealing, I destroy the concept of private property, which in turn destroys the concept of stealing.

HUMANS AS "ENDS IN THEMSELVES"

That is the basic point of Kant's ethics. He proceeds to draw some interesting conclusions from his Categorical Imperative. In a puzzling passage he claims that the Categorical Imperative can also be stated as follows:

> So act that you treat any human being, whether yourself or any other, always as an end and never merely as a means. (p. 429)

What does this have to do with the previous statement? And what exactly does this mean, and how does Kant prove this? As I have shown in detail elsewhere, Kant seems to have meant something like this: All rational beings are in a deep sense the same. Since they are all seeking what is universally true, and since there is only one universal truth, it is absurd to talk about different rationalities in different individuals the way we talk about different personalities. We can talk about different *degrees* of rationality; clearly, Donny Osmond has not actualized his rationality to the same degree that Albert Einstein has, but fundamentally, both have the same *kind* of rationality. As such, they have the same ultimate "end" or goal or nature. For a rational being, the ultimate goal and the ultimate object of value is the exercise of rational function.

Let us examine this point. There must be some "end" to all our actions, or else we are in the position of a dog chasing its own tail. That is, we seek, for example, to increase our wealth. Do we do it for its own sake? Surely not. Wealth is a tool; as philosophers put it, it has only *instrumental value,* value as a *means* to something else, not *intrinsic value,* that is, we do not seek it for its own sake. But for Kant (as for Aristotle), for a rational being rational functioning is an end in itself and does have intrinsic value.

We can now see how Kant arrives at his claim that to be moral involves treating other humans as ends in themselves. If rationality is the same kind of thing in all humans, it would be absurd for one human rational being to treat another human rational being in a way that simply uses the other person as a means to some immediate goal, say, wealth. For as rational beings, we are seeking rational activity as our end or ultimate purpose or goal. Since others are striving for exactly the same goal, and all rational activity is the same, it is *irrational* for us to use them; rather, we are obliged to nurture them in their attempt to accomplish that which we ourselves are and ought to be trying to achieve.

ANIMALS AS MEANS

It is for this reason that Kant concludes that only rational beings are "ends in themselves," that is, are not to be used as means to achieve some immediate or long-term goal. Many of us who do not read much philosophy may nonetheless be familiar with this notion from recent popular discussions of sexual ethics. Many sexologists take as basic the idea that what determines the rightness or wrongness of a given sexual activity is not the "normalcy" of the activity, but rather whether or not one's sexual partner is being seen simply as a tool, or means, to gratifying one's lust, rather than as an end in himself or herself. On this view, even "normal," "missionary position" sexual intercourse between married people can be grossly immoral, if one partner is simply using the other as a release, seeing the other as a body alone, without love and without concern for his or her individuality and unique needs as a person.

In any event, it follows clearly for Kant that since only human beings are rational beings, only human beings fall within the scope of moral concern. As far as animals are concerned, they have only instrumental value; that is, any worth they may have stems from their usefulness for humans. In his *Lectures on Ethics,* Kant actually says this:

Animals are . . . merely as means to an end. That end is man. (p. 239)

Kant does assert that we should avoid cruelty, but only for the reasons mentioned earlier, that cruelty to animals can lead to cruelty toward humans, or that an animal is human property, and to damage that animal is to harm a person.

This then is a sketch of the argument that thinkers in the tradition of Kant might advance to justify excluding animals from the scope of moral concern. We must now show the connection between all this and the possession of language. When we have done this, we can turn to our attempt to refute this pervasive and influential argument.

LANGUAGE AND REASON

It is clear from the *Critique of Pure Reason* that Kant, like Plato, Aristotle, Aquinas, Descartes, and innumerable other thinkers, equated reason with the possession of language and denied linguistic ability to animals. The basic pattern of argument seems to be this. In order to reason, one must be able to deal with generalities, with what philosophers call "universal judgments" and "general terms." Almost all reasoning involves some statement—or as Kant put it, judgment—that refers to some general feature of the world, and all reasoning follows some universal pattern.

Consider a very elementary piece of reasoning:

Premise 1: All pentagons have more sides than do squares.
Premise 2: All squares have more sides than do triangles.
Conclusion: Therefore, all pentagons have more sides than do triangles.

Notice in the above piece of reasoning that each of the premises as well as the conclusion are *universal statements.* The first one asserts, for example, that anything in the universe that is a pentagon will have more sides than anything in the universe that is a square. We make this assertion about *all pentagons* and *all squares* that exist now, in the past, or in the future, or even those that *could* exist or that we can imagine. Our ability to do this stems from the fact that we have *concepts,* or general terms, that refer to types of things expressed by words in our language. A proper name like "President Harry Truman" refers to only one individual, whereas a word like "square" or "fire" refers to an indefinite number of entities. Without such general concepts, we could not reason, nor could we communicate our reasoning to others. What allows us to have such general concepts, which we can put into general statements, is language. In language we use particular symbols, for example, the printed word "SQUARE," to stand for a general concept. Thus, language allows us to deal with generalities as well as particulars. Also through language, we can deal with highly abstract notions, like good and bad, which refer to things we do not perceive with our senses.

So reasoning is made possible by language, which allows us to deal with past and future as well as present, generalities as well as particulars, possibilities as well as actualities, abstractions as well as concrete things we can see, hear, feel, touch, and smell. Only through language, then, can we reason. Animals, it is further argued, clearly do not have a language. They can communicate, they do have and apprehend, as we mentioned earlier, signs; but they do not have symbols. The difference lies precisely in the universality we have been discussing. And thus, according to this theory, animals cannot reason, nor can so-called "wolf-children," children brought up in isolation or by animals.

The difference between humans and animals with regard to reason and language postulated by a Kantian sort of theory can be expressed in the following way: Imagine an animal, say a dog, signaling to another dog a threat, and the second dog responding with submissive behavior, for example, rolling over and showing its throat. Here we clearly have a case of understanding and communication, but not of reasoning. It is not reasoning, a Kantian would say, because the dog's behavior is tied to the particular stimuli confronting him and, furthermore, can be totally explained by tracing the process of cause and effect leading from the first dog's growl to the second dog's submission. The first dog's growl is analogous to my pushing the "off" button on my television set. Just as a set of purely mechanical steps fully explains the set's going off, so the growl leads to the submission by a series of purely mechanical steps, presumably through the brain and central nervous system. When animals respond, they do so because their "switches" are activated by direct causal processes in their immediate environment, and the *full meaning* of their reaction can be explicated simply by tracing these steps. (Note the tie between this account and Descartes's view of animals as machines.)

Not so, it is argued, with humans. With a rational being, while it may indeed be possible to specify the causal steps going on in the brain and nervous system when a universal judgment or sentence involving a concept is uttered or apprehended, the *meaning* of that event is not given by listing these causal processes. For no set of particular causal processes can explain, in our earlier example, that our sentence manages to refer to *all* pentagons. Meaning must be sought beyond the purely mechanical. In other words, language has this unique feature: while the processes that make language possible in a human being are indeed bodily activities happening at a specific time in a specific place, the resulting linguistic statements have meanings that transcend that place and time. When I utter the statement about pentagons, the actual utterance is indeed a localized event that can be described in terms of brain activity, neural transmission, vocal chord vibrations, etc. But the meaning of the statement, and the fact that it refers to all pentagons that have existed in the past, do exist now, will exist in the future, or could exist, or for that matter, the fact that it also refers to purely abstract mathematical objects that can't exist in the physical world, cannot be accounted for simply by a description of what is happening in my body.

Let us summarize by contrasting two cases as the Kantian position would see them. Imagine a dog seeing a fire and fleeing. According to this argument, the sight of the fire in some way triggers an avoidance reaction.

On the other hand, consider a father telling his young son, "All fires are dangerous." In the first place, he can utter this without any fire being present to stimulate that utterance. Second, the meaning of that utterance cannot be explained by reference to what is going on either in his or in the child's brain, since what is happening there is some set of specific events happening at a certain time, whereas the sentence makes reference to any possible fire, anywhere, at any time.

This sort of argument enjoys a great popularity and is held by many and probably by most linguists, psychologists, and philosophers. One can find this argument in the writings of Noam Chomsky and Jonathan Bennett, to name two very clear recent expositors of this position. It is neatly summarized in the following poem by Edwin Muir:

THE ANIMALS

They do not live in the world,
Are not in time and space.
From birth to death hurled
No word do they have, not one
To plant a foot upon,
Were never in any place.

For with names the world was called
Out of the empty air,
With names was built and walled,
Line and circle and square,
Dust and emerald;
Snatched from deceiving death
By the articulate breath.

But these have never trod
Twice the familiar track,
Never never turned back
Into the memoried day.
All is new and near
In the unchanging Here
of the fifth great day of God,
That shall remain the same,
Never shall pass away.

On the sixth day we came.

In any event, we have finally presented the major philosophical stance that has been used to exclude animals from moral concern. In summary, this Kantian position argues that rationality is required for something to be an object of moral concern (as well as to be a moral agent). The essence of rationality is the ability to universalize and transcend mere particulars. Only a being with language can be rational, because rationality requires concepts. Animals lack language, are tied to stimulus and response, are not, therefore, rational beings, and for this reason do not enter into the scope of moral concern. We have spent a good deal of time on this argument, and it is quite complex, but it is also very important. Most people, I suspect, when pressed as to why they exclude animals from moral concern, will fall back upon some such claim as "animals can't speak." Furthermore, even in a nonmoral context, language is usually used (as it is by Chomsky) to draw a clear-cut gulf between humanity and the rest of nature; so it is of great importance to understand the rationale behind this position.

THE ORDINARY NOTION OF RATIONALITY

Is the Kantian account a persuasive reason for excluding animals from moral concern? I think not, for a variety of reasons. In the first place, I am not sure that Kant has even clearly captured what is ordinarily meant by rationality. While it is certainly the case that the ability to universalize and generalize is a major aspect of what we call "rational," there are many cases of rationality in which we do not make even implicit reference to universalization. For example, we speak of the rationality of a man's swerving into a snow bank to avoid colliding with a truck, or we speak of the rationality of one's giving up in a fight when the opponent has clearly outmatched him. Interestingly enough, animals such as dogs can and do engage in this sort of behavior, and, in this sense, seem to behave perfectly "rationally." In point of fact, we regularly speak of animal behavior as being rational, not only in ordinary discourse, but in our scientific works on animal behavior. In fact, a good deal of our psychological research that studies the learning behavior of animals is based on an implicit assumption that human cognitive behavior bears significant analogies to animal intellectual processes.

DO ANIMALS BEHAVE RATIONALLY?

It is interesting to note also that many philosophers do not share Kant's view that reason is unique to humans. Philosophers like David Hartley or David Hume, who are in the empiricist tradition, and who tend to stress the importance of experience rather than pure thought as the basis of knowledge, do not hesitate to assert that when man reasons about the world, he does so in exactly the same way that animals do. As we said before, for Hume all reasoning about the world is based on habit or conditioning. Thus, there is for Hume no real difference between a dog's expecting to get fed when you pick up his dish, and a scientist's expecting an atomic pile to explode when it reaches critical mass. True, the scientist makes reference to laws of nature, but according to Hume these laws are just experientially based habits! I am not intending here to decide which account of rationality is correct—that is far too deep a philosophical issue to decide conclusively, and fortunately, it is not necessary for our purposes. My only point is to show that there do exist alternative views of reason, ones that do attribute reason to animals, and that these views are in many ways persuasive. If it is even plausible to suggest that animals do reason, it seems to be irrational to deny them entrance into the scope of moral concern on the basis of an undecided and controversial theory of reason. It is especially odd now that Lana, a young gorilla, has scored eighty-five on a standard IQ test, higher than some humans.

In point of fact, I am quite certain that almost everyone reading this book has probably seen at firsthand or on film or heard of or read of some cases of animal behavior that they would be prepared to call reasoning. In my own reading on dog behavior and in my own work with dogs, I have come across many such cases. For example, I had a highly intelligent German shepherd that I acquired when he was an adult. One extremely hot day, while my wife was filling the horses' tank from a high-pressure hose, the dog approached her, clearly wanting a drink. Not having a bowl handy, she turned the hose towards the ground, and the dog attempted to drink but was thwarted by the extreme pressure. Undaunted, he proceeded to dig a hole beneath the stream, allowed the water to pool, and drank his fill.

One of the best stories I have ever run across in this area was told by a German trainer of police dogs. He relates that he had trained a police dog in Berlin to apprehend suspects and hold them by the arm unharmed until the officer arrived. Only if the suspect resisted was the dog to bite, and then only to disable the offensive arm. On the dog's first day at work, he was patrolling a large public park along with his handler. They came upon a robbery in progress, being perpetrated by two men. When the men caught sight of the dog, they broke and ran towards a fork in the path, where both took off in different directions on the theory that the dog could not pursue both. The dog chased one suspect up the left fork, apprehended him, disabled his leg, left him, proceeded up the right fork, and held the second man by the arm, unharmed. The dog had never been trained to attack the leg.

As I said, anyone who has lived with animals can tell such stories, and many such incidents have been filmed and documented. It seems to me only common sense to call such behavior rational and to say that such animals reason. We all know, of course, that common sense is often wrong, as when it tells us that the earth does not move. But still, in order to abandon common sense, one needs strong counterevidence or powerful philosophical or scientific arguments that demonstrate its inadequacy. And to my knowledge, such evidence and argument have not hitherto been forthcoming. This point is discussed at length in my *Unheeded Cry: Animal Consciousness, Animal Pain and Science.*

ARE ONLY HUMANS "LANGUAGE-RATIONAL"?—
DO ANIMALS USE CONCEPTS?

Perhaps a holder of the Kantian position would be quite prepared to admit the plausibility of everything we have just said. Very well, he might say, you have indeed shown that as the words "reason" or "rationality" are ordinarily employed, animals can indeed be said to be "rational" or to reason. But still, what is interesting and morally relevant is not the ordinary use of the word, but Kant's very special sense, which expresses the idea of universalizing, language- or concept-using rationality. It is this idea, which in German could be put into one long word, that is the basic way of distinguishing humans from animals with regard to the scope of moral concern. After all, Kant's argument does show the relevance of this restricted sense of rationality to morality. In short, Kant might say that there is no reason to believe that animals have concepts or general notions, since they lack the linguistic marks of those concepts.

One very obvious answer we may tender to the Kantian is this: It is by no means clear that even this restricted concept of rationality applies to humans alone. For one thing, there does seem to be reasonable evidence that animals do have something like concepts, or general notions, or else how could they learn? My dog knows that my puttering around his food dish means that he is likely to get fed. He knows this even though on different days I am wearing different clothes, atmospheric conditions are different, and sometimes it is light outside and sometimes it is dark. The claim that an animal acts only mechanically by stimulus and response loses plausibility as we vary the stimuli markedly, and yet the animal continues to react appropriately. He even knows it if I use a completely different dish, in a different place. Does not any animal recognize certain visual perceptions as being marks of water, even though these perceptions differ widely from time to time? Surely this sort of activity bespeaks some general notions, or concepts, as do the examples of animal reasoning discussed in the last section.

The major obstacle to accepting the idea of animals having concepts is of course their lack of language. First of all, we see no overt obvious marks of their possession of concepts. But there is an even deeper philosophical problem that some philosophers have raised against the idea that a nonlinguistic being could have concepts. This is called "the private language argument" and was developed by the great twentieth-century philosopher Ludwig Wittgenstein. To have a concept, the argument goes, there must be *publicly checkable rules* for the use of the concept. That means that there must be ways in which I can conceivably *misapply* the concept and be detected and corrected. This is only possible when the vehicles of the concept are public, accessible to others who can see how you are using the concept, and who can correct deviations from proper use. Thus consider a child, learning the concept of "dog." In his mind, he may wish to group a cow with dogs. But when he calls the cow a "dog," there is someone available to correct him. On the other hand, in the absence of a public way of expressing the concept and of being corrected, what is to stop him from using it differently each time? What criteria does he have for deciding whether the concept does or doesn't apply to some new case? Such a state, says Wittgenstein, is comparable to a game where you make up the rules as you go along. Without some fixed, externally checkable rules, the activity is not really a game at all.

This is indeed a strong argument. But does it really count against animals having concepts? Let us see. A person has words for his concepts. These words can be checked against what other people say. This is supposed to be different from the animal who presumably only has some ideas in his head or perhaps certain perceptions to use as marks of his concepts. For example, the animal has only some memory of the appearance of water or the visual appearance of the water itself (for example, its shimmering) to serve as a mark of his concept.

Is there ultimately a difference between the two situations? On the surface, yes. But in a deeper sense, perhaps not. According to the private language argument, the animal must rely on memory and thus has no way of being shown to be wrong. But suppose, as we all know happens, a puppy sees me rattling a martini shaker and approaches me, thinking that it is about to be fed. I say "No, that's not for you," and fail to feed him. In such a way, his initial concept of "dish rattling—food time" *is* corrected, and I see no relevant difference between this case and the case of the child who calls a cow a "horse." Nor does this process of public correction require a human being at all. Let us return to the visually shimmering perception serving as the visual sign of water. An animal may see shimmering on asphalt and believe it to mean water (even as we do), but he is "publicly" corrected by approaching the road and finding there is no water there at all.

If the private language theorist is persistent, he might say, "But how does the animal know the next time that he is using the sign or idea in anything like the way he did before? The animal has only memory; we at least have other people." The answer is simple. If we can be skeptical about memory, we can also be skeptical about other people's memories and ask how do we ever really know that they are using the word or concept the way they did before? So public checks don't really help in the face of extreme skepticism.

This discussion has, of course, presupposed that animals can remember without language. Aside from the fact that behavioral evidence supports this claim, it is obvious that we humans must be able to remember without language, or else we could never learn language in the first place.

There is an even deeper philosophical response to the private language argument. The possibility of publicly checking linguistic concepts itself depends on my leaving certain linguistic concepts unchecked. For example, let us return to the case of the child who wants to group a cow under his concept of dog. He is corrected when he points to the cow and says "dog," for example, by a parent who says "No, cow." The presupposition here is that the child's concept of "No" is correct. How do we check that publicly without presupposing some other concept that we cannot check without presupposing some other concept, etc., *ad infinitum?* We do not, of course, worry about this—we take the correct behavior as evidence that the child does have the concept correct. Well, if that is so, why do we not take the animal's correct behavior in context as evidence that it, too, has concepts? Its concepts are, as Berkeley said, learned from the language of nature and are certainly not as complex or abstract or variable or precise as ours, but they still seem to be concepts, that is, some sort of intellectual capability that allows the creature to recognize repeatable features of the world.

So perhaps we may conclude that animals have something like general notions or concepts. But even so, the Kantian would say, the animal cannot make universal judgments because it has no language. In the first place, it is not so clear that this is so, for reasons very similar to the ones just given in our discussion of denying concepts to animals. Animals do seem to make judgments, at least as evidenced by their behavior. A watchdog seems to judge, for example, that strangers are a danger until proven otherwise. Furthermore, it is not so clear that the difference between language (a system of artificial signs) and a system or set of natural signs such as animals have is a difference in kind, rather than merely a difference in degree of complexity. In my own book, *Natural and Conventional Meaning,* I have tried to show, contrary to the belief of most philosophers, that there is no clear-cut line between the two. But I do not wish to rest on that here, for there are a number of other points more directly relevant.

ANIMALS AND HUMAN LANGUAGE

The reader may be surprised that I have not yet mentioned the remarkable research that has been done on teaching language, or at least what seems to many scholars to be language (sign language, computer language), to chimpanzees, gorillas, and orangutans. This work is indeed fascinating and certainly, to my mind, supports the claim that no hard and fast line can be drawn between human reason, thought, and sign apparatuses and that of animals. My view is shared by many evolutionary theorists, even those who think that humans are "at the top" of the evolutionary pyramid, since all of evolutionary theory strongly suggests the absence of sharp breaks in the chain of life. But I fear that this research will have little effect on those people who hold to a sharp cleavage. If a person believes that language creates a sharp gulf between humans and animals, and such a person is shown that the higher primates have language, he or she will tend to respond not by obliterating the unbridgeable gulf between humans and animals, but by moving the higher primates from the realm of animals to the realm of humans and saying that if these animals indeed have language, they, too, should fall within the scope of moral concern, but that this has nothing to do with the animals that do not have language. So it is unwise, I think, to rest too much upon primate language research when trying to show that animals fall within the scope of moral concern.

MORAL CONCERN AND NONRATIONAL HUMANS

No, to rest a great deal on the attempt to prove that animals do have language is to ignore our earlier warning about the moral relevance of criteria used to distinguish humans from animals. And herein lies the source of our major direct objections to the Kantian position. For we will now show that rationality and language do not explain the scope of moral concern. If indeed, as the Kantian argument suggests, only rational and linguistic beings fall within the scope of moral concern, it is once again difficult to see how we can allow infants, children, the mentally retarded, the insane, the senile, the brain-damaged, the autistic, the comatose, etc., to be considered legitimate objects of moral concern. We do consider them such objects; yet they lack rationality and/or language. This shows that rationality and language do not represent a necessary condition for moral concern. Perhaps one might try to answer this objection by saying that it is because the human species as such is characterized by rationality that these nonrational individuals fall within the scope of moral concern. But this is inadequate, if only because such an argument would make the species the object of moral concern and not individuals at all; yet it is individual and not species considerations that are the focus of our moral reasoning, as we shall later discuss.

Is it then the fact that such people are *potentially* rational? This might work for infants and children, but certainly not for the senescent and the hopelessly brain-damaged or insane, who are not in fact potentially rational. If one were to argue that perhaps future scientific progress might allow for these (or such) people to be made rational, the same might be said for animals. In this fanciful sense, all animals are "potentially" rational, as indeed they are in the long-term evolutionary sense as well. (Squirrels might evolve into rational beings!)

It has been suggested that the analogy between animals and "marginal humans" is misguided, because such deficient humans are in fact not direct objects of moral concern. In a move reminiscent of the St. Thomas-Kant argument prohibiting cruelty to animals because of its potential for harming people, some philosophers have suggested that deficient humans are treated morally not for their own sakes, but because they are enmeshed in a tissue of relationships with real humans, and not treating them morally would cause pain to these *bona-fide,* 24-karat humans.

Such an argument clearly will not do the job. Surely there could be marginal humans that no "real humans" care about, or that "real humans" positively loathe. It would then presumably follow that we had no moral obligations to such people, and we would then be free to do invasive research on them, cook and eat them, or test for product safety using their eyes. (Since they are physiologically a much higher fidelity model for normal humans than animals are, research done on them would surely be of far greater scientific value than research done on animals.) But the fact is, we are not out there determining which marginal humans are of concern to real humans and which are not, and happily exploiting the latter.

Furthermore, the argument contains the seeds of its own undoing, for it cannot distinguish marginal humans from animals even in its own terms. As we all know, animals are enmeshed in a web of relationships with "real humans," the most obvious case being pet animals, but the point would hold of almost every other imaginable kind of animal as well. Many antivivisectionists, for example, feel deeply for laboratory animals, both in a general sense and *vis-à-vis* specific animals they know. And doubtless, if one took the trouble, one could find people willing to establish relationships with any animals about to be used invasively. If the argument we are discussing is correct, then we surely would (or ought to) exhibit the same degree of concern for such animals as we do for marginal humans; so we are back, via a different route, at our initial point.

OUR CONCERN FOR NONRATIONAL HUMAN INTERESTS

The chief criticism of Kant's theory, however, is far more basic and, in fact, points us towards resolving the general problem of candidacy for moral concern. The Kantian position suggests, as we have seen, that rationality is necessary and sufficient for considering something to be a moral agent, that is, to be held responsible and accountable for its actions. With this we have raised no disagreement, and, in fact, this is a common assumption of moral practice. On the other hand, we have been asking the question of why rationality is the criterion for entrance into the arena of moral consideration. And we readily note that Kant's theory does not in this respect accord with our fundamental moral intuitions and practices. Very simply, we may ask, if the Kantian theory is an adequate account of why people are objects of moral concern, namely, because they are actually or potentially rational beings, why do we extend our moral concern, attention, deliberation, and consideration beyond the strictly rational aspects of human life and activity? Why do we concern ourselves morally with human activities that have nothing to do with our rational side? Is it only because these other aspects of life, our daily pleasures and pains, hopes, fears, aspirations, and desires, all ultimately affect our rational activity? Surely this is not the case. Most of what we worry about in our moral thinking about other people has nothing to do with the fact that they are rational beings. In fact, if Kant is correct, it seems impossible to explain why any human interests that admittedly have nothing to do with a person's nature as a rational being ought to figure as at all morally relevant.

　　Why, according to the Kantian theory of morality, are there any prohibitions against harming a rational being in ways that demonstrably do not harm his or her rationality? Why do we feel any obligation to nurture and assist those aspects of human life and activity that are irrelevant to rationality? Let us consider some extremes that bring this point home. Suppose we discover that a certain amount of physical torture, regularly administered, is biologically conducive to developing a person's rational abilities. It seems that the Kantian theory would not only allow such torture, but would actually make it obligatory! On the other hand, suppose that we discover that taking candy from a baby, or misleading or tripping a blind person, does not at all impede their rationality. It is difficult to see why the Kantian ethic would in any way forbid these obviously unacceptable actions. In short, if the Kantian approach to morality through rationality is correct, then those aspects of human nature that are independent of our rational abilities necessarily fall outside of the scope of moral concern. Yet this is clearly a major inadequacy in a moral theory, since surely most of our moral concern for people has nothing whatever to do with their rational aspects. A good deal of our moral concern toward people is oriented toward alleviating unnecessary suffering, whatever its effect on their rationality. We would not, for example, wish to have people cold and hungry all the time even if it became known that this sort of torment fueled their intellectual capabilities; so rationality alone does not seem to delineate the sphere of moral concern.

THE MORAL RELEVANCE OF PLEASURE AND PAIN

Of course, as we said earlier, a moral theory often does cause us to change our intuitions. But I do not think that this is the case here, because the Kantian theory flies in the face of far too many intuitions and excludes far too much of what we take to be central to morality. Frankly, most of us do not worry excessively about rationality in our moral deliberations— we consider pleasure and pain to be far more important criteria of concern. So important are pleasure and pain to our intuitions about morality that some philosophers have made the ability to suffer the sole criterion for admittance into the sphere of moral concern. For example, Jeremy Bentham, the great English utilitarian who argued in his *Principles of Morals and Legislation* that the test of rightness and wrongness of actions was whether they produced the greatest amount of pleasure (or least possible amount of pain) for the greatest number, argued that in calculating this total amount of pleasure and pain, we needed to take account of all creatures capable of suffering, including animals. Certainly this theory accords far better with our intuitions than does Kant's, and it furthermore serves greatly to increase the scope of moral concern. (It does not, for example, suggest that retarded persons or the insane ought not to be legitimate objects of moral concern.) And most recent discussions of the moral status of animals that have attempted to draw our attention to the fact that animals ought to be included within the scope of moral concern have begun by taking pleasure and pain as basic requirements of moral consideration. This, for example, is the argument of Peter Singer in his pioneering work, *Animal Liberation.*

Although we are perhaps a good deal closer to an adequate theory when we consider pleasure and pain, I do not believe that this gives us the complete picture. We can readily see the problems involved in this view by pursuing the same line of criticism we leveled against Kant. If pleasure and pain are the determining characteristics that make something an object of moral concern, in the way that rationality is for Kant, it is difficult to see why those actions that do not touch pleasure and pain have any bearing on morality. Yet a moment's reflection makes us aware that we have strong moral intuitions about all sorts of activities toward people that do not directly touch pleasure and pain. In fact, we may begin by drawing from Kant's insight. I believe that we would all consider it wrong to impede a person's intellectual or rational development, even if we cause him or her no suffering. Self-fulfillment is a good quite independent of pleasure. Or consider the sort of situation vividly described in Huxley's *Brave New World,* a situation where people are kept in a state of happy idiocy by the use of drugs. Even though they are not suffering and are indeed feeling considerable pleasure, we still find such a society to be immoral and monstrous. Clearly, we tend to think of freedom, for example, as in many instances more important than pleasure and lack of pain. We consider it immoral to restrict a person's freedom even if we can ensure that they will be happier (or experience less pain) without that freedom. Thus medical schools permit a student to apply for admission year after year, even though they know he or she will never be accepted. We resist things done "for our own good." Very often, we do not consider it right to withhold the truth from a person, even if the truth will "hurt." We do not consider it right for the mass media to manipulate people's desires and actions even if they are not pained by it. And so forth.

Nonetheless, even though concern for pleasure and absence of pain does not capture all of our intuitions about our moral concern for people, it certainly captures a good many of them. And concern for pleasure and pain, taken in conjunction with Kant's concern for rationality, gives us a much better theoretical purchase on our morality *vis-à-vis* people. Certainly, using pleasure and pain as additional criteria for candidacy for moral concern would not allow us to exclude animals from moral concern, at the very least the "higher" animals who evidence pain behavior and for whom we have good, sound, neurophysiological evidence that they have nervous systems relevantly similar to ours.

SCIENTIFIC IDEOLOGY AND THE DENIAL
OF ANIMAL PAIN AND CONSCIOUSNESS

Ordinary people would never dream of denying that animals think and feel. If anything, common sense sometimes errs by going to excess in the other direction and attributing to animals (most often pets) total understanding of human speech, preferences in television programs, etc. Even David Hume, the most skeptical of philosophers, who was prepared to call into question the existence of mind, body, persistence and externality of objects, causality, identity, scientific rationality, and cosmic intelligibility, considered the presence of thoughts and feelings in animals an indubitable truth. As he asserted in his *Treatise of Human Nature:*

> Next to the ridicule of denying an evident truth, is that of taking much pains to defend it; and no truth appears to me more evident than that beasts are endowed with thought and reason as well as men. The arguments are in this case so obvious, that they never escape the most stupid and ignorant. (p. 74)

The belief in animal mentation thus seems firmly ensconced in common sense, so much so, indeed, that it has been pointed out by psychologist D. O. Hebb that we simply could not deal with animals if our license to talk in these terms were revoked. As such, this belief hardly needed support from mainstream science, which support, however, it nonetheless garnered unequivocally with the advent of Darwinism. For Darwin himself, and for the nineteenth-century biologists (at least in England and America) who carried forth his ideas, thought and feeling in animals was an inevitable consequence of phylogenetic continuity. If morphological and physiological traits are evolutionarily continuous, so, too, are psychological ones. Thus, in the *Descent of Man,* Darwin affirmed that "there is no fundamental difference between man and the higher animals in their mental faculties," and that "the lower animals, like man, manifestly feel pleasure and pain, happiness, and misery." In the same work Darwin in fact attributed to animals the full range of human subjective experience, and took it for granted that one could scientifically gather data about such experience. In a work which brazenly hoists a middle finger at the Cartesian tradition, *The Expression of Emotions in Man and Animals,* Darwin detailed his conclusions concerning animal feelings, and in later work, both his own (Darwin 1896) and that which he entrusted to his colleague, George Romanes, he explored the cognitive dimensions of animal experience, even including the problem-solving abilities of earthworms!

One might conclude, then, that animal mentation, buttressed as it was both by common sense and by the foundational theory of modern biology, enjoyed a secure position ensconced in the studies and concerns of the mainstream scientific community in the twentieth century. In fact, nothing could be more erroneous than such a conclusion. By the 1930s one would be hard pressed to find a psychologist, biologist, or medical scientist willing to talk openly of animal thought and feeling, though most continued to think of themselves as Darwinians. Talk of animal thought and feeling, and most relevant for our discussion, talk about animal pain and suffering, had gone the way of talk about life-force, entelechies, essences, absolute space, or spirits—banished from the legitimate purview of scientific inquiry. The persistence of this legacy is manifest even today. One must still search extensively if one wishes to find a respectable scientist willing to echo Darwin's unequivocal statements quoted earlier.

To what can we attribute the abandonment of what appeared to late-nineteenth-century science to be a legitimate, rich, nonproblematic, empirical domain of inquiry, susceptible to investigation by standard scientific methods? A study of the history of science reveals that the view of animals having thought and feeling was neither empirically disconfirmed nor shown to be conceptually flawed, which are the only ways science recognizes that scientific ideas are superseded. In actual fact, as I have shown in detail in my recent book, *The Unheeded Cry: Animal Consciousness, Animal Pain and Science,* the belief in animal mind vanished because of new philosophical ideas that seized the scientific community in the first two decades of the twentieth century, and dominated scientific thought and practice for some fifty years.

Though science tends to ignore its philosophical basis, it should be recalled that every human activity with any intellectual component whatever, from geometry to law, from art to science, must rest on certain assumptions that are almost always taken for granted by practitioners of the discipline.

As in the paradigmatic case of geometry, one must begin with certain notions that cannot be proved, for it is on them that all proof rests, although most fields do not neatly and explicitly articulate their assumptions as well as does geometry. As Aristotle pointed out, to prove our basic assumptions in a given area, one would need other assumptions, which in turn would require proof *ad infinitum.* In practice, one's assumptions are as invisible to one's daily activities as the air one breathes, although one could not function intellectually without such assumptions, just as one could not function biologically without air.

What is often forgotten is that although assumptions in a given area are rarely questioned—practitioners in the area are too busy advancing the discipline on the basis of assumptions to question them—assumptions are, in principle, subject to questioning, and are in fact often flawed. To question such assumptions is the task of philosophic or conceptual activity, for it is of necessity nonempirical. The philosophic questioning of such assumptions can become the basis for major scientific revolutions, as in Einstein's critique of foundational concepts of Newtonian physics, or Newton's conceptual critique of the Aristotelian assumption that the science of motion must be qualitative.

In the case of scientific activity for most of the twentieth century, certain general assumptions have ossified into an invisible dogma so taken for granted by most scientists that I have termed it the *common sense or ideology of science,* because it is to scientific activity what ordinary common sense is to daily life. Not surprisingly, the common sense of science may and does conflict with ordinary common sense, just as science conflicts with common sense. The philosophical roots of scientific common sense lie in the movements known as *positivism* and *behaviorism* that evolved in the early twentieth century.

For purposes of our discussion of pain in animals, two components of the common sense of science are especially worthy of note. The first is the widespread belief that, in and of itself, science has nothing to do with values in general and with ethics in particular—the usual slogan is that science is value-free. This is assumed because science deals with what is objective, verifiable by experiment, observation, and data gathering, that which is intersubjectively confirmable. Because value judgments cannot be so verified, they are said to be outside of the purview of science itself. Hence, the common sense of science sees ethics as a subjective matter of taste and personal preference—as matters of emotion, not reason. Scientists who worked on the Manhattan Project and have said that they did not consider the development of the atomic bomb except as a scientific question—ethics was for the politicians—epitomize the belief that science is value-free.

Other evidence of the common sense of science's view that science is value-free is manifest. Few scientific textbooks explore ethical issues inherent in their subject matter—indeed many basic textbooks stress in their introductory chapters that science is value-free. For a good part of the twentieth century scientific use of human subjects was largely unconstrained; witness the widespread use of disenfranchised human beings, i.e., convicts, the retarded, and the aged, for invasive research without informed consent. Note that I am not here referring to the moral monsters such as Josef Mengele. I am rather focusing on generally accepted practices that bespoke a widespread belief in a clear schism between science and ethics.

By the same token, one may cite the remarkable dearth of arguments and discussions in biomedical research circles and publications on the complex moral questions associated with animal research. (Ordinary people immediately see the moral issues involved.) Until recently, and still to a large extent, such discussions tended to be defensive reactions to criticism or long lists of the benefits to human beings produced by such animal use.

As a result, since scientific ideology turned a blind eye to the moral questions associated with inflicting pain on animals, there was no moral pressure to concern oneself with morally relevant mental states in animals.

The second component of scientific ideology that blocked concern with animal pain is the claim that animal consciousness—what an animal thinks and experiences—was outside of the purview of scientific inquiry, since mental states were not subject to observation and experimentation. This positivistic component, in tandem with a new movement in psychology called behaviorism that was launched in 1913 by J. B. Watson, banished consciousness from the scientific arena. In its pure form, behaviorism denied the knowability and reality of consciousness in human beings or in animals. We do not really have thoughts, we only think we do, said the behaviorists in essence. And so psychology became the study of behavior, specifically of learning, not of mentation. The scientific acknowledgment of mental states in animals was dealt a death blow. By the 1940s virtually all psychologists in the United States were behaviorists.

So strong was the positivist flame that it consumed talk of consciousness in animals in Europe as well, where Konrad Lorenz and Tinbergen were opposing behaviorism with the fledgling science of ethology, on the grounds that behaviorism ignored genetic and evolutionary determinants of behavior. Nonetheless, ethologists also denied the legitimacy of talking about consciousness in animals, the one point in which they stressed their agreement with behaviorists. Lorenz spoke of appetite-behavior in animals, not of appetite, to stress the need for eschewing mentalism; behavioral psychologists spoke of aversive behavior and negative reinforcers, not of felt pain; biologists were carried along by the same current.

These two components of scientific ideology, the denial of values in science and the methodological elimination of talk about consciousness, naturally reinforced each other and were in turn buttressed by other factors. In particular, the philosophical denial of scientific reality to thought and feeling in animals helped allay reservations that scientists might have had about hurting animals in the pursuit of scientific goals. Interestingly enough, as we mentioned earlier, the same thing had occurred in the seventeenth century when Descartes declared that animals were machines with no souls, minds, or feelings, thereby reconciling in one master stroke the demands that animals not have souls with his belief that biology is a part of physics, and with the demands of a growing science of physiology forced in its quest for knowledge to do what common sense called painful procedures to animals without anesthetics. No need to control the pain, said Cartesian physiologists, because it is not really experienced pain, merely mechanical response. And so, too, in the twentieth century, the study of animal pain became the study of mechanical responses, not of felt hurt. Similarly, stress became a catchall for what ordinary common sense would call suffering and misery of a variety of forms, and then was described purely mechanistically in terms of activation of the hypophysis (pituitary)–adrenal axis and its effects, with any notion of experienced suffering suppressed as scientifically illegitimate.

Furthermore, while ordinary common sense never denied the reality and knowability of animal pain, and thus was shocked by the common sense of science (when it knew about it), it was not morally shocked. For although ordinary common sense never denied pain and suffering in animals, it did not care a great deal about them either. Too much of ordinary practice and economic life depended on inflicting pain and suffering on animals to devote much moral attention to animal pain and suffering. This cavalier disregard for the moral relevance of animal suffering was of course mirrored in the legal system, which accorded animals the status of property, and, as we shall shortly discuss, proscribed only overt and usually intentional cruelty, which might endanger human beings, and turned a blind eye to "necessary," expedient, and usual suffering. By the same token, although turn of the century veterinary medicine was certainly Darwinian in not denying pain to animals, its sense of moral responsibility for controlling it was as limited as and was reflective of that of society in general, as the following quotation from a 1906 surgery text illustrates:

> In veterinary surgery, anesthesia has no history. It is used in a kind of desultory fashion that reflects no great credit to the present generation of veterinarians. . . . Many veterinarians of rather wide experience have never in a whole lifetime administered a general anesthetic in performing their operations. It reflects greatly to the credit of the canine specialist, however, that he alone has adopted anesthesia to any considerable extent. . . . Anesthesia in veterinary surgery today is a means of restraint and not an expedient to relieve pain. So long as an operation can be performed by forcible restraint . . . the thought of anesthesia does not enter into the proposition. (Merillat, p. 223)

Thus, for most of the century, ignoring animal pain, suffering, and the ethical dimensions of animal research was buttressed not only by a general social disregard for animal pain and suffering, and by a hard-fought tradition of academic freedom and freedom of inquiry, but also by a ubiquitous and powerful ideology that said that science had no truck with values and that talk of animal mentation was operationally, empirically, and scientifically meaningless. Only in such an environment could routine use of paralytics without anesthesia for some surgery (e.g., horse castration) flourish uncriticized, as it indeed did in research and veterinary practice.

Until about five years ago, little was known concerning analgesia in laboratory animals; more papers have been published in this area in the past few years than in the previous century, although the literature is still scanty. There still exist no textbooks of veterinary analgesia; the subject is rarely covered in depth in veterinary schools; the average research worker has little if any knowledge of good analgesia protocols; and even board-certified laboratory animal veterinarians and their journals have not made laboratory animal analgesia a major concern.

Ironically, although virtually all analgesics have been screened in rodents, rodents used in painful procedures are almost never the recipients of analgesics. Only in the last few years have people turned to the voluminous data base that has been gained in the course of screening analgesics for human use, with an eye toward abstracting information from that data that can be used to control pain in rodents.

The papers presented at the first conference ever held in the United States on animal pain, convened in 1982, and later published as *Animal Pain* by the American Physiological Society, were, with a few notable exceptions, by and large aimed at exploring what I call the plumbing of pain—mechanisms of pain response—and tended to circuit moral issues involved in pain infliction and control and the fundamental morally relevant experiential dimension of pain, that is, the fact that the animal hurts.

Later on in our discussion of animal research, we shall explain how scientific ideology is changing in virtue of new social moral concerns about animals and the laws which follow in their wake. Here, however, it is appropriate to sketch the philosophical critique of scientific ideology which I presented in great detail in *The Unheeded Cry*.

A CRITIQUE OF SCIENTIFIC IDEOLOGY

Scientific ideology must be shown up for what it is: bad philosophy. In the first place, science is neither value-free nor free of ethical judgment. Indeed, the very notion of what will count as a fact, as a legitimate object of investigation, or as data relevant to a given question, rests squarely on valuational presuppositions. Consider, for example, the Scientific Revolution, when the common-sense, experience-based physics and cosmology of Aristotle were replaced by the rationalistic, mathematical, geometrical physics of Galileo and Newton. The discovery of new data is not what forced the rejection of Aristotelianism; on the contrary, empirical observations all buttressed Aristotle's idea of a world of qualitative differences. What led to the rejection of Aristotelianism was essentially a change in value, a discrediting of information provided by the senses, as Descartes does so well in his *Meditations,* and a correlative valuing of the rational and mathematically expressible over the empirical, of Plato over Aristotle, so nicely expressed in Galileo's claim that in essence an omniscient deity would have to be a mathematician, and create a mathematical unity underlying apparent diversity.

In the same way, the adoption of the behavioristic/positivistic view of science as incapable of dealing with animal consciousness earlier this century, as a replacement for the Darwinian view that animal consciousness was a legitimate object of study, was a change not forced by new facts or by the discovery of logical incoherences in the older approach. Rather, it was a change in how philosophical approaches are valued, one that was defended in valuational terms about what science ought to be, and in terms of the benefit to society coming from a science of psychology aimed at controlling behavior.

Biomedical science, too, is based in valuational assumptions. The key concepts of health and illness of disease in human or animal medicine rest on valuational notions. One cannot have a concept of illness without a concept of health; yet any concept of health must rest in valuational assumptions. No set of facts, including the fact of statistical normalcy, forces us to call an organism healthy or sick. Thus the recent—and questionable— United States medical community's proclamations naming obesity and alcoholism as diseases rather than conditions leading to disease, and child or wife abuse as sickness rather than badness, all bespeak debatable moral and other valuational assumptions. We will discuss this in greater detail later.

A second piece of bad philosophy is the common sense of science's shibboleth that ethics is subjective and not rationally adjudicable. Such a view is incorrect. One is free to choose one's own use of the English language, but certain uses are incorrect. Similarly, one can be wrong in one's moral positions. One cannot logically be a Christian and a moral relativist at the same time, though many people believe they are. One cannot commit oneself to fairness as a moral principle and discriminate against others on the basis of skin color. One cannot rationally be a libertarian and support censorship.

One cannot hold the moral principles we all implicitly share in virtue of living in the same society under the same set of laws and not be logically committed to the notion that animals are more than tools for our use, although most people fail to draw these conclusions unaided by philosophical dialogue. Therefore, the invasive use of animals for research does raise moral valuational questions intrinsic to science and does require making inescapable moral commitments. As soon as one has admitted that animals can be hurt in ways that matter to them, or admitted even that animals are entitled to humane care and treatment, or that unnecessary animal suffering is wrong, one has implicitly but inescapably presupposed that animals are in the moral arena, that it makes sense to talk about them in the moral tone of voice, that one can be morally wrong in how one uses or treats animals, none of which one would say of chairs or wheelbarrows.

The common sense of science's claim that one cannot know animal mental experience is bad philosophy. The same positivism that would exclude talk of animal consciousness from science would also exclude talk of an external world existing independently of perception, talk of other minds (or pain!) in human beings, and the knowability of the past. Evolutionary continuity and neurophysiological and behavioral analogies across species militate in favor of the claim that animals experience pain, and the fact that the failure to feel pain is biologically disastrous in human beings so born or suffering from conditions like Hansen's disease is ample evidence that animals also feel pain and do not merely exhibit the pain mechanisms and pain mitigation responses that are remarkably similar in all vertebrates.

Stress is not simply a catchall nonspecific response, but is in fact under the control of and modulated by the animals' cognitive and emotional and thus mental states. In addition, although we cannot directly perceive thoughts and feelings in animals, we cannot directly perceive quanta and black holes either; all are postulated theoretical entities that are presumed to exist because they provide us with the best explanations for certain phenomena, and enable us to predict features of those phenomena.

In sum, then, despite its pervasiveness, the scientific ideology that denied the knowability and studiability of animal thought and feeling throughout the twentieth century cannot be defended.

Nonetheless, when the first edition of this book appeared, it was quite common to encounter researchers who espoused the skeptical position on animal pain. This, for example, could be found expressed in the *Bulletin of the National Society for Medical Research*, a lobby group that attempted to block legislation that would in any way place restrictions on biomedical research. Or let us cite some more personal examples. In the early 1980s I debated a prominent neurophysiologist whose field of specialization is pain. During the course of his presentation, he brought forward an elaborate argument purporting to show that since the electrochemical activity in the cerebral cortex associated with pain is different in animals and human beings, animal pain is not *really* like human pain, since the cerebral cortex governs higher intellectual activity. My rebuttal was brief. I pointed out to him that his actions belied his rhetoric, since his own area of research was pain, and he used animal subjects and extrapolated the results to people!

In the same vein, I challenged a wildlife biologist who had flatly asserted to his students that fish don't feel pain. I pointed out that evolutionary evidence, neurophysiological analogies, and behavioral evidence, including the fact that fish can be conditioned to swim in certain directions by electroshock, all militate against his claim. His reply was telling: "Well, these sorts of questions are like the existence of God." In a deep sense, this is true. None of us can feel anyone else's pain, man or animal. But if this is what this man believes, he is certainly not in a position to categorically deny that fish feel pain! We shall return to this point.

It is also worth noting some remarkable recent scientific discoveries that have direct bearing on the question of animal pleasure and pain. Most ordinary people have been willing to attribute pain (and pleasure) to mammals and birds and, perhaps to a limited extent, to fish. Although a child will suggest that a worm being put on a hook is suffering, we tend to dismiss this as immature anthropomorphism or sloppy sentimentality. In 1979, however, four Swedish researchers reported in *Nature* that earthworms possess β-endorphins and enkephalins. Other researchers have found α-endorphins. These chemicals, which have been the subject of much research in human beings, are hormones produced by the brain that are similar to morphine, and whose pain-killing properties are many times more powerful than that of morphine. It has been theorized that release of these chemicals is responsible for the masking of pain after severe injury. It has also been suggested that endorphin release is triggered by acupuncture, thus explaining the latter's anesthetic effects. In any event, the presence of these chemicals in invertebrates strongly suggests that these creatures do feel pain, and thus the child's concern for the worm may well be vindicated. It also suggests that something like pain is a valuable evolutionary device across the entire evolutionary scale, and that what has hitherto been dismissed as "anthropomorphism" may just be plausible extrapolation from behavior to sensation. One of my colleagues at Colorado State University, physiologist Dr. Jay Best, is convinced that consciousness pervades the entire evolutionary ladder, and that even planaria (or flatworms) possess some rudimentary "mind." Best and others have performed experiments in which planaria are taught to take certain routes and avoid certain foods by the use of electroshock, once again suggesting that the animal is capable of experiencing some unpleasant sensation that we might as well call pain. And in a fascinating article, famed Cambridge entomologist V. B. Wiggelsworth has argued that insects most likely experience visceral pain, as well as pain elsewhere, caused by heat and electric shock.

It is indeed ironic that in physiology, as in cosmology, contemporary thought has come full circle. It was the mechanical model of Descartes that led to the claim that animals do not feel pain, and that they should be studied as physico-chemical machines. But as we become more and more conversant with the physiology and biochemistry of the animal and human bodies, we find ourselves led back to a rejection of Descartes. For if the human body possesses a biochemical mechanism that serves only to mask pain, is it reasonable to deny the sensation to a "lower" creature possessing the same mechanism?

Incidentally, it is also important to recall that animals can feel pleasure and enjoy all sorts of positive sensations and experiences. While it has been known for a long time that fear, frustration, anxiety, etc., can induce various diseases and lesions in animals, it is only recently that the other side of the coin was studied. (This is in itself a revealing fact about our attitude toward animals.) In an article in *Science* (June 27, 1980), researchers have shown dramatically that love and affection can make a major difference to the physical health of experimental animals. In this study, two groups of rabbits were fed a 2 percent cholesterol diet. One group of rabbits was handled, cuddled, petted by the researchers; a control group was not. The rabbits who had received the love and attention had 60 percent fewer cholesterol-induced aortic lesions! (It is sad and ironic that the researchers had to kill the rabbits to establish this important fact.*)

We must also recall, as just mentioned, that we have no way of knowing what another person suffers as compared with what we suffer, when put in certain circumstances. For instance, it is perfectly possible that a Marie Antoinette, with a sensitivity refined by years of high living, may have suffered more from being deprived of her truffles than a clod like me would suffer from being deprived of food altogether! In short, if we become too skeptical about our ability to know that animals suffer pain, we have no real reason to avoid extending that skepticism to other people. While it might be argued, as it was by Descartes, that at least people can communicate their pain linguistically, it is worth remembering that the most eloquent signs of pain, human *or* animal, are nonlinguistic. A scream tells me much more about pain than does a long-winded description of symptoms. We shall shortly return to this question of language.

It may be suggested that while animals may indeed feel pain, human pain is always infinitely greater, because humans have the ability to anticipate and fear and remember the pain, as when we go to the dentist. In response to this, two points must be made. In the first place, even if human pain

---

*It is also known that animals, as well as humans, recover and heal more quickly when routinely given postsurgical analgesia.

is always greater than animal pain, that is irrelevant to our basic question, namely, what beings enter into the scope of moral concern. If animals feel pain at all, and feeling pain is legitimate grounds for entering into the moral arena, then animals should be objects of moral concern. Second, there is good behavioral evidence that animals do anticipate and remember pain. After all, the dog fears the stick and trembles at the rage in his master's voice. Finally, let us note that the argument cuts both ways. If animals indeed cannot anticipate or remember, then an animal in pain cannot anticipate an end to pain, or remember a time without pain, as we can. The entire horizon of its universe is filled with pain, whereas we can see an end to suffering. If this is the case, perhaps animal pain confers even higher claim to moral concern! In contrast to the poem by Muir quoted earlier, and in order to illustrate the current point that animal pleasure and pain may be more deep than human, the following poem by Robinson Jeffers is worth citing:

THE HOUSE DOG'S GRAVE

I've changed my ways a little; I cannot now
Run with you in the evenings along the shore,
Except in a kind of dream; and you, if you dream a moment,
You see me there.

So leave awhile the paw-marks on the front door
Where I used to scratch to go out or in,
And you'd soon open; leave on the kitchen floor
The marks of my drinking-pan.

I cannot lie by your fire as I used to do
On the warm stone,
Nor at the foot of your bed; no, all the nights through
I lie alone.

But your kind thought has laid me less than six feet
Outside your window where firelight so often plays,
And where you sit to read—and I fear often grieving for me—
Every night your lamplight lies on my place.

You, man and woman, live so long, it is hard
To think of you ever dying.
A little dog would get tired, living so long.
I hope that when you are lying
Under the ground like me your lives will appear
As good and joyful as mine.
No, dears, that's too much hope: you are not so well cared for
As I have been.

And never have known the passionate undivided
Fidelities that I knew.
Your minds are perhaps too active, too many-sided . . .
But to me you were true.

You were never masters, but friends. I was your friend.
I loved you well, and was loved. Deep love endures
To the end and far past the end. If this is my end,
I am not lonely. I am not afraid. I am still yours.

VARIABILITY OF PAIN EXPERIENCE IN HUMANS AND ANIMALS

Unquestionably, animal pain responses are not always the same as ours—compare a horse's wincing rather than crying out when hurt—but, for that matter, human pain responses vary across different cultures and subcultures and among individuals. While the pain-detection threshold (that is, the minimum stimulus that, when applied to a person or an animal, gives rise to the perception of pain) is relatively uniform across human beings, the pain-tolerance threshold (that is, the maximum pain that a subject can endure before the stimulus is perceived as unbearable) varies widely from individual to individual, depending on a number of factors. Indeed, it varies widely even in the same individual, depending on the context of the pain, the person's mood, anxiety level, and so on. Athletes are notoriously good at ignoring great pain. What else would one expect when locker rooms are festooned with giant signs declaring "No pain, no gain" and quoting from football great Johnny Unitas that "If pain bothers you, you have left your game in the locker room."

Ordinary observation, as well as classical research, supports the view that socio-psychological and socio-cultural factors loom large in shaping the experience of pain in humans. Compare, for example, the way in which middle-class New York Jewish children are sometimes encouraged to express pain and are reinforced when they do so when they fall down as toddlers, in contrast to children raised on ranches in the West who are taught to ignore the pain and get on with their business. Research has shown that northern Europeans are less susceptible to painful stimuli than southern Europeans—that is, have a higher pain-tolerance threshold—and this is explained by cultural, rather than biological, differences. Stoicism, control, and keeping emotion in check are valued among northern Europeans; volubility, effusiveness, and emotional display are accepted and encouraged among southern Europeans. Other studies show similar results. When told that Jews are less able to tolerate pain than Christians, Jewish subjects were found to increase their pain tolerance significantly; but when told that Jews can take more pain than Christians, they showed satisfaction with the status quo and did not increase their tolerance. Other studies indicate that Jews are much more concerned about future pain than Italians, whose concern tends to be with immediate relief and who forget about the pain after it has been relieved, while Jews continue to complain even after the pain is alleviated. This is explained by the notion that Jews tend to be culturally future-oriented, as well as pessimistic. This dovetails with the well-known fact that fear and anxiety increase pain, and indeed may cause it.

In his now classic work, H. K. Beecher showed in 1956 that wounded front line soldiers required less analgesia than nonmilitary surgical patients, even though the injuries they sustained were more massive. He explained this by reference to the fact that the soldiers saw real benefit in the wound— that is, no longer having their lives at risk on the battlefield—whereas the surgical patients focused more on their pain. Facts like these have sometimes been used to claim that animal pain is qualitatively different from human pain because it is unaffected by psychological and cultural factors. However, clinical veterinarians and common experience dispute this. A wounded animal seems to suffer less pain in the presence of its owner, less when treated at home or in familiar surroundings and when reassured, less when a rapport is established with the clinician, less when stroked, and so on. "Cultural" differences appear here as well. Dogs accustomed to rough treatment and minor injury (like athletes) show far less pain behavior than highly pampered lap dogs—even members of the same breed, poodles providing a notable example. In addition, various breeds of dogs or other animals selected for certain purposes appear to tolerate pain better than others selected for other purposes. Thus, pit bulls, bred for fighting, seem to tolerate pain better than lap dogs. Furthermore, it is widely known that dogs learn to utilize pain behavior to manipulate people; Fox and others have reported feigned injury by animals that is clearly designed to elicit better treatment.

I myself experienced this vividly in a Great Dane I had when living in New York. After a day of romping in the park, she developed a severe limp, which my wife and I proceeded to overtreat with massage, heating pad, treats, and a great deal of attention. Predictably, I now realize, she continued to limp until, ten days later, we took her to a major veterinary hospital, where she was diagnosed as having degenerative cartilage disease that would inevitably cripple her permanently and that required immediate surgical intervention. I decided to take her to the park for what could well be her last run with her friends. We slowly made our way down the hill to Riverside Park, she limping bravely and pathetically at my side. We finally arrived at the park. The dog spotted her playmates and began to wag her tail. Choking down my emotion and steeling myself to the inevitable pathetic scene, I slipped off her leash and—to my utter amazement—watched her take off like the proverbial "bat out of hell" to join her peer group. That was the end of the limp forever, with one notable exception. Two years later we were in the Canadian North Woods, and, spotting a rabbit, the dog took off, heedless of my demands that she come and heel. Twenty minutes later, she bounded back to confront her enraged master. As I roared "Bad dog!" she suddenly began to limp pathetically, desisting as soon as I convulsed with laughter. Melzack and Scott have provided another interesting example of "social" influence on animal pain. They showed that puppies raised in total social isolation did not react to painful stimuli like burns and pinpricks as if they felt pain.

All this raises an important, often neglected point about animal pain. As with humans, one should not forget about individual differences; what hurts one person significantly may seem irrelevant to another, even one closely related. (This is equally true, of course, of what gives pleasure to humans or animals.) Hereditary and environmental factors are both operative here; even "macho" dogs like pit bulls can be rendered very sensitive to pain if pampered. Thus, if one wishes to be able to recognize pain in animals, or humans for that matter, one can try to develop general criteria that apply to the type of creature in question. But one must also know the individual animal (or human). One needs to know some people quite well to become aware that extreme quiet, rather than voluble outcry, is a sign of pain in that person. (In the same way, excessive cheerfulness can be a sign of depression in certain people.) All of which leads to an inevitable result: namely, that to be morally responsive to pain in animals, one must ideally know animals in their individuality.

The practical problems involved in doing this in research colonies or feedlots are obviously monumental. In fact, I believe that these practical barriers are a greater obstacle to recognizing pain in animals than the epistemological ones posited by the common sense of science. Farmers or caretakers (uninfected with scientific ideology) who deal with small groups of animals have no problem identifying pain in their animals. But one can conjecture that the large numbers of animals dealt with today in science, animals identified by number not name, have contributed to the hold of the ideology of science. The animals become as indistinguishable as grains of sand, which in turn weakens both our sensitivity to signs of pain and our moral response. This is what happened in the concentration camps; shaved, starved prisoners, identically dressed, lacked individuality in the eyes of their captors and were thus more easily perceived as part of an endless flow of clones, about which one need not feel moral concern.

INTEREST IN SURVIVAL AND FREEDOM

In any case, pain and pleasure have still not given us a complete account of moral candidacy, because, as we have seen, there are aspects of our treatment of people that we consider immoral even if we are not causing pain. And this would similarly be true of animals. It would seem to me paradigmatically immoral to kill a person for no reason, even if it were done painlessly, and even if we had reason to believe that the remainder of the person's life would bring him more suffering than pleasure. (Most of us probably will have more suffering in our lives than pleasure.) By the same token, it seems to be wrong to do this to an animal. We shall discuss this in more detail later. It is true that we do regularly kill animals to forestall their suffering, but we are usually thinking of great suffering, as in the case of a severely injured animal, or of sacrificing a few for the sake of the majority, as in the case of a starving deer population. And in any case, it is not at all clear that such practices are moral, on examination. After all, if our criterion for moral concern is amount of suffering, yet we consider it immoral to kill people painlessly to forestall future suffering, it is difficult to see why we allow it for animals, since we have not given a *morally relevant difference* between people and animals. (On the other hand, some people have argued that we ought to euthanize humans who are suffering uncontrollable pain—and justify this claim by appealing to what we do with animals.)

It would also seem to be clearly wrong for us to take an animal that was by nature free-roaming, say a gazelle or tiger or, more dramatically, an eagle, and condition it to prefer living in a tiny cage and to abhor or fear open space. Even though we were producing no pain in the animal, and possibly even conditioning it to feel a good deal of pleasure at being in its cage, we would consider such an action to be monstrous for moral reasons having nothing to do with pleasure and pain, namely, violating the animal's nature and dignity. This same intuition may explain the repugnance we feel at watching bears ride bicycles, even when we are assured that they have not been trained using negative reinforcement and are, in fact, well-fed and well-cared for. The concept of an animal's nature is crucial here, and we shall shortly discuss it in detail.

MORAL CONCERN AND CREATURES WITH INTERESTS

The moral of the story so far is that neither rationality nor ability to experience pain and pleasure nor even both taken together gives us an adequate account of what makes a being an object of moral concern. Certainly the presence of rationality and the ability to suffer are relevant for entrance into the moral arena, but they do not seem to give us the whole story. In order to arrive at what is missing, let us engage in what philosophers and scientists call *thought experiments,* imaginative exercises designed to help us understand our concepts better. We can certainly imagine a nonrational being falling within the scope of moral concern; indeed, we have already discussed the case of infants, children, the insane, the comatose, the senescent, etc. But even more interestingly, we can imagine something happening to a whole group of people, say some strange mutation that rendered them incapable of suffering and of feeling pleasure and pain. We certainly would not feel that it would be moral to do whatever we wished to such people. It would certainly be immoral to starve such a person, even if he didn't suffer while we were doing it.

One more thought experiment will help supply the missing piece to our puzzle. Let us imagine a totally powerful, indeed, omnipotent being who is totally self-contained and has no needs, desires, goals, interests, etc., that depend on anyone else or can be at all affected by anyone else. (Some accounts of the Judeo-Christian God fit this description.) Now let us ask ourselves if this being would enter into our scope of moral concern. I would argue that it would not, since anything we did or did not do would be totally irrelevant to it. This in turn leads me to argue that what makes something fall within the scope of moral concern of a being capable of moral action is the presence of needs, desires, goals, aims, wants, or, more generally, interests, which that being has and which the being capable of moral action can help, ignore, or hinder. Thus rationality and the ability to suffer are not *in themselves* what make the creatures who have them fall within the scope of moral concern—it is rather the fact that rationality and the feeling of pleasure and pain are interests for those beings that can be helped or hindered by those of us who act. They are *examples* of interests. I am thus suggesting that there could be and indeed are other interests that make something worthy of moral concern besides reason and the ability to suffer. In our previous discussion, it seems that freedom, for example, is such an interest. And going back to our thought experiments, a perfect rational being would not be an object of moral concern, because what we did or did not do would make no difference to it.

INTERESTS, LANGUAGE, AND NATURAL SIGNS

But what exactly is an interest? And what things can be said to have interests? Quite clearly, as in the case of our uses for all moral concepts, our exemplars derive from human beings. And we can have little reason to doubt that other human beings have desires, aspirations, wants, goals, needs, and intentions, objectives that they strive to achieve in order to survive, to avoid suffering, to increase pleasure, and to actualize their nature. This is certainly the paradigm case of interests. First of all, we impute something like our own mental lives and experiences to others. More important, as we acquire language and linguistic abilities, we become increasingly aware of the needs and goals of others. In point of fact, it is through language that we impart to others an awareness of our needs, desires, goals, and intentions and discover that they can impede, ignore, or nurture them, and this in turn spurs our sensitivity to them and to their linguistic expressions of needs. This, it seems to me, contrary to the Kantian argument, is the link between the possession of language and counting as an object of moral concern. It is not that linguistic ability is constitutive of rationality, which in turn is the chief criterion for entrance into the moral arena. Rationality is, after all, one interest among many. It is rather that through language we become aware of the needs, wants, aspirations, goals, and intentions of others, often with unambiguous clarity. Hence Descartes's exaggerated claim that language is the only evidence of the presence of a mental life at all, as given in a letter to Henry More:

Language is the one certain indication of latent cogitation in a body, and all men use it, . . . whereas on the other hand not a single brute speaks, and consequently this we may take for the true difference between man and beast. (Quoted in Rosenfield, p. 16.)

Now certainly no one can deny the importance of language as a vehicle for communicating needs, goals, desires, etc. But it is equally important to realize that language is not the only source of such information—even among human beings. In fact, our earliest and in many ways most eloquent communication of needs occurs between infant and mother, long before the baby has even begun to actualize its linguistic potential. And throughout our lives, some of the subtlest communication among human beings, some of the clearest expression of needs and desires, occurs nonlinguistically, through what have traditionally been called *natural signs*. Certainly the best clues to another's emotional and psychic pain, and indeed physical pain, comes about in spite of the breakdown or failure of language. As poets and lovers have always been aware, language breaks down at the most emotionally critical junctures, and communication is best achieved by a glance, a touch, an expression, or even, as Merleau-Ponty has shown, by silence.

When this is called to our attention, none of us would wish to deny it. Yet when the argument is extended to other creatures, across species, it is resisted as "anthropomorphism." But this is not cogent. If I can deny that the whimper and limp of a dog are signs that the animal is in pain, why can I not deny that your telling me that you are in pain is a good sign that you are? If it is anthropomorphic to read the natural sign as pain, why is it not, to coin a phrase, ego-morphic to assume that what you feel is similar to what I feel? Indeed, although veracity is a presupposition of discourse, as Thomas Reid pointed out, and we should always assume that a person is telling the truth unless we have reason to believe otherwise, people do frequently lie, and linguistic communication is always suspect in this regard. Animals, on the other hand, *typically* do not, though dogs, as we saw, for example, have been known to feign a limp for sympathy or to avoid punishment, and certain mother birds, killdeers, will feign a broken wing to lead predators away from their nest. Recent research has shown that primates, too, will engage in deliberate deception.

The point of all this is clear. We allow linguistic or conventional signs to serve as evidence of human need and interest. We allow natural signs to serve as evidence of human need and interest. Why, then, are we skeptical that natural signs can serve as evidence of animal need and interest? Surely the more we study animals and their behavior, the more sensitive we are to signs of their needs. Perhaps one might argue that natural signs among human beings can always be checked against linguistic vehicles of communication, which are somehow a higher order of things; for example, if your expression indicates to me that you are depressed, I can always ask you, "Are you depressed?" But such an argument is essentially ill-grounded for it rests upon a dogma as old as human thought itself, to which we alluded earlier, the dogma that there is some mysterious, ultimate, metaphysical schism or gulf between natural and conventional signs or vehicles of communication.

For as long as philosophers have thought about humans and about communication, they have attempted to separate humans from the rest of nature by the assertion that linguistic or conventional signs are somehow unbridgeably set apart from the signs that are to be found in nature: clouds signifying rain, smoke signifying fire, the cry of an animal signifying pain. In fact, as I indicated, it was an examination of this alleged dualism that led me to an interest in the moral status of animals. For try as I might, I could find no clear-cut line between linguistic or conventional signs and the natural signs that fill the natural and animal world. In my book, *Natural and Conventional Meaning: An Examination of the Distinction,* I tried to show that the perennial attempt to draw such a line is ungrounded and doubtless stems from an attempt to hold humans apart from nature in a nontheological way.

Be that as it may, few of us, upon reflection, are prepared to deny that we can recognize, at least in the case of the higher animals, the presence of needs, wants, desires, goals, and even perhaps intentions, which qualify them for admittance into the moral arena. And undoubtedly, as philosophers like Singer and Bentham suggest, the most compelling and undeniable signs that inform us of these characteristics in animals are those of pain and suffering. We are prepared to assert that the hungry animal has a want and need for food because in the absence of food it exhibits signs of discomfort, with which we can empathize and identify. But it would be a mistake, though a tempting one, as we indicated earlier, to identify needs and interests solely with pleasure and pain, and thus to restrict the scope of moral concern to the scope of pleasure and pain.

LIFE AND AWARENESS AS THE SOURCE OF INTERESTS: THE *TELOS* OF LIVING THINGS

Pleasure and pain are, in the final analysis, tools: tools by which a living thing capable of experiencing them can ensure its survival and the fulfillment of its needs. But it is the interests that it has in virtue of its being a living being, and our ability to nurture or impede fulfillment of these interests, not the pleasure and pain, that make it enter the moral arena. In fact, seeking of pleasure and avoidance of pain are themselves interests! We can easily imagine human beings evolving to a point where they do not feel pleasure and pain, or perhaps some humans being affected by a strange malady that renders it impossible to feel pleasure and pain. Under these circumstances, these humans would still have interests and needs and would still be objects of moral concern, even if they no longer experienced pain and pleasure. And it is this that broadens the scope of moral concern beyond pleasure and pain to the essential characteristics of conscious life itself. This is far from clear and far from obvious, and it is to the defense of this claim we must now turn.

Let us consider three categories of things, a rock, a machine, and an animal. For the sake of simplicity, let us look to a living thing—say, a spider—whose pleasure and pain many people feel is at least highly questionable for us to discuss. Clearly, in the case of the rock, it is senseless to speak of any real intrinsic unity to its being, or any needs. If the rock is split or eroded, it remains a rock. If it is ground into sand, it is perhaps no longer a rock, but there is nothing to tell us that it has jumped a metaphysical barrier and become a totally different sort of thing, nor would we say that something undesirable has happened to the rock. There is nothing about a rock that resists the change to sand—the change is from dead matter in one form to dead matter in another form.

In contrast, consider the spider. It has an intrinsic nature connected with being a spider, one that requires that it be alive. When it ceases to be alive, it is like the rock, and there is little difference between a crushed dead spider and a dried-up dead spider. The change from living to dead is far more profound than the change from rock to sand, and it is sensible to call it undesirable from the point of view of the spider. But when the spider is alive, it has what Aristotle called a *telos,* a nature, a function, a set of activities intrinsic to it, evolutionarily determined and genetically imprinted, that constitute its "living spiderness." Furthermore, its life consists precisely in a struggle to perform these functions, to actualize this nature, to fulfill these needs, to maintain this life, what Hobbes and Spinoza referred to as the *conatus* or drive to preserve its integrity and unity. This is not of course to suggest that the spider or any animal need be conscious of its nature and of all of these needs, any more than a man need be conscious of his need for oxygen or calcium. It surely makes sense to speak of nonconscious needs. (Even wants and intentions perhaps need not necessarily be conscious—many analytical psychologists speak of unconscious wants and intentions, though whether this is sensible or not is the subject of much philosophical debate.) It is enough that we, as moral agents, can sensibly assert that the spider has interests, which are conditions without which the creature, first of all, cannot live or, second of all, cannot live its life as a spider, cannot fulfill its *telos.* And thirdly, and most important, as we shall shortly discuss, it is necessary that we can say sensibly of the animal that it is *aware* of its struggle to live its life, that the fulfilling or thwarting of its needs *matter* to it. (Once again, we must stress that a man may not be conscious of his need for oxygen, but thwarting that need certainly *matters* to him. This sort of talk is senseless *vis-à-vis* a rock.) Further we are aware that it is in our power to nurture or impede these needs and even to destroy the entire nexus of needs and activities that constitute its life. And once this is recognized, it is difficult to see why the entire machinery of moral concern is not relevant here, for it is the awareness of interest in living (human) beings that we have argued is constitutive of morality in the first place. We may of course decide that the interests of the spider are insignificant compared with our desire for a spider-free living room, but the key point is that such a decision logically must be considered a moral decision, quite unlike sweeping up a pebble one finds in the living room. (We are, of course, not here considering the actual details of the moral decision, simply pointing out that as a living creature with interests, the spider enters the arena of moral concern.)

Contrast this with a machine. Someone might argue, cleverly, that machines, too, have a *telos* or functional nature and, correlatively, have needs. The *telos* of a thermostat is to regulate the temperature in a room;

the *telos* of a car is to run. Connected with this *telos* are needs; the car needs oil, gas, antifreeze, air in its tires, and so forth. Must we assert, then, that cars fall within the scope of moral concern? If so, the entire theory must collapse under its own weight, for it violates our basic moral intuitions to consider a car in itself an object of moral concern.

There is, happily, a difference between an animal and a machine, between spider and car. The *telos* of the spider is its own, imposed upon it by nature, encoded in its genetic blueprint, and protected by a thousand activities that evidence a struggle to actualize that *telos* and preserve its life. The *telos* of the car is extrinsic to it, imposed by the mind and hand of man. The car is a tool of man, invented and built by man to be used by man, to be, as Heidegger says, "ready-at-hand." There is no more intrinsic unity in the car than there is in the glove box or wheel. When removed from the human point of view and use, any part of the car is as much or as little a unity as is the car itself. In itself, there is as much *conatus* in a piece of the fender as there is in the car as a whole, in a real sense more, for the car is held together by our ministrations. Each organ and cell of the spider, while indeed evidencing a function of its own, does so as an organic component of the life of the spider as a whole. When the spider dies, so do its cells. When the car is abandoned, the nuts and bolts endure.

INTEREST AND AWARENESS

But even more important than having an intrinsic versus an extrinsic *telos* is that the needs of the animal fall into that special category of needs we call *interests*. We have thus far tended to be somewhat imprecise in our tendency to use "needs" and "interests" synonymously. There is a major difference between these notions, one that is clear even in ordinary language. As stated earlier, it makes perfect sense to talk of cars as having needs—needs for gas, oil, and so on. But it does not make sense to say that a car has an interest in being gassed or oiled. Similarly, in the case of a lawn, it would not make sense to say that it had an interest in being watered, though it is, of course, perfectly correct to refer to it as needing water.

What is the difference marked by these terms? Very simply, "interest" indicates that the need in question *matters* to the animal. In some sense, the animal must be capable of being aware that the thwarting of the need is a state to be avoided, something undesirable. As suggested earlier, any animal, even man, is not explicitly conscious of all or probably even most of its needs. But what makes these needs interests is our ability to impute some conscious or mental life, however rudimentary, to the animal, wherein, to put it crudely, it seems to care when certain needs are not fulfilled. Few of us humans can consciously articulate all of our needs, but we can certainly know when these needs are thwarted and met. Pain and pleasure are, of course, the obvious ways these facts come to consciousness, but they are not the only ones. Frustration, anxiety, malaise, listlessness, boredom, anger are among the multitude of indicators of unmet needs, needs that become interests in virtue of these states of consciousness. Thus, to say that a living thing has interests is to suggest that it has some sort of conscious awareness, however rudimentary.

What sort of evidence counts for the existence of such a consciousness? Obviously, as we discussed earlier, there is evidence from a variety of sources. First of all, neurophysiological evidence—the presence of a nervous system in an animal—certainly suggests that these structures perform a function similar to that performed in humans. Second, biochemical evidence—we have already discussed the presence of endorphins and enkephalins in earthworms. The presence in an animal of a biochemical mechanism that is similar to a mechanism in man that regulates some conscious state is evidence for something like that state in the animal. Third, behavioral evidence—when an animal yelps or thrashes or shows avoidance behavior in the presence of a stimulus known to be harmful to the animal or unpleasant to men—that is evidence for awareness in the animal. Fourth, the presence of sense organs—finding eyes, organs for hearing, and organs for touch, taste, etc., in an animal—certainly suggests that the animal enjoys some kind of consciousness. Finally, we may cite all of the above in the context of evolutionary theory. Given that evolutionary theory is at the cornerstone of all modern biology and evolutionary theory postulates continuity of all life, it is even more implausible to suggest that a creature that has a nervous system displaying biochemical processes that in us regulate consciousness, or that withdraws from the same noxious stimuli we do or from other dangers, and that has sense organs, does not enjoy a mental life. In fact, evolutionary theory suggests that we need not be so strict as to demand all of the above at all levels in order to project some form of consciousness. Thus, protozoa will approach noxious substances and swim away from them, and some protozoa also possess rudimentary sense organs, such as an eyespot. While it is possible to say that everything that happens to such a creature is simply mechanical, it is perhaps just as plausible to suggest a continuum of consciousness. If a creature has a sense organ, would not evolutionary continuity suggest that the animal senses, not only reacts?

For a long time, as we have just discussed, an emphasis on psychological behaviorism led us to ignore human and animal consciousness and concentrate on behavior. This was supposed to make psychology more "scientific," since it would deal only with observables. The crude view of science upon which this theory is based is no longer tenable—even physics, the master science, deals with entities and processes that are beyond observation. As psychology realizes the sterility of behaviorism, it must return to the proper study of mind in humans and animals, rejecting the bias against talking about consciousness. Happily, this movement has already begun, and increasing numbers of biologists, psychologists, and philosophers are willing to talk about consciousness in animals. (This is discussed at length in my *Unheeded Cry.*) In his excellent book *The Question of Animal Awareness,* for example, ethologist Donald Griffin explores the questions of animal consciousness we have touched upon and projects a future science of cognitive ethology, what he calls a possible "window on the minds of animals." Such a science has obvious implications for our moral awareness of animals and can facilitate the moral gestalt shift we will discuss in the next section.

For the moment, the question of when an animal can be said to have an interest, i.e., to have sufficient awareness that its needs matter to it, cannot be given a precise answer. In each case, the evidence must be looked at in terms of reasonableness. For example, no reasonable person would deny that dogs or monkeys are aware in the sense we are discussing. The presence of pain in an animal obviously would be a sufficient condition for asserting that it has interests, though a creature could have interests without the ability to feel pain, as long as it had some needs that mattered to it. (Pain is, of course, only biologically useful if a creature can be aware of it and bothered by it.) The presence of a nervous system, pain behavior, and endorphins in a creature are useful evidence for the presence of pain. This would take us down, as we saw earlier, at least to insects, worms, and perhaps planaria as animals with interests. There are obviously many cases where we cannot even begin to say whether the animals have interests. But hopefully, these cases will be illuminated by future research, especially research such as Griffin suggests, which is guided by an open mind, and which does not reject the possibility of consciousness in advance at any level of the animal kingdom.

We can thus provide an answer to the question often asked of theorists who argue for animal rights: "What of plants? What of bacteria?" The answer is simple. Although plants, bacteria, viruses, and cells in culture are alive and may be said to have needs, there is no reason to believe that they have interests. That is, there is not a shred of evidence that these things have any awareness or consciousness, and consequently, we cannot say that the fulfillment and thwarting of these needs "matters" to them anymore than getting oil matters to a car. There has of course been a good deal of lurid popular misinformation concerning the ability of plants to feel pain, or communicate with their owners, or respond to "friendly and hostile vibes." This research is not reproducible and also does not prove what it claims to. (Just because the mechanical effects on the bush of cutting off a rose can be translated into noises that sound like screams does not mean that the rose is screaming.) But if someone were to come up with good evidence for plant awareness—though it is difficult to know what that would be like—it would of course put the matter in quite a different light.

MORAL THEORY AND OUR WORLD VIEW

Thus we have tried to argue that any living thing, insofar as it evidences interests, with or without the ability to suffer, is worthy of being an object of moral concern. Insofar as we can inform ourselves of the interests of a creature, we must at least look at that creature with moral categories. Certainly, from a psychological point of view, those creatures whose interests are most readily understood by us, and that are most like ours, will be most readily granted moral status. On the other hand, we must recall that this is also the case in ordinary human morality—we are powerfully inclined to favor people to whom we are related, or whom we know, or who live in our neighborhood or state or country, or who dress and look as we do. And though rational reflection can provide no defense for these inclinations, we persist in them.

Certainly, visible signs of the ability to suffer, which betoken in the creature conscious negative correlates of thwarted needs, will always most readily seize our imagination and empathy. This leads to an important point: the limits of what we are *psychologically* capable of being concerned about must serve as a curb on the pretensions of any moral theory, else our arguments degenerate into merely scholastic exercises or intellectual oddities, much like McTaggert's proof that there is no such thing as time. Few philosophers have made this point, since our psychological abilities are changeable and variable, and philosophers seek eternal verities. The one exception is perhaps Hume, who stressed the importance of sympathy and fellow-feeling for moral theory. And it is certainly difficult for a person of our era to have much fellow-feeling with a spider. Yet it is precisely because human empathy can change that we must stress the vast range of creatures that must enter within the scope of moral concern, for only in this way can we hope to effect changes in what human psychology can accept as morally palatable.

The much used notion of *gestalt shift,* drawn from gestalt perceptual psychology, is of great relevance here. A gestalt shift is a change in perspective on the same data, as when we suddenly see a person in a new light or realize we have a crush on the girl next door. This can be illustrated with a familiar example. I propose to show you a figure that illustrates one cube perched upon two:

You examine it, and realize what I am showing you:

I then point out to you that it also depicts two cubes perched upon one:

You are puzzled at first, but suddenly make the perceptual or gestalt shift and realize that both perspectives were there, even though you failed to notice them.

A remarkably similar thing happens with considering animals as objects of moral concern, as many people can verify from their own experience or from the experiences of friends. We all know people who have stopped hunting when they suddenly realized that they are *killing a living thing for amusement,* rather than merely innocently participating in a sport. Or people who have stopped hunting when they first hear a wounded animal's exclamation as a *cry.* It is not that they have discovered some new fact, unavailable to them before. Rather, they have suddenly seen the same data in a new way, much as I suddenly realize that the girl next door is incredibly desirable, though I have seen her a thousand times. I can recall one of my own gestalt shifts in this regard. After moving to Colorado, I immensely enjoyed hiking into the mountains and trout fishing. I found the fight that the trout gave me exhilarating and therapeutic, a test of my skill and an outlet for tension, much like negotiating a motocross course on a motorcycle. One day, for no obvious reason, I suddenly realized that the good fight that fifteen-inch rainbow trout was giving me was its struggle to survive, born of pain and fear. My perception shifted; I could no longer fish for fun.

I also recall a conversation I had with a well-known parasitologist, who does much research with protozoa. We were discussing my ideas on the moral status of animals when he turned to me and somewhat hesitatingly, as if he were somehow ashamed, confessed that the more he worked with protozoa, the more he understood their *telos* and their life, the more he could *empathize* with them, and the more loath he was to destroy them. This embarrassed him because, as we shall discuss later, such empathetic understanding is foreign to current scientific practice. But the fact is, he had undergone a gestalt shift and was seeing the protozoa as objects of moral concern, not merely as things in test tubes.

Another interesting example concerns the scientist mentioned earlier who works with planaria or flatworms. As he became more and more aware of their behavior, and studied them in greater detail, he began to see them, in his words, as "little men in worm suits." This example illustrates an important point. Perhaps this sort of anthropomorphism is in some cases psychologically necessary as a stage in developing moral consciousness, for it provides us with a fulcrum for our gestalt shifts. Eventually, one can put the human connection aside and value the creature in its own right, but before this can take place, it is possible that we must move them from the realm of things to the realm of people. It is for this reason that anthropomorphic depictions of animals, as in Disney movies and cartoons, are not necessarily bad as a first step in education. They are pernicious only if a child does not transcend them and appreciate the creature in terms of its *telos.* For eventually, he or she will see through the anthropomorphism and realize that dogs do not understand English and write messages with their paws, and that woodpeckers do not converse with hunters. If he has not learned to value the creature for what it is, he may move in the opposite direction, dismissing any concern for the animal as "childish" since it has, after all, turned out to be totally unlike a person.

This, then, is one task of a moral philosophy, whether it argues for extension of rights to people who are enslaved, or whether it argues for extending the scope of moral concern to other creatures. It serves not to effect changes in behavior overnight; such hopes would be utopian. But it does serve to prepare thinking people for the moral gestalt shift that is a necessary prerequisite to any genuine and enduring change in conduct. No one can be argued into morality, any more than one can be argued into religion. But argument can prepare the ground and plant the seeds that may grow into new moral viewpoints and show anomalies in one's ordinary perspective that ready us for the possibility of a new, revolutionary shift in attitude. Any thoughtful individual must either refute our arguments or else, however hesitatingly, begin at least to think about applying his or her moral discourse to nonhuman beings.

DO ANIMALS HAVE "MORAL RIGHTS"?

Does this mean then, that animals have "moral rights"? As philosophers know from trying to deal with the question of human rights for thousands of years, the notion of rights is extremely complex and extremely elusive, so much so that some philosophers have suggested that we abandon all talk of rights altogether. I do not endorse this extreme position, partly because, as I shall try to show in later discussion, the notion of *legal rights,* which is much easier to define, is intimately connected with the notion of moral rights. And I shall stress very strongly the need for legal rights for animals. But even more importantly, I think that we all do have some fairly clear sense of what we are talking about when we speak of moral rights, as when we claim that humans have a right to be free, a right to worship (or not worship) as they please, a right to express themselves, etc. So we must now come to grips with the question of what our argument has shown about "animal rights" from a moral point of view.

THE RIGHT TO MORAL CONCERN

It is important to make a basic distinction here about what our argument has been designed to do. So far, we have not been asking any *specific moral questions* about animals. Such questions are questions like "Is it wrong to experiment on animals for human benefit?" "Is it wrong to kill animals for food?" We have been addressing an issue far more basic and fundamental than any such specific problems. For it has been our concern to raise the problem of whether it makes any sense to raise moral questions about animals in themselves at all. This question, it will readily be seen, requires an answer before one can sensibly begin to deal with particular problems. If someone denies that animals are objects of moral concern, one cannot debate with him about the moral evaluation of how we treat animals, except, perhaps, by showing him that he has intuitions that belie his general position, for example, a reluctance to torture his own dog. Our primary concern has not been a question *in* moral theorizing; it has been a question *about* moral theorizing and what it applies to, a question in what Kant called the metaphysics of morals, or the basic notions of morality and their range of application.

We have attempted to answer this question by arguing that there are no defensible grounds for excluding animals from moral concern and the treatment of animals from moral discussion if we grant, as do most people, that *people* are legitimate objects of moral concern. We have tried to show that there is no difference between people and animals relevant to excluding animals from moral discussion. In our presentation, we have argued that entrance into the moral arena is determined by something's being alive and having interests in virtue of that life, interests and needs that can be helped or harmed by a being who can act morally. It is important to stress that our argument does not depend so far on any specific moral theory about what specific sorts of things are right or wrong when done to people *or* to animals. We have attempted to show that regardless of what moral theories one holds, regardless of one's principles of right and wrong, one is logically compelled to apply these theories and principles to animals.

Just as Kant's theory attempted to define the scope of moral concern and concluded, as we saw, that only rational beings enter into the realm, so our refutation of Kant and subsequent arguments have tried to show that all living creatures *must* be considered as subjects of moral discourse, whatever moral "language" one happens to speak. Thus, to put our conclusion in the language of "rights," we have established that animals have a very basic right, a right that is on a higher level than any particular right, namely, *the right to be dealt with or considered as moral objects by any person who has moral principles, regardless of what those moral principles may be!* In philosopher's terminology, we may call this a "meta-right." It is another way of saying that animals are objects of moral concern, with a legitimate claim to such concern. As we shall see, it is the only absolute, invariable, and inalienable right.

We have also argued that getting people to recognize this right involves, in many cases, getting them to change their gestalt. It necessitates, for example, ceasing to see one's pets merely as property, or one's experimental animals as tools, analogous to test tubes or laboratory equipment, whose only value is economic. In a real sense, this is the major purpose of this book: getting people to shift their intellectual and emotional gestalts on animals.

THE RIGHT TO LIFE

Can we go any further on the basis of our arguments? I believe we can. If we have been successful in our account of the features that make up an object of moral concern, namely, the possession of life and interests that are associated with that life, we can draw some further conclusions. If being alive is the basis for being a moral object, and if all other interests and needs are predicated upon life, then the most basic, morally relevant aspect of a creature is its life. We may correlatively suggest that any animal, therefore, has a *right to life*. This is not necessarily to suggest, as philosophers put it, that this right to life is *absolute*. An absolute right would be one that would always be wrong to violate, regardless of the situation. Many moral theories suggest that rights are not absolute, that is, they can be violated on occasion for morally relevant reasons. For example, most of us feel (and our Constitution and Declaration of Independence officially assert) that humans have a right to freedom. But few of us feel that this is absolute. Few of us feel the right to freedom means that we ought to be morally allowed to drive on any side of the road that we choose, or spit in someone's face. Thus we feel that the right to freedom is limited by such moral considerations as the general welfare, other people's right to freedom, etc. In fact, one of the key problems in political theory and practice is balancing these competing moral factors.

When we look at moral theory and practice, as applied to humans, we find that the right to life is considered most basic. Typically, it is not considered absolute. Most of us (and most moral theories) recognize some situations in which it is not wrong to take a human life: in war, to stop a homicidal maniac or a terrorist, in self-defense. Indeed, in such cases, we often feel that it is wrong *not* to take the life. Clearly, the right to life is considered violable only for the gravest of reasons. Even those of us who deny that the right to life is absolute would not be prepared to say that it is morally defensible to take a human life because we do not like the person's body contours, or because it would make many people happy, or enrich the public coffers. On the other hand, some people have argued that the human right to life is absolute and that it is always wrong to take a life for any reason. Some Christians and some pacifists have historically taken this tack.

What of animals' right to life? The point seems clear. If one takes the position that human right to life is absolute, then one must show a morally relevant difference between human and animal life that justifies denying that an animal's right to life is absolute. Interestingly enough, this point has often been historically recognized, for many people who have argued that humans have an absolute right to life have extended this claim to animals as well. Among such groups were certain of the Pythagoreans in Greece, the Jainists in India, and certain Tibetan Buddhists. (A colleague of mine, who is an expert in Indian culture, informs me that on one occasion an American AID expert was completely devastated by the unwillingness of an Indian Buddhist community to drain a swamp because of the resulting death for millions of mosquitos!) On the other hand, if one takes the position that the right to life is not absolute in the case of humans, but that strong moral reasons must be given in defense of any violation of that right, one must hold a similar position *vis-à-vis* animals. I personally do not take the right to life to be absolute but require careful dialectical analysis and justification whenever it is abrogated. Thus, for example, we might argue that killing a terrorist who is holding hostages with a bomb is justifiable because failure to kill him would result in extensive loss of innocent life. Similarly, it seems that our argument thus far forces us to that point with regard to animals. Thus the traditional vegetarian argument presents itself quite powerfully, namely, that humans can live and live well without taking animal life; therefore the taking of animal life for food is unnecessary and correlatively unjustifiable, and our mere gustatory predilection for meat does not serve as sufficient grounds for violating the basic right to life. If one wishes to refute that argument, one need supply strong morally relevant grounds that outweigh the presumptive right.

To say for example, as some have argued, that since oftentimes an animal would have had no life at all were it not for us (as, for example, in the case of dogs or cows, because we have bred them), we can kill these creatures as we see fit is not morally relevant. By parity of reasoning, parents could always take the life of children! Or suppose I discover a woman who is about to have an abortion. I pay her a large sum of money to bear the child and turn it over to me. I then raise the child, house it, feed it, educate it, cap its teeth, give it tennis lessons. When it turns sixteen, I decide that I am going to cook it and eat it, or use it to study the effects of asbestos inhalation on the lungs. After all, without me it would have no life at all. Obviously, this is a silly position when applied to people or to animals.

On the other hand, many thoughtful, compassionate philosophers concerned about the treatment of animals do feel that there is a morally relevant difference between humans and animals that militates against ascribing the right to life to most animals. This difference grows out of the idea that since animals (unlike humans) have no concept of life or death, termination of an animal's life (if done without causing pain or fear) does not matter to the animal. An animal can be concerned about being hurt, confined, deprived of food or water, etc., but lacks the ability to be concerned about dying or living. To the claim that animals seem to stuggle mightily to survive, such a philosopher would respond by affirming that what matters to the animal is to eat or drink or escape the traps, all of which are indeed essential to continuing its life, but that the animal aims at alleviating pain or hunger or thirst, not at life or avoidance of death, for it lacks such notions. In short, while an animal's actions may ultimately be aimed at survival, it does not understand this, and thus survival in and of itself does not matter to it. A person who takes such a position is still likely to oppose meat-eating, not on right-to-life grounds, but on the grounds that current confinement animal agriculture produces great amounts of animal suffering.

On the other side, one can argue that even if an animal does not understand the notions of life and death, killing it is still morally problematic, for by killing it one closes the door on its current and future positive experiences. This is certainly buttressed by ordinary intuitions, which find euthanasia of suffering pet animals morally acceptable, but which are not comfortable with euthanasia of healthy pet animals for frivolous reasons, even if painless. (We shall discuss euthanasia of pets in detail later.)

I find myself unable to directly respond to the argument about animals having no concept of death. If, indeed, most animals do not understand the concept of death, that would seem *prima facie* to be a morally relevant difference between humans and animals regarding their right to life. (Empirical study is certainly relevant to this claim, for example, the reports of elephant behavior pertaining to death which suggest that elephants may have some notion of death.) On the other hand, I do not think that it allows us to conclude that killing animals is not morally problematic. After all, many marginal humans and small children have no concept of death either, and we would not accept painless killing of them. Also, since we cannot be sure whether or not life and death in themselves matter to animals, perhaps we should give them the benefit of the doubt, and not be cavalier about animal life, even when the life is taken "painlessly." It does appear, however, that killing an animal is not the worst thing one can do to it; keeping an animal alive under conditions which violate its *telos* in significant ways appears to me far more problematic. And certainly from the political point of view of social change, it is far more important that we focus on the harm and suffering we perpetrate on animals while they are alive and aware than on painless killing. In any case, relatively little killing of animals is truly painless; most killing involves stress, pain, and fear.

THE VIOLATION OF RIGHTS

How does one decide whether one has given a good, morally relevant reason for violating a right? This is indeed a profound and difficult problem but one that is, in the final analysis, no more problematic for animal rights than for human rights! Upon a moment's reflection, we realize that we all engage in this sort of moral weighing and deliberating, without being aware of it, as a regular part of life. For example, parents feel that children have a right to express themselves, but must constantly limit that right for a variety of reasons. Admitting that animals have rights would simply extend that dialectical activity into an area from which it has been withheld, but no fundamental changes in our conceptual apparatus would be required.

Consider, for example, taking seriously the animal's right to life. This would not mean that one could not justifiably shoot a rat about to bite one's child. But perhaps it would mean that it is wrong to poison the rabbits eating one's garden lettuce when one can trap them without harm and deposit them elsewhere (conceivably, in someone else's garden!). It would certainly mean reconsidering the moral acceptability of shooting animals solely for fun, as is done in pigeon shoots around the country. The key point is that the moral reasoning involved in making such a decision utilizes exactly the same weighing of principles and consequences that our moral deliberation about human rights does. Many people who have already experienced a gestalt shift on animals do precisely this sort of weighing as a matter of course. One of my colleagues, for example, who does organic gardening, tells me that she will kill insects, but only when they pose a danger to the ecosystem. As a result, she has killed only six grasshoppers during one growing season that was literally infested with them. Incidentally, she enjoys as good a crop yield as do people who make massive use of pesticides, without the expense or the danger. This illustrates that adopting the moral point of view toward animals does not necessarily entail making great sacrifices—sometimes the moral gestalt shift and rational self-interest go hand in hand, as we shall see later in discussing research. As another similar example, we may cite the use of nonlethal insect control as against poisoning. One of these methods involves releasing sterile male insects into the population, who then compete with fertile males for the favors of the female. This is demonstrably effective: it cuts down on insect birthrate, it eliminates the vast dangers that insecticides pose to the ecosystem and to human life, and it respects the animal's right to life. As humans have learned to their detriment, many if not most animal problems are not solved by wholesale extermination, for we cannot project the ecological consequences of such monumental action. (We all learn as children that killing spiders causes us more harm than good, since spiders keep down the number of flies and mosquitos.)

Other relevant examples of adopting the moral gestalt are easily found. Many people will chase a stinging insect, such as a bee or wasp, out of the house rather than kill it. In this case, the person clearly sees the animal's right to life as trumping their own danger of being stung. On the other hand, such an act would scarcely be obligatory for a person who is violently allergic to bee stings. Or again, seeing animals as moral objects rather than merely as valueless pests does not mean that one lets the coyote eat the sheep indiscriminately. It does, however, mean one seeks some method of discouraging the coyote short of explosive traps or poisons. One of my colleagues, Dr. Phil Lehner, has had some success using large Komondor dogs to guard sheep flocks.

The point is now hopefully clear. Respecting an animal's rights does not mean subordinating one's own interests to those of animals, any more than respecting human rights means letting other people take advantage of one. It does mean looking for ways of resolving conflicts of interests that consider the animal's interests, especially the interests essential to its nature. Sometimes it may perhaps mean subordinating or sacrificing some of one's own interests, if reflective analysis tells one that they do not outweigh the interests of the animal, as, again, many people feel to be the case in the instance of meat eating. In such cases, extramoral incentives are often necessary to buttress the moral gestalt shift, as, for example, reflection on the price of meat, or on the dangers of cholesterol, or on the ecological consequences of confinement agriculture.

ANIMALS AS ENDS IN THEMSELVES

The general point we have been trying to make can be put in terms of notions that arose in our discussion of Kant's ethics. It will be recalled that Kant argued that only rational beings are "ends in themselves"; that is, only rational beings, and therefore human beings, have intrinsic value or ultimate worth. This meant for Kant that we must always treat human beings as "ends in themselves," not merely as means. As we saw, that meant we should value human beings simply for their function as rational beings and respect that function for its own sake, independently of their usefulness for us. We should never treat a person solely as a means or instrument to some end we happen to have. That is not, of course, to suggest that according to Kant we can't ever think of a person as a means. Obviously, when I go to the dentist, I see him primarily as a means to alleviate my pain. Kant's point is that I must never treat him *solely* as a means but must always realize that, as a rational being, his end (or function) is of value independently of what instrumental value he happens to have for me on that occasion. I should thus do nothing that will infringe on the dignity and worth he has simply by being rational. All this, of course, followed from the fact that, for Kant, rationality and intelligence were the only criteria for admittance into the sphere of moral concern.

We have been arguing that it is not rationality that makes something an object of moral concern but rather conscious life itself, and the interests and needs that are associated with life. As such, if we wish to use Kantian terminology, we must say that *any living thing with interests is an end in itself,* worthy of moral consideration merely in virtue of its being alive. That in turn means that even if we use another living creature as a means, it must never be *merely* as a means, but we should always keep in mind a respect for its end, that is, its life, and the interests and needs associated with that life which matter to it. Just as we use the dentist as a means to some end provided we don't consider him only as a means; just as we may have sexual relations to alleviate our biological needs as long as we do not treat the other person simply as an outlet; so if we use animals as means, we must never forget that they are also intrinsically valuable, and that they and their ends (life and its interests) are objects of moral concern that must always be kept in mind. For something to be and end in itself, then, what we do to it must matter to it, whether or not it is rational.

A perfect example of this perspective is provided by the Old Testament. It will be recalled that the Bible was written primarily for an agrarian culture, for people who did use animals for such purposes as plowing. Clearly, the Bible recognizes that animals are used as means. But the Bible also recognizes that they are ends in themselves, with value and function of their own, independent of the uses to which we put them. It is for this reason that in the Sabbath regulations promulgated in the Ten Commandments it is required that animals be granted a day of rest along with humans. Correlatively, the Bible forbids "plowing with an ox and an ass together" (Deut. 22: 10–11). According to the rabbinical tradition, this prohibition stems from the hardship that an ass would suffer by being compelled to keep up with an ox, which is of course far more powerful. Similarly, one finds the prohibition against "muzzling an ox when it treads out the grain" (Deut. 25:4–5), and even an environmental prohibition against destroying trees when besieging a city (Deut. 20: 19–20). These ancient regulations, virtually forgotten, bespeak an eloquent awareness of the status of animals as ends in themselves. How ironic, indeed, in the face of such passages, that the Bible has most often been used as a justification for man's using animals and nature as he chooses, in virtue of the "dominion" passage in Genesis. Clearly, "dominion" does not entail or allow abuse, any more than does the dominion a parent enjoys over a child.

SPECIFIC RIGHTS AND ANIMAL NATURE

We can now return to our main question, the rights of animals. We have thus far argued that animals have a right to enter into the scope of moral concern, and to be morally considered by any person who weighs his or her actions morally. We have further discussed the question of a right to life, stemming from the fact that it is life and the interests associated with life that make something an object of moral concern. Now we may proceed further and argue for the identification of more specific rights.

We have tried to show that any living thing with interests is an end in itself and should never be looked at simply as a means. Now, as we have been stressing, any such life has associated with it a set of interests, needs, desires, wants, proclivities, and aversions, and so forth. Indeed, in a real sense, one can see the entire set of needs and wants a creature has as constitutive and definitive of life itself. To live is to function in certain ways, and associated with these functions are needs and interests. With Aristotle, we may speak of a particular *telos* for each sort of living thing, a nature that sets it apart from other things. This nature is defined by the functions and aims (not necessarily conscious aims) of the creature in question, so in a real sense, what a thing is is what it does. (Aristotle puts this in his philosophical terminology by saying that the *formal cause* [essence] of a living thing is its final *cause* [end, what it does].) If the life of an animal has intrinsic value and should be weighed in our moral deliberations, so, too, should its interests, which is to say its nature or *telos*. Indeed, it is the existence of interests that makes something a moral object in the first place. So I am now explicitly suggesting that the essence of our substantive moral obligations to animals is that any animal has a right to the kind of life that its nature dictates. In short, I am arguing that an animal has the right to have the unique interests that characterize it morally considered in our treatment of it. As we shall show later, in a deep sense its *telos* is its life.

As a very simple example to which most people would agree, we might point out that a captive giraffe has a right to a cage in which it can stand straight up. (Assume for the moment that we have a right to keep animals captive at all.) Or a bird surely has a right to fly, and keeping a bird captive in a small cage that prevents this is immoral in much the same way as is not allowing a person to express himself or herself verbally (humans being linguistic beings by their nature).

As we said before, such a position, of course, does not require that a right be absolute. Obviously there are conditions for which the giraffe could morally be kept cramped: for example, if this were required for treatment of an illness. But nonetheless, what we are suggesting is in many ways quite radical, for it has implications for our "use" of animals in research, in agriculture, in teaching, as food, in zoos, and even as pets. We are suggesting that such use must always take cognizance of the animal's nature. Thus it would be immoral to raise a social animal in isolation, to keep an active animal under conditions where it could not exercise, etc. Later we shall discuss some specific problem areas in more detail. But for the moment, it is enough to be aware that our theory commits us to animals having certain rights based on their nature. Taking these rights seriously could be costly in terms of our comfort, convenience, and life style, but this is always the price to be paid for acknowledging rights, be they the rights of blacks, children, women, or animals.

It is worth noting that the notion of *telos* or essence or nature has often historically been used to justify various forms of oppression—"It is the nature of blacks to be servants and slaves"; "It is the nature of women to raise families and keep house"; "It is the nature of Jews to make money." But just because the concept of *telos* may be or has been abused does not make it illegitimate! It is true that people have seen the nature of women as domestic, and thus have seen women as totally unsuited for any other activities. But this was a prejudice, based on tradition and superstitious encrustations rather than upon sound empirical evidence, or even upon sympathetic observation. Maintaining this prejudice required active filtration from one's experience with women of the multitude of evidence militating against it. The notion of *telos* is testable and compatible with modern biology and ought always be open to revision. Clearly, slave owners would *see* only that behavior of black people that fit their prior conception of black "nature," in much the same way that bigots do today. But this is a criticism of those who misuse the concept of "nature," not of the concept itself. I recall working in a warehouse, loading trucks and boxcars, where the employees were essentially dyed-in-the-wool bigots, much given to analyzing the "nature" of various minorities. "All niggers are lazy by nature," I was told. As it happened, one of our most popular co-workers was a black man (the only black man in the warehouse), beloved by all. "What about Joe," I said. "He's black, and he's not lazy." With nary a moment's hesitation, I was informed that that was because he "hung around with us"! This anecdote well illustrates the dangers of talking about "nature," but also illustrates that the dangers are in principle avoidable by rational individuals.

TELOS AND ETHOLOGY

But how does one know, it might be asked, what the nature of an animal is? Is not such a concept, with its Aristotelian roots, an outmoded, mystical, metaphysical category? After all, we don't even know what human nature is—the discussion of that question fills libraries. Indeed, some thinkers have denied that humans even have a nature.

This is not an objection to be lightly dismissed. But it can, I think, be answered. Perhaps the sort of essence or nature that Aristotle envisioned, one that could be neatly expressed in a pat formula, is not readily forthcoming. Clearly, the classic Aristotelian approach cannot be taken literally by anyone who accepts modern biology. Whereas Aristotle sees species as fixed, immutable, eternal, and unchanging, and hence sees their essences as at least in principle fully graspable, we post-Darwinians see a world far more dynamic, with species being mere momentary stages along the ever-changing route taken by developing life. All this may be granted, for it amounts to little more than the realization that biological knowledge does not have the certainty that mathematical knowledge does, and that living things are not numbers. But most of our knowledge is subject to correction and revision; that does not mean that it is not knowledge. On the other hand, biology gives us a powerful incentive to accept the idea of a nature. The genetic code of a given species provides us with a clear, scientific, testable, physicalistic locus for *telos*. And it is clear that this code determines behavioral, psychological, and social aspects of a creature's nature as well as physical ones—this is the message of sociobiology. To understand the nature of an animal in a way that is relevant to ethics is not a great or profound epistemological problem; it involves only sympathetic observations of the animal's life and activities. Those of us raised on farms—family farms, not factory farms—or in other contexts that bring us in close touch with nature come by such knowledge as easily as we breathe, as did the American Indians. Indeed, few cultures have understood animals better or have had more respect for them as ends in themselves than some hunting cultures, for whom the hunted animal is often an object of moral concern (but not always—witness the Indians who ran buffaloes off cliffs), and often even an object of reverence. This illustrates our earlier point that having a moral gestalt on animals must not necessarily entail always refusing to kill them.

Those of us not fortunate enough to have been brought up with an understanding of the natural world can gain this sort of awareness simply through a sympathetic observation of creatures around us: dogs, cats, ants, and even flies and spiders. Far too little natural history is included in our formal educational systems; we are too busy studying the creature's body to know the creatures—as Tennyson said, "we murder to dissect." Those who cannot observe for themselves can read and be enlightened by the marvelous, captivating accounts of Goodall, Eiseley, Lorenz, Tinbergen, Mowat, Köhler, Von Frisch, Fox, Von Uexküll, and myriad others. Animal nature is simpler than human, and though we may despair of knowing human nature, animal nature seems in principle more accessible. In point of fact, as we shall see, despite the notorious difficulties involved in getting clear about human nature, we have, in Western democracy, built a system of legal safeguards to protect the rights that we wish to extrapolate from what concept of human nature we do have—freedom of speech based on the idea that man is a talking, thinking being, freedom of assembly based on the idea that man is a social being, etc.

There are, of course, additional problems that are initially puzzling. What of the domestic dog or cat or the farm animal whose nature has been (and continues to be) molded by human beings? It is easy to raise apparent paradoxes here: Is the "true" nature of the dog to be feral and to kill caribou along with a pack of other dogs? Common sense prevails here and shows us that we have selected artificially over thousands of years against such traits. Can we imagine a ravening pack of chihuahuas savaging a caribou? (Or lest we think that size is the relevant factor in my example, substitute English sheepdogs!) Similarly, we have drastically modified the nature of the domestic bovine as against her wild cousins. But that does not mean that the domestic animals do not themselves have a *telos,* genetically encoded and deserving of moral concern. Again, we need the guidance of those ethologists and biologists who study the behavior of domestic animals. As we shall see, this is especially poignant regarding the pet animal.

As a simple example, consider the sexual urge relative to the domestic dog. Whatever we have done to the dog in the course of our symbiotic development, we have not bred the sex urge out of its nature. On the other hand, our needs militate strongly against allowing the dog to breed freely. We have responded to this by spaying and neutering. Clearly, given the technological capability that we in fact now possess, it would be much less of an infringement upon the animal's nature to sterilize it and allow it the pleasure of copulation. We are still tampering with its reproductive nature, of course, but that at least can be morally justified, in terms of advantage to the dog gained from living under human guardianship, the impossibility of its living among humans if allowed to reproduce freely, the fact that no specific pleasures are aborted, etc.

We may thus conclude that there exists a dual moral imperative that militates in favor of the study of ethology in addition to the study of biology, and its inclusion in science curricula. (Indeed, we shall see later that such study can provide a much needed counterforce to pernicious elements currently dominant in the training of scientists.) For those who recognize animals as objects of moral concern, the study of ethology essentially teaches the proper way to actualize that concern, in keeping with the animals' natures. For those who do not see animals as part of the moral sphere, the study of ethology, especially field work, which of necessity brings a person into close contact with an animal and its needs, can serve to effect the gestalt shift we spoke of earlier. As we saw in the case of my friend the parasitologist, familiarity and understanding can breed concern. Unfortunately, as ethology becomes more "scientific," i.e., quantitative and "dispassionate," the empathetic dimension tends to disappear. It is sometimes rewarding to look at the books of the nineteenth-century writers on natural history who did not hesitate to punctuate their descriptions of animal behavior with original poetry. One can find this even in books on insects; witness the classic Kirby and Spence's *Entomology.* Happily this tradition is kept alive by the ethologists mentioned above. Michael Fox, for example, in one of his textbooks, intersperses his scholarly discussions of wolf-pack behavior with lyrical poems that sing of his sheer joy at the wonders these creatures display.

With such knowledge, such empathetic understanding, with the willingness to see, can come this gestalt shift. It is easy for most of us to step on a spider when it is seen simply as a foreign body on the floor, to be thrown away like tracked-in mud. We do not look, nor listen, nor see. But I recall being ill one day and watching a little spider spin its web and catch its prey. And suddenly it became difficult for me to snuff out that life, terminate those functions, for no good reason. I also recall a funny yet profound incident that occurred when I was a graduate student. One of my fellow graduate students lived in a small, airless, cheerless basement room. The pressure of a demanding doctoral program in philosophy at an Ivy League university was felt by all of us and left its mark on us in different ways. In my friend's case, he had become reclusive, reading and writing furiously, but rarely leaving his little room. One evening I visited him to study together for an examination. As we pored over the texts, I saw that a cockroach had fallen into his teacup, and he was too engrossed to notice. Horrified and disgusted, I yelled at him that there was a roach in his tea, expecting him to pour the whole mess into the sink or toilet. Gently, with infinite patience, he removed the little struggling creature from the teacup, wiped it off on his sleeve, deposited it tenderly on his carpet, and drained the tea. As I reddened and sputtered, he smiled at me and gently said, "They are my friends." In this case, loneliness was the road to empathy.

In the final analysis, we can understand the wants, needs, desires, and interests of other creatures. Perhaps in a deep sense we can understand these better than we can understand the needs of other humans despite language, because there are apparently so few layers of deception in animals. Perhaps we can understand them even better than we can understand our own everchanging needs. Human needs, after all, are socially, culturally, and historically determined and thus subject to far greater variation than those of animals. This empathetic understanding should be nurtured in ourselves and taught to our children, not only for the moral reasons we have discussed, but because of the infinite richness and texture it brings to our own lives and to the world that we see. But in any case, given the argument we have developed, we are morally bound to understand the lives upon whom our actions have profound and considerable effect, for only through such understanding can come a respect for their rights.

Incidentally, the perceptive reader may feel that there is a tension between my denial of a clear-cut line between the natural and the conventional, and my insistence on the concept of *telos* or nature as basic to morality. I do not believe that this is the case. Nothing I have said precludes my using the concept of nature—I have only said that there is no clear-cut line between the natural and the conventional. And in point of fact I believe, as I implied earlier in this section, that what we consider the nature of a given animal (or for that matter, of man) will depend in part on the scientific theories and conceptual schemes (biological, ethological, genetic) current at a certain time and place, which theories involve elements of what is traditionally called conventional.

WHERE DO YOU DRAW THE LINE?

This theoretical account of the moral status of animals and of their rights is open to a number of obvious and serious objections that will doubtless have arisen in the mind of the reader, and that must now be considered. The first objection that invariably materializes in a discussion of animal rights may be termed the "where do you draw the line" problem. "If your claim is correct," goes the argument, "where do you draw the line? Are you suggesting that we not swat flies, that we worry about stepping on cockroaches, that we give up mouthwash because we are killing germs? Must we worry about plants? If you are suggesting that, the argument is absurd. If you are not suggesting that, what criteria do you use to make a division?"

This objection in fact is ambiguous since it really contains two questions. In the first place, the objector is inquiring about whether one can give some grounds for distinguishing what is an object of moral concern from what isn't. In the second place, the objector is asking whether my position entails that one cannot swat flies or kill germs.

With regard to the first question, I believe that the answer is clear. We have argued quite unambiguously that if something is alive and has interests, it falls within the scope of moral concern, i.e., is worthy of moral consideration. Now there may indeed be a problem here, in the sense that we cannot draw a very clear-cut division between the living and the non-living, or between what does and does not have interests, i.e., needs it is in some sense aware of, or the thwarting of which matters to it. But such a problem is relatively trivial. Consider: One cannot draw a clear-cut line between what feels warm and what feels cool. There are certain borderline cases we can always debate about, but we are certainly aware of the extremes. Insofar as we are clearly aware of some things that are alive and have interests, those things fall within the scope of moral concern. In fact, for practical purposes, I would be quite happy to set aside all cases where the slightest question exists and concentrate only on things that everyone clearly judges to be alive and to have interests.

What of the other related question? Am I seriously saying that one ought not swat flies or kill lice? No, I am not suggesting that, unless the reader wishes to hold to the belief that the right to life is absolute. What I am suggesting is that harming anything—even an insect—does involve making a moral decision and does demand moral justifications and the giving of moral reasons. It is not difficult to come up with a moral justification for killing parasitic organisms that make us ill. I would be prepared to argue that harming anything for absolutely no defensible reason is *always* wrong, even crushing an insect. Most of us who swat flies, for example, would be prepared to argue for that on morally relevant grounds. One swats flies because they carry disease, or bite, or something of the sort. By the same token, it is significant to notice our ordinary characterization of sadists and paradigmatically cruel people as "those who pull the wings off flies."

HOW DO WE DEAL WITH COMPETING INTERESTS?

A closely related objection is also invariably forthcoming and goes like this: "Life involves, by its very nature, conflict; conflict of interests, competition for survival, nature red in tooth and claw. How are you going to decide between the interests of two creatures, say a dog and his fleas, or between human interests and an animal's interests? Are you going to stop snakes from eating mice, predators from devouring prey?" Again, this objection is ambiguous. First of all, it is raising the question of how we decide when we encounter competing interests. Second, it is asking whether our theory requires that we morally police all of creation.

The question of competing interests is indeed a profound one, but in point of fact, no more of a logical problem when we broaden the scope of moral concern to include animals than when we are dealing exclusively with people. We do (or implicitly should) face these sorts of questions daily: ought I give charity to cancer research or to an orphanage; ought I deny myself a Twinkie so that a starving child can eat at all? There are familiar patterns of argumentation we employ in such cases: which contribution will do the most good, will the child die anyway, etc.

Doubtless there are additional problems when deciding between competing animal interests. For example, I think that all of us would share the following intuition. In doing research, it would be better to perform an experiment on a living thing that does not feel pain than on one that does. What is the principle behind this intuition? Presumably something like an awareness from our own experience, as well as from commonsense observation, that pain matters to us more than interests not associated with pain, or perhaps this is better put by saying the more painful something is, the more it matters to us. So one could adopt as a general principle that in cases where we must choose between competing animal interests, say between the dog and his fleas or between experimenting on a frog and experimenting on a cat, we choose the alternative that results in minimizing pain, even though both alternatives involve thwarting some interest or taking life. I would not adopt as a universal principle always favoring the "higher" animal—for example, if the choice came down to a quick death for the higher animal versus a slow, lingering death for a lower animal, one should presumably choose the death of the higher animal. This makes us realize that we cannot simply resolve conflicts by adding interests. It might be tempting to say that if we must choose between the lives of two creatures, one of whom has interests a,b,c,d, and the other of whom has interests a,b,c,d, and e, we always favor the latter since, after all, our morally relevant swing point is interests. But this is too simple, for clearly we need to consider not only number of interests, but also quality and intensity of their satisfaction and frustration. Here as elsewhere in ethics, moral problems do not admit of simple accounting solutions.

This latter case, incidentally, indicates that a presumptive right to life can be qualified by circumstances that render the quality of life distinctly undesirable. Hence our willingness to euthanize even the most beloved of animals when we feel their life has become sufficiently unpleasant to exclude positive satisfaction of those functions constitutive of life. Thus the basic right to life may seem in principle to conflict with the demand of the *telos*. But this is not the case, for *real* life *is* functioning in accordance with the *telos*. It is performing those functions and satisfying those interests that in a real sense form the essence of life. Hence our reluctance to keep a creature "alive" on a respirator when it has effectively ceased to have any hope of really actualizing that life. We do not wish to prolong a life without awareness—for then the creature in question has no interests. We also do not wish to prolong a life that is in gross and hideous violation of the creature's *telos,* even if the creature is conscious and not suffering. (Consider the totally paralyzed person who does not want to live, even though he is not in pain.)

Incidentally, this point is an instructive example of how the study of the moral status of animals can illuminate dark areas of human ethics. Most people would consider it monstrous *not to provide* euthanasia for a horribly suffering, terminally ill, or totally dysfunctional dog. On the other hand, many of us who hold that position would also deem it monstrous *to provide* euthanasia for a suffering, terminally ill human, even if the person has requested it. A realization that there is no clear-cut defensible gap between humans and animals from a moral point of view might help us deal with this basic incoherence. It is indeed ironic that we make more subtle distinctions between mere life and quality of life in terms of function in the case of dogs than we do in the case of humans. Many people would euthanize a cat simply because it lost a leg, or a dog simply because it was getting old. In the case of humans, doubtless for reasons provided by the Judeo-Christian tradition, we treat life as if its value were totally independent of function or even of awareness, as if its value endures after the cessation of all function and awareness. In the case of animals, we seem to recognize that life artificially sustained or totally dominated by suffering is not an object of value; we seem loath to accept this point *vis-à-vis* humans. Realization that animals are not separated by ontological chasms from people might well help us to come up with a more rational, less tradition-bound approach to such human problems.

In any case, this discussion reflects back on our earlier discussion of the right to life. We need stress that the upshot of our analysis is this: the right to life must be cashed out in terms of the interests and functions constitutive of that sort of being. We do not respect the right to life of a gazelle by keeping it alive and even conscious by machinery in a laboratory while its life as a gazelle—a running creature—has been essentially and irrevocably terminated. We must be careful to distinguish always (whether dealing with animals or with people) between life as function, satisfaction of interests and *telos,* and protoplasmic existence. A human body on a respirator in an irreversible coma is not a human person since it has no awareness and thus no interests; a canine body on a respirator is not a dog; a human body *totally* consumed by pain is not a human person, a canine body *totally* consumed by pain is not a dog. In the latter cases, the only end or interest that remains is the cessation of pain.

On the basis of our earlier discussion, it would seem that more basic than number of interests, and as important as the quality of their satisfaction, is the degree of awareness of the animal in question. We have argued that it is awareness, or "mattering to the animal," that transforms a need into an interest. In the case of an intestinal parasite, we do not have good evidence that things matter to them, even pain. In the case of the dog, we have much better evidence. So if we are faced with this choice, the answer is clear. This accords with our commonsense intuition that the more complicated the mind of the animal, the more intense its awareness, and the more valuable it is. On the other hand, we must be careful with this principle as well, for it is extremely difficult to apply. We argued earlier that even though humans have more complicated lives than animals, it does not follow that their pain is more intense; in fact, more complex awareness may actually mitigate pain (through hope, self-control, etc.). Furthermore, the principle does not tell us how, if animals have a right to life, to weigh the choice of killing a creature with low awareness against thwarting some interest of a creature with higher awareness: For example, if the flea is mildly debilitating to the dog, why ought we kill it? Is the life of a rabbit worth more or less than the lives of three frogs? Ultimately it appears that these cases must be decided dialectically, on a case-by-case basis.

As far as the problem of human interests competing with animal interests is concerned, the answer is also far from clear. I know that our official, publicly articulated morality would unhesitatingly assert that human interests should predominate. But I'm not at all sure that this is something we really believe; nor am I sure that it is even defensible. All of us who have pets and spend money on pets that could be spent for human welfare have implicitly made the decision that the interests of certain animals, at least, supersede the interests of certain humans. And I believe that many and probably most people, if specifically confronted with having to choose between the life of the family dog and the life of a nomad in Central Asia, would choose the dog. This does not of course entail that such a decision is morally *correct,* but it at least helps to show that we are not all committed to humanity above all else. It seems to me further that there are cases—including the one just mentioned—where it is quite meaningful and cogent to argue that animal interests *ought* to predominate. Consider the following: imagine a newly discovered drug that could possibly check a raging epidemic. Suppose, for esoteric reasons, that it could be tested with equal validity either on members of a species of higher primate or on humans. Testing it on the primates would require the risk of slow, agonizing death for hundreds of primates, whereas it could be adequately tested on only a few humans, who would endure a quicker death. Barring legal constraints, I would submit that it would be more defensible morally to test it on child-murderers awaiting execution, whose right to life has already been preempted by society, than it would be to test it on the innocent primates. Such a claim sounds monstrous, mostly because of the sanctimonious hypocrisy of our official morality. Yet I believe that a strong case can be made in its favor. The strongest case against it, I think, would be an argument from the danger of setting a precedent of using people against their will, not from the greater intrinsic worth and moral value of the individual men in this case. In fact, prisoners often wish to serve as volunteers in experiments in a desire to atone, and are not permitted to do so. At least we could give them the choice. It is ironic that no one ever raises the question of the animal's will or wishes!

In general, without an argument that shows that humans are always of more value than animals, each potential situation of conflict cannot be decided in advance, any more than we can decide in advance the rules governing a "lifeboat situation" concerning humans, where there is only room on the lifeboat for ten people and there are twelve survivors. As another example, it was certainly not clear that the economic interests of Newfoundland seal hunters are to be preferred to the baby seals' right to life; the Newfoundlanders could survive without killing (and we could survive without seal coats), whereas the cost to the seals is significant. Indeed, society has recently determined that the animals' interests outweigh the human, and has banned the hunt.

MUST WE POLICE CREATION?

As to the second part of the objection, must we stop predators from killing prey or is such killing *wrong,* the answer seems to be this: Certainly it is not "wrong" for the predator to kill prey, since animals acting in this way are not ordinarily seen as moral agents, any more than it is "wrong" for an avalanche to kill things in any sense of "wrong" other than the trivial one that it would be a better universe if nothing killed anything. Perhaps the dog who has been taught not to steal food from the table but sneaks over to do so is an object of blame. Perhaps the elephants, porpoises, and the other cases mentioned earlier qualify as cases of animal moral agency. But certainly when an animal kills for food or defense, we have no reason to believe that it has any concept of right or wrong. Is it our duty to stop predators from killing prey? That is more difficult. It is in the animal's nature to kill by predation, it does so to survive; so though it would be a better universe if this were not the case, it is not clearly typically within the scope of our moral duties to correct what has been called natural evil. (On occasion, of course, we do check natural evil, as when we try to prevent impending avalanches in areas frequented by skiers. This raises interesting questions about the moral obligations of governments to citizens, since it is not at all obvious to me that a government that failed to do this would be immoral, as long as the skiers were cognizant of the risk.) On the other hand, it seems plausible to suggest that we have a duty to stop a well-fed house cat from killing a bird, in the same sense that we have a duty not to drive our car over a bird's nest for no reason. (True, the cat may have an interest in killing because killing behavior is natural to it; on the other hand, this doesn't seem to trump the bird's more basic right to life.)

DON'T ANIMALS KILL EACH OTHER?

In this context, it is worth dealing with another related objection to the suggestion that animals have moral status and rights. It is often said that animals kill each other as a routine part of nature and, therefore, why shouldn't we kill animals? In a related argument, meat eaters often respond to vegetarian arguments by pointing out that we have evolved for meat eating. This objection, in addition to being false, ignores the fact that as moral agents, we make moral choices according to principles of right and wrong and need not operate simply by instinct in our eating behavior. To justify meat eating by such an appeal is to ignore totally our moral natures. We can shape our natures according to right and wrong and, in any case, do not require meat either to live or to live well.

THE NONLIVING ENVIRONMENT

Another possible currently popular objection to our arguments is that we have talked only of individual living beings and have made no mention of the inanimate environment as an object of moral concern. To this, I would simply respond by agreeing. I do not believe that nonliving things have rights. If we have duties to the environment, it is because of its instrumental value to living things. In and of itself, the physical environment has no interests and is therefore not a direct object of moral concern.

This is not, of course, to denigrate the importance of environmental issues or to suggest that preservation of tropical rainforests, endangered plant species, wetlands, rivers, wilderness areas, clean air and water, habitat for animals, etc., is not of paramount concern. Rather, I am arguing that one cannot found an environmental ethic on the same basis as we have founded our ethic for sentient creatures, namely by logically extending our consensus social ethic to beings who cannot be excluded from the application of that ethic to them for any morally relevant reason. But inanimate nonsentient entities such as plants or rivers, or abstract entities such as species, are not the sort of things our ethic can logically encompass. To suggest that "rocks have rights" is to trivialize the notion of rights, since what we do to rocks does not matter to them.

Many leading environmental ethicists have attempted to do for nonsentient natural objects and abstract objects the same sort of thing I have tried to do for animals—namely, attempted to elevate their status to direct objects of intrinsic value, ends in themselves, which are morally valuable not only because of their relations and utility to sentient beings, but in and of themselves. To my knowledge, none of these theorists has attempted to claim, as I do for animals, that the locus of such value lies in the fact that what we do to these entities matters to them. No one has argued that we can harm rivers, species, or ecosystems in ways that matter to them. Wherein, then, do these theorists locate the intrinsic value of these entities? This is not at all clear in the writings, but seems to come down to one of the following doubtful moves:

1. Going from the fact that environmental factors are absolutely essential to the well-being or survival of beings that are loci of intrinsic value to the conclusion that environmental factors therefore enjoy a similar or even higher moral status. Such a move is clearly fallacious. Just because I cannot survive without insulin, and I am an object of intrinsic value, it does not follow that insulin is, too. In fact, the insulin is a paradigmatic example of something having instrumental value.

2. Going from the fact that the environment "creates" all sentient creatures to the fact that its welfare is more important than theirs. This is really a variation on (1) and succumbs to the same sort of criticism, namely, that this reasoning represents a genetic fallacy. The cause of something valuable need not itself be valuable and certainly not necessarily more valuable than its effect—its value must be established independently of its result. The Holocaust may have caused the state of Israel; that does not make the Holocaust more valuable than the state of Israel.

3. Confusing aesthetic or instrumental value for sentient creatures, notably humans, with intrinsic value and underestimating aesthetic value as a category. We shall return to this shortly, for I suspect it is the root confusion in those attempting to give nonsentient nature intrinsic value.

4. Substituting rhetoric for logic at crucial points in the discussions and using a poetic rhetoric (descriptions of natural objects in terms such as "grandeur," "majesty," "novelty," "variety") as an unexplained basis for according them "intrinsic value."

5. Going from the metaphor that infringement on natural objects

"matters" to them in the sense that disturbance evokes an adjustment by their self-regulating properties, to the erroneous conclusion that such self-regulation, being analogous to conscious coping in animals, entitles them to direct moral status.

In short, traditional morality and its theory do not offer a viable way to raise the moral status of nonsentient natural objects and abstract objects so that they are direct objects of moral concern on a par with or even higher than sentient creatures. Ordinary morality and moral concern take as their focus the effects of actions on beings who can be helped or harmed, in ways that matter to them, either directly or by implication. If it is immoral to wreck someone's property, it is because it is someone's; if it is immoral to promote the extinction of species, it is because such extinction causes aesthetic or practical harm to humans or to animals or because a species is, in the final analysis, a group of harmable individuals.

There is nothing, of course, to stop environmental ethicists from making a recommendation for a substantial revision of common and traditional morality. But such recommendations are likely to be dismissed or whittled away by a moral version of Occam's razor: Why grant animals rights and acknowledge in animals intrinsic value? Because they are conscious and what we do to them matters to them! Why grant rocks, trees, or species, or ecosystems rights? Because these objects have great aesthetic value, or are essential to us, or are basic for survival. But these are paradigmatic examples of objects with *instrumental* value. A conceptual confusion for a noble purpose is still a conceptual confusion.

There is nothing to be gained by attempting to elevate the moral status of nonsentient natural objects to that of sentient ones. One can develop a rich environmental ethic by locating the value of nonsentient natural objects in their relation to sentient ones. One can argue for the preservation of habitats because their destruction harms animals; one can argue for preserving ecosystems on the grounds of unforseen pernicious consequences resulting from their destruction, a claim for which much empirical evidence exists. One can argue for the preservation of animal species as the sum of a group of individuals who would be harmed by its extinction. One can argue for preserving mountains, snail darters, streams, and cockroaches on aesthetic grounds. Too many philosophers forget the moral power of aesthetic claims and tend to see aesthetic reasons as a weak basis for pre-serving natural objects. Yet the moral imperative not to destroy unique aesthetic objects and even ones that are not unique is an onerous one that is well ingrained into common practice—witness the worldwide establish-ment of national parks, preserves, forests, and wildlife areas.

Rather than attempting to transcend all views of natural objects as instrumental by grafting onto nature a mystical intrinsic value that can be buttressed only by poetic rhetoric, it would be far better to nurture public appreciation of subtle instrumental values, especially aesthetic value. People can learn to appreciate the unique beauty of a desert, or of a fragile ecosystem, or even of a noxious creature like a tick, when they understand the complexity and history therein and can read the story each life form contains.

It is important to note that the attribution of value to nonsentient natural objects arising simply out of their significance (recognized or not) for sentient beings does not denigrate the value of natural objects. Indeed, this attribution does not even imply that the interests or desires of individual sentient beings always override concern for nonsentient ones. Our legal system has, for example, valuable and irreplaceable property laws that forbid owners of aesthetic objects, for example, a collection of Vincent van Gogh paintings, to destroy them at will, say by adding them to one's funeral pyre. To be sure, this restriction on people's right to dispose of their own property arises out of a recognition of the value of these objects to other humans, but this is surely quite sensible. How else would one justify such a restriction? Nor, as we said earlier, need one limit the value of natural objects to their relationship to humans. Philosophically, one could, for example, sensibly (and commonsensically) argue for preservation of acreage from the golf-course developer because failure to do so would mean the destruction of thousands of sentient creatures' habitats—a major infringement of their interests—while building the golf course would fulfill the rarefied and inessential interests of a few.

Thus, in my view, one would accord moral concern to natural objects in a variety of ways, depending on the sort of object being considered. Moral status for individual animals would arise from their sentience. Moral status of species and their protection from humans would arise from the fact that a species is a collection of morally relevant individuals; moral status also would arise from the fact that humans have an aesthetic concern in not letting a unique and irreplaceable aesthetic object (or group of objects) disappear forever from our *Umwelt* (environment), in addition to a prudential concern for the benefits these objects might carry (obscure plants may be a source of cancer-fighting drugs). Concern for wilderness areas, mountains, deserts, and so on would arise from their survival value for sentient animals as well as from their aesthetic value for humans. (Some writers have suggested that this aesthetic value is so great as to be essential to human mental/physical health, a point perfectly compatible with my position.)

Nothing in what I have said as yet tells us how to weigh conflicting interests, whether between humans and other sentient creatures or between human desires and environmental protection. How does one weigh the aesthetic concern of those who oppose blasting away part of a cliff against the pragmatic concern of those who wish to build on a cliffside? But the problem of weighing is equally thorny in traditional ethics—witness lifeboat questions or questions concerning the allocation of scarce medical resources. Nor does the intrinsic-value approach help in adjudicating such issues. How does one weigh the alleged intrinsic value of a cliffside against the interests of the (intrinsic-value-bearing) homebuilders?

Furthermore, the intrinsic-value view can lead to results that are repugnant to common sense and ordinary moral consciousness. Thus, for example, it follows from what has been suggested by one intrinsic value theorist that if a migratory herd of plentiful elk were passing through an area containing an endangered species of moss, it would be not only permissible but obligatory to kill the elk in order to protect the moss because in one case we would lose a species, in another "merely" individuals. In my view, such a case has a less paradoxical solution. Destruction of the moss does not matter to the moss, whereas elk presumably care about being injured or perhaps about living. Therefore, one would give *prima facie* priority to the elk. This might presumably be overridden if, for example, the moss were a substratum from which was extracted an ingredient necessary to stop a raging, lethal epidemic in humans or animals. But such cases— and indeed most cases of conflicting interests—must be decided on the actual occasion. These cases are decided by a careful examination of the facts of the situation. Thus, our suggestion of a basis for environmental ethics does not qualitatively change the situation from that of current ethical deliberation, whereas granting intrinsic value to natural objects would leave us with a "whole new ball game"—and one where we do not know the rules.

Although it is nonsensical to attribute intrinsic value or direct moral value to nonsentient natural objects, they nonetheless must become (and are indeed becoming) central to our social moral deliberations. This centrality derives from our increasing recognition of the far-reaching and sometimes subtle instrumental value these objects have for humans and animals. Knowing that contamination of remote desert areas by pollutants can destroy unique panoplies of natural beauty, or that dumping wastes into the ocean can destroy a potential source of antibiotics, or that building a pipeline can have undreamed-of harmful effects goes a long way toward making us think twice about these activities—a far longer way than endowing them with quasi-mystical rhetorical status subject to (and begging for) positivistic torpedoing.

DON'T WE HAVE ENOUGH PROBLEMS
WITH HUMAN MORALITY?

Finally, we may mention a very common set of pragmatic arguments against animal rights. It might be said that we have more than enough problems with managing moral theory and practice when we consider only humans; to admit animals into the scope of moral concern is to stir up already troubled waters. To this I would respond by saying that this is quite true but morally irrelevant. It is a safe guess that our moral deliberations and decisions would be a good deal simpler if we excluded from the scope of moral concern women, children, and nonwhite people, but this does not make it right to do so. We have hopefully given strong arguments for saying that animals do have rights and ought to be morally considered; it is a *non sequitur* to protest that this is a difficult thing to do.

ISN'T ALL THIS UTOPIAN?

Second of the pragmatic arguments, and in a deep sense most important, is the claim that all our theorizing is utopian. People will not consider animals morally, theory will not change practice, and none of this will make any practical difference. In the first place, this sort of cynicism is unfounded. Moral theory has made incalculable practical differences; witness the teachings of Moses, Jesus, Buddha, Marx, Hitler (who was a moralist, albeit an evil one), Gandhi, and King, to name but a few salient examples. True that theorizing about animal rights will not change things overnight. But it will make people think just a little differently, perhaps change their gestalts, bring these issues to public airing and dialectic, make them ordinary topics of conversation. Plato, in the *Republic,* considers the objection that his ideal state will never come to pass. Quite probably, he replies, but it gives us a measure for evaluating actual states, and for suggesting improvements. The same point can be made with regard to theorizing about animal rights; it provides us with grounds for criticizing current practice, and most important, it provides a wedge for making a very immediate and direct impact on social and individual conduct through legislation and education that have, in turn, direct and practical ramifications on our treatment of animals and our attitudes toward them. It is the connection between morality and law, and the implications that this has for animals that we must now consider, and to which we shall turn in the next chapter. For it is here that we will realize the full implications of "rights" talk and of our argument that animals must be included in such talk. If it is the case that animals ought to enjoy a place within the scope of moral concern, as we have argued, while many of our institutions, practices, and habits are firmly entrenched in their disregard for the rights of animals, then these rights must be safeguarded, publicized, and pressed through the law. Moral rights must be translated into legal rights for, in a deep sense, the two are organically connected.

Later on in this book, we shall examine in great detail with regard to animals used in research how one tries to tie the moral theory we have developed to the demands of our real, socio-cultural situation. We shall see that the theory must indeed serve as an ideal in Plato's sense. But we shall also see that we must be prepared to accept less than the ideal when seeking the intersection between pure theory and the pressures of reality, in order to achieve anything at all.

2

Animal Rights and Legal Rights

HOW ARE LAW AND MORALITY CONNECTED?

What, precisely, is the connection between law and morality? In his classic treatise on legal theory, Professor Wolfgang Friedmann wrote, "There cannot be—and there never has been—a complete separation of law and morality." But this insight is ambiguous. Does it mean that law and morality are what philosophers call *logically inseparable,* such that one cannot understand one without necessarily referring to the other? For example, the concept of parent is logically inseparable from the concept of child—if one is to understand what it is to be a parent, one must make reference to the notion of child. Is it the case, then, that we cannot understand what law and legal rights are without bringing in concepts of morality and moral rights? Or, on the contrary, are the two in principle separable, so that one can fully explicate, analyze, and define the concept of law without bringing in moral concepts? Is the connection between the two simply one of *causal influence,* with laws affecting morality and morality affecting laws, but with no conceptual connection between the two?

Quite obviously, laws often do affect public morality, and public morality determines laws. This is very clear when we think of our laws governing prostitution, pornography, obscenity, drugs, wet T-shirt contests, and so forth. For example, if everyone (or most people) in a given society holds a strong moral position against prostitution, it is quite likely that the laws will reflect that moral position and will also serve to reinforce that position in subsequent generations. Sometimes laws are designed to effect a change in widespread public morality, as was the case with Prohibition laws, or the laws concerning the fifty-five-mile-per-hour speed limit, or the civil rights laws. On the other hand, public morality often forces changes in laws that have ceased either to reflect or influence that public morality—Sunday "blue" laws, those laws which required that all shops be closed on Sunday, are a good case in point. But this sort of connection between law and morality is ultimately *causal,* and it does not tell us whether the two concepts are *logically* inseparable in the sense discussed above.

NATURAL LAW THEORY

There is a very old tradition that asserts that morality and law are logically inseparable, that moral notions and ideals are part and parcel of law, that law in society must ultimately embody and be based on certain absolute, unchanging, and presuppositional notions of right and wrong, else it is not really law. This is called *natural law theory* and goes back to the ancient Greeks—it can be found in Plato, Aristotle, and the Stoics. It is probably most closely associated historically with the Roman Catholic tradition. According to the standard natural law position, certain principles of right and wrong are absolutely true and do not change from place to place or time to time. For the Catholic tradition, of course, these moral principles ultimately find their source in the commands of God, or in the Bible, and much (but not all) of natural law theory in the West has customarily been theologically based. According to natural law theorists, law of any society must embody these moral truths—if it fails to do so, it is *not really law!* Obviously, on this view, law and morality are inseparable. In the view of natural law theorists, laws passed in Nazi Germany are not true laws. Although they are written down in law books, passed by legislatures, adopted by parliaments and so forth, they are not genuine, binding laws because they contradict the basic moral law, and thus people are not morally obligated to obey them (even though they may of course be *forced* to obey them). Such "laws" are not legitimate, and one is morally obligated to disobey them because they fly in the face of the moral law.

NATURAL RIGHTS

Closely connected with the natural law theory is the notion of *natural rights,* the idea that human beings have *by nature* (however that is interpreted, most usually by appeal to God) certain rights that governments cannot legitimately violate, and that political law must respect. Any government that does not respect these rights loses its legitimacy and is not *morally entitled* to obedience, though, of course, it may force obedience on citizens. It will be recalled that this notion of natural rights was one of the key theoretical concepts behind the American Revolution and, later, the French Revolution. It was claimed that the ruling governments had lost any claim to legitimacy, any entitlement to be obeyed, by their failure to respect these fundamental and absolute rights that flowed from the natural law. This sort of view is what underlies conscientious civil disobedience—freedom rides, nuclear facility sit-ins, etc. Though such concepts sound terribly mystical to many of us today, their historical importance cannot be underestimated. This theory provides, of course, the conceptual basis for the American Constitution and is clearly heralded in the Declaration of Independence:

> We hold these truths to be self-evident; that all men are created equal, that they are endowed by their creator with certain inalienable rights, that among these rights are life, liberty, and the pursuit of happiness.

A related statement of natural rights and law can be found in the Virginia Declaration of Rights of 1776:

> All men are *by nature* equally free and independent and have certain *inherent rights,* of which, when they enter into a state of society, they cannot by any compact deprive or divest their posterity [Italics mine].

Obviously, on this view, these rights are logically independent of any social contract. Once again, the French Declaration of the Rights of Man and of Citizens of 1789, adopted by the French Assembly of 1789 and prefixed to the French Constitution of 1791, makes the same point:

> The end of all political associations is the preservation of the *natural and imprescriptible* rights of man; and these rights are liberty, prosperity, security, and resistance of oppression [Italics mine].

And even in the twentieth century, this idea remains very much alive and is implicit in the United Nations 1948 Universal Declaration of Human Rights.

But despite the undisputed historical importance of the theory of natural law and natural rights, there are many obvious problems associated with it. How do we prove that there really are natural rights and that there really is a natural law? How do we know what this law and these rights are? Clearly, in a highly theologically oriented setting, such as obtained in medieval Catholic Europe, these questions do not present fundamental difficulties, for the source of natural law is held to be God, and its content defined through revelation. Even in the passages quoted above, God often provides the ultimate justification for claims about natural rights. But as belief in God and certainty about our knowledge of His Law waned in all areas of life and thought, including political theory, some thinkers began to deny the existence of natural rights and natural law altogether, and to see talk about them as just so much mystical nonsense. These thinkers felt that such ideas simply cloud the real issues in political and legal theory and attempted to abandon all reference to natural rights. Thus Jeremy Bentham, in commenting on the French Declaration of Rights in his *Anarchical Fallacies,* declared resoundingly that "Natural rights is simple nonsense; natural and imprescriptible rights, rhetorical nonsense,—nonsense upon stilts" (p. 501).

THE REJECTION OF NATURAL LAW
AND NATURAL RIGHTS: LEGAL POSITIVISM

The Bentham idea that talk about natural rights and natural law was lofty "nonsense upon stilts" grew into an important movement in legal theory that has dominated British and American legal thinking for well over one hundred years, the position called *legal positivism,* eloquently developed by men like Bentham and John Austin. According to the legal positivists, we can know nothing of natural law or rights; the only laws and rights that exist are those specifically adopted by legislatures and that can be found in statutes. Legal positivism, as we shall see, does not deny the notion that law is causally influenced by moral considerations, as we discussed earlier. In fact, none of the positivists mentioned above denies that the law is and ought to be motivated and assessed by moral criteria. In point of fact, these positivists have been highly articulate utilitarians, arguing that the ultimate *purpose* of the law is the advancement of the general welfare, or the "greatest good or happiness for the greatest number." What positivism does deny is that talk about law and legal rights is logically inseparable from notions of moral law and moral rights. The grounds for positivism are empiricistic—we can clearly discover what the positive law is while the content of moral law is endlessly debatable. The content of positive or actual law is fully and exhaustively specified by the explicit set of rules that are adopted by a community or society according to a certain procedure (vote of an assembly, decree of a king, etc.). Thus, moral rules are clearly distinguishable from legal rules by some test of origin that provides us with, in H. L. A. Hart's term, a "rule of recognition" for the latter, a clear-cut, empirically verifiable test that will tell us whether something is or is not a law simply by looking at how it was adopted. It is correlatively meaningless on this view to speak of rights that antedate their *explicit enunciation* according to the explicit procedures by which legal rules are created.

THE REVIVAL OF NATURAL RIGHTS

This neat separation of law and morality, while still dominant, of late has been challenged by a variety of thinkers seeking to revive the notion of natural rights and natural law, the notion that basic moral principles are the skeleton of all proper law and that these principles do not change even though public attitudes change. Such thinkers are trying to show that what is legal and what is moral are *logically inseparable.* Not surprisingly, some of these theorists have attempted to revive the natural law tradition without appeal to God, so as to avoid charges of mysticism and nonsense. One of the most interesting of these thinkers is Professor Ronald Dworkin, holder of the Chair of Jurisprudence at Oxford, who has brilliantly argued for the unity of law and morality in the series of papers published in book form as *Taking Rights Seriously.* Dworkin's attack on legal positivism has been two-pronged. First of all, contrary to positivist doctrine, he has demonstrated that no rule of recognition, no test of origin, can provide a criterion for demarcating the positive law from moral rules, and thus no clear-cut line can be justifiably drawn between the legal and the moral. Second, Dworkin has attacked the positivist claim that utilitarian moral concerns, considerations of what produces the greatest good or happiness for the greatest number, are the only moral notions relevant to the law. He does this by showing that once it is recognized that moral notions are inseparable from positive law, it becomes clear that among these moral notions falls the extremely important concept of individual rights, which essentially serves as a moral check *against* utilitarian considerations.

Let us see how Dworkin argues for these points. According to Dworkin, any attempt to specify a procedure that will explicitly demarcate the law by demarcating legal rules is doomed to failure. In addition to explicit rules, the reading of almost any case shows us that laws contain *principles,* moral notions that are invoked regularly by judges in resolving cases for which no explicit rules or statutes exist. We all know, of course, that much of the law is made by judges when they interpret statutes and decide their application to hard cases. No statute can possibly cover all possible cases; this is why we need judges and not computers to apply and interpret the law. In deciding hard cases, judges appeal to principles that are not arbitrary commands whimsically chosen by the judges, but are normative moral standards, notions of right and wrong that are consulted in order to apply the law to new cases. A principle, according to Dworkin, is a standard to be observed "because it is a requirement of justice or fairness or some other dimension of morality" (p. 22). These principles were never adopted by legislatures; yet they form implicit parts of our legal system. In fact judges often use such moral principles to overturn certain rules that *were* explicitly adopted by law-making bodies or government agencies. Consider, for example, the use by the Supreme Court of the moral principle that "separate is inherently not equal" in the landmark school desegregation case, *Brown* v. *Board of Education.* Or consider the principle cited by the court in *Riggs* v. *Palmer,* in which the court was compelled to decide whether a man named in his grandfather's will could inherit after he murdered his grandfather. The court appealed to the moral principle that "no one shall be permitted to profit by his own fraud, or to take advantage of his own wrong, or to found any claim upon his own iniquity, or to acquire property by his own crime." In other cases, judges have appealed to the principle that "courts will not permit themselves to be used as instruments of iniquity and injustice." Directly germane to the topic we are discussing is the principle enunciated by the court in the *U.S.* v. *Sisson,* a case dealing with a nonreligious conscientious objector. The judge declared that "when the state through its laws seeks to override reasonable moral commitments, it makes a dangerously uncharacteristic choice. The law grows from the deposits of morality. . . . When the law treats a reasonable, conscientious act as a crime it subverts its own power."

It is precisely these principles that prevent judges from being totally arbitrary and making capricious decisions in unprecedented cases, i.e., in cases not explicitly covered by existing statutes or precedents. Even more dramatically, as we indicated, appeal to principles often serves as grounds for the overthrow of legal rules that have been explicitly adopted, as in the *Brown* v. *Board* school desegregation case. Rights that are granted to individuals on the basis of these principles (for example, the right to conscientious objection to military service on moral grounds) are as much a part of the legal system as are those whose origin results from the usual explicit manner of adoption of legal rules and rights. Once a case is decided using principles, of course, the resolution may then stand as an explicit rule of law, but this does not vitiate the important role of principles in deciding the next hard case. Dworkin's conclusion is compelling and yet quite shocking to those schooled in legal positivism:

It is wrong to suppose . . . that in every legal system there will be some commonly recognized fundamental test for determining which standards count as law and which do not. No such fundamental test can be found in complicated legal systems like those in force in the United States and Britain. *In these countries no ultimate distinction can be made between legal and moral standards* [Italics mine]. (p. 46)

Thus, the important point to note is that our legal system is inextricably tied to a set of moral principles that guide, limit, constrain, and influence the explicit laws that are adopted. So it follows that moral principles can and do serve as grounds of legal rights and obligations in the same way that explicit legal rules do.

Most important, perhaps, among the moral principles that stand at the base of the legal system is the notion of *moral rights* possessed by persons. These moral rights follow directly from our recognition of persons as direct objects of moral concern, as entities worthy of moral consideration, as loci of intrinsic value, or, in Kant's terminology, as ends in themselves. Once we become aware that individual persons are ends in themselves, we feel that we must publicly acknowledge that certain aspects of their nature or *telos* must be shielded and protected from possible abuse, even when such abuse could be in the general interest. We say, then, that human beings have moral rights in virtue of being moral objects, these rights follow from their nature, and from these rights flow claims by individuals against the state that ought and do enter into judicial and legal reckoning. In Dworkin's words:

A man has a moral right against the state if for some reason the state would do wrong to treat him a certain way, even if it would be in the general interest to do so. (p. 139)

RIGHTS ARE A PROTECTION FOR THE INDIVIDUAL AGAINST THE GENERAL WELFARE

A right is a safeguard of the moral status of the individual and his or her human nature or *telos* against the pressures of social convenience or general welfare that might otherwise tend to submerge his or her individuality and crucial interests. As the legal positivists pointed out, most of our public decision-making morality is utilitarian; that is, the decisions that are considered desirable are those that will produce the greatest benefit for the greatest number of people. This is not surprising, and in many ways it is a fair way of setting policy. The basic assumptions behind utilitarianism are the same assumptions that underlie much democratic theory, free enterprise, egalitarianism, and individualism: namely, that each person counts for one, for purposes of public policy all citizens are equal, and the fairest decision procedure is one that yields the highest net benefits across the sum of these individuals. If all people are equal, no particular individual or group should have his, or her, or its interests favored, each person's interests count equally, and conclusions are drawn by simple addition.

In a sense, of course, this is very fair—everyone has had a chance to express his preferences and to have his interests considered. But in another sense, it can be very dangerous because the interests, preferences, and concerns of *any given individual* often become submerged under the crushing weight of the common good. For example, if the majority would benefit by preventing an unpopular speaker from expressing himself, strict utilitarian considerations make it easy to allow his being silenced, since not letting him speak will benefit most people, and letting him speak can lead to disturbance, friction, and expense.

It is here that the notion of rights becomes significant. For the notion of rights builds protective fences around the individual and declares that there are certain things that cannot be done to him even for the general benefit, and even when he stands alone. Even if he has no power to resist the majority, even if his activity leads to general inconvenience, there are certain areas where he ought not be touched or stifled, despite the cost to the majority, *simply because he is a moral object,* and those areas are essential to him. Such a right, to take a salient example, is freedom of speech. This freedom is held to be sacred because it is at the heart of a person's status as a human being and, correlatively, as an object of moral concern. It is an essential feature of the human essence or *telos.* (The Greek word for reason, in fact, was *logos,* which means "word.") Our system protects the right of the holder of unpopular views to air them even if he or she offends, antagonizes, and upsets everyone else. As we all know, taxpayers pay a great deal of money for police to protect unpopular speakers, even if everyone in the community would like to see them silenced. The same holds true, of course, for freedom of religion and assembly (rights that again reflect features we take to be essential to the human *telos*). The notion of rights is based on the basic moral idea that ultimately the *individual* is the fundamental object of moral concern and attention, that the individual has intrinsic value, and that there are certain interests that are inseparable from his or her being and, hence, themselves have intrinsic value. It is the solution to the basic problem of democracy, reconciling majority rule with the inescapable value of the individual. Rights protect the individual moral being from what has been called "the tyranny of the majority." They set the ground rules that utilitarian social policies can violate only for the gravest of reasons, such as the survival of the society as a whole. (The fact that they can be violated under some conditions shows that rights are not absolute, but are *presumptive.*) So, in summary, a right is a morally based notion that serves a major political, legal, and social function—the function of protecting the individual object of moral concern. It allows individuals to demand certain kinds of treatment, not as a gratuity based on benevolence, but as their due as moral objects, possessing a certain nature. Rights mean we don't have to depend on the unreliable goodwill of others.

HOW RIGHTS ARE ESTABLISHED

The Constitution of the United States, of course, lists some of the major and most obvious rights that belong to human beings in the Bill of Rights, but this is not meant to be a complete list of all rights, or even to state fully the content of the rights listed. Let us recall the Ninth Amendment:

> The enumeration in the Constitution of certain rights shall not be construed to deny or disparage others retained by the people.

But if that is the case, how do we establish *other* rights, or define the content of the rights which *are* enumerated? The answer is simple. In order to establish a right in legal cases, as was done in the civil rights cases, the desegregation cases, the conscientious objector cases, and so forth, one must use *moral arguments;* one must present moral reasons and discussion. According to Dworkin, this possibility is built into the Bill of Rights. Rather than attempt to cover every possible sort of case that could come up that is relevant to the enumerated rights, the Bill of Rights was instead designed to provide broad moral schemata that can be interpreted and applied to particular cases through a dialectical process of moral argument and discussion. Thus, for example, the "separate is not equal" argument advanced for school integration in the 1950s represented an application, through moral argumentation, of the equal protection clause of the Bill of Rights. Says Dworkin, summarizing this view:

> The difficult clauses of the Bill of Rights, like the due process and equal protection clauses, must be understood as an appeal to moral concepts rather than laying down particular conceptions. Therefore, a court that undertakes the burden of applying these clauses fully as law must be prepared to frame and answer questions of political morality. (p. 147)

So, to establish a right, one must utilize moral arguments, oftentimes to flesh out and interpret constitutional locutions and oftentimes to extend them. Constitutional law and, for that matter, all law, is thus in a real sense logically inseparable from moral philosophy. What this in turn means, as our legal history clearly shows, is that one cannot separate questions of law from questions of right and wrong, that is, from morality. (Incidentally, it is clear that violating a right for grave reasons, like survival of the society or health and safety of a large number of persons, also requires a moral argument.)

If Dworkin is correct, the legal positivists are wrong on two counts. In the first place, they are wrong to suggest that law is logically and clearly separable from morality. In the second place, they are wrong in suggesting that even though law and morality are two distinct things, the morality by which law is to be constructed and assessed is exclusively utilitarian. We have seen clearly that this is not the case, that, in fact, the key notion of rights is designed to serve as a check against the extremes of utilitarianism, which might submerge the individual object of moral concern and his or her nature.

HOW DOES THIS RELATE TO ANIMALS?

What is the connection between all this and animals? We have just shown that fundamental legal/moral rights, which override utilitarian considerations, follow from our recognition that a person is a legitimate object of moral concern or end in itself. We have further shown that those rights follow from the nature or *telos* of the human person. Freedom of speech, for example, is a direct consequence of the fact that humans are by nature rational, social beings with opinions they wish to express. But now let us recall the entire force of our previous argument. We showed in the first place that there is no morally relevant difference between humans and animals. Second, we showed, by independent argument, that being an object of moral concern, being an end in itself, and having rights, follow from being alive and having interests that are essentially constitutive of that life and its *telos*. In any case, the conclusion of both of these arguments is that animals are objects of moral concern, just as humans are, and are ends in themselves. But we have just seen that enjoying legal rights follows and is indeed inseparable from enjoying moral status. So it also follows that animals ought to be considered as recipients of legal rights. Furthermore, it will not do to cite utilitarian arguments against granting legal rights to animals, because the entire point of rights considered from a social point of view is anti-utilitarian. If rights are designed to protect objects of moral concern from the excesses of utilitarianism, it certainly won't do to launch utilitarian arguments against rights! In fact, one can muster a compelling argument to the effect that animals are, in one sense, even more deserving of such legal rights than humans. We have argued that purely utilitarian laws and decisions are morally inadequate even when the interests of all of the individuals who will be hurt by those decisions have been counted in calculating the net benefit. In other words, even if your interest has been considered in utilitarian calculation, and your interest has been outweighed by the majority, the notion of rights insures that certain aspects of your individual interests, fundamental to your *telos,* cannot be violated. If utilitarian laws and policies are inadequate when the interests of all human beings have been weighed, what are we to say of such laws and policies when they do not weigh the interests of all objects of moral concern? And we certainly do not weigh the interests and benefits of animals when passing laws and policies. Their interests do not enter into our utilitarian calculations. How exigent, then, that *their* intrinsic value and interests stemming from their being legitimate candidates for moral concern be protected by legal rights! We are arguing, then, that we are morally compelled to grant legal rights to animals, to protect essential features of their *telos.*

DON'T ANIMALS HAVE LEGAL RIGHTS NOW?

Whenever I lecture on this subject, be it before humane groups, philosophers, scientists, veterinarians, or college students, I invariably encounter the same objection. "Surely," it is asserted, "animals *do* have legal rights. They *are* protected by laws—anticruelty laws have been in existence for many years. Why proliferate legislation unnecessarily in a society that already has far too many laws!" This is a serious and cogent objection and must be carefully considered.

In the first place, in and of themselves, animals do not have legal rights. They are not "legal persons" in the eyes of the law in the way adults, children, ships, municipalities, and corporations are. Rather, animals are *property*. Domestic animals—dogs, cats, cattle, etc.—are personal property, much like automobiles or television sets. If someone kills your dog, he has committed a crime against *you,* not against your dog. Until very recently, in fact, such a person was only liable for the actual value of the dog. (Recently, courts have begun to hear suits that raise the question of the sentimental value of the animal and of the pain and anguish suffered at its loss, but this does not change the animal's status as property.) By the same token, so-called "wild" or "stray" animals are the property of the public, or the state. (Note, by the way, how naturally we fall into language like "wild" and "stray," language that defines the animal's status in a way that is relative to and dependent upon human beings.) In any case, property has no rights, as consideration of even well-treated slaves makes clear.

In Colorado, as in many states, a farmer can shoot a dog that crosses his property line as a potential threat to livestock. Ironically, in most states, a householder may not shoot a burglar or robber unless he has reasonable grounds for believing that his life is threatened.

DO ANIMALS NEED RIGHTS? THEIR LEGAL STATUS TODAY

But perhaps animals do not need rights; don't the animal protection or anticruelty laws suffice? Sadly not. An examination of these laws will make our point quite clear. We must note, in the first place, that these laws take the people who own or use animals as primary objects of moral concern, rather than the animals themselves. Consider, for example, the legislative declaration introducing the Colorado Nongame and Endangered Species Conservation Act in my home state:

> The general assembly finds and declares that it is the policy of this state to manage all nongame wildlife for *human enjoyment and welfare, for scientific purposes, and to insure their perpetuation as members of ecosystems* [Italics mine].

It ought to be quite clear that moral concern toward the animal is not even mentioned. Rather, it is directed toward humans, knowledge, and the environment. Things are much worse when we examine the anticruelty laws. Again, let us look at the Colorado statute, which in fact has the most harsh penalties of any such law in the United States associated with it. The law says:

> A person commits cruelty to animals if, except as authorized by law, he overdrives, overworks, tortures, torments, deprives of necessary sustenance, unnecessarily or cruelly beats, needlessly mutilates, needlessly kills, carries in or upon any vehicles in a cruel manner, or otherwise mistreats or neglects an animal.

At first blush, this law may seem to be quite adequate, since it addresses itself to all sorts of abuse. But a moment's reflection leads us to the conclusion that it is self-emasculating. The problem is, of course, the use of words like "needlessly" or "unnecessarily," and through this loophole, the interests of humans pour and submerge the moral status of animals. One discovers that it takes very little to blunt the edge of this law. Subsequent cases that tested this law made this point quite clear and resulted in a ruling that asserts that:

> Not every act that causes pain and suffering to animals is prohibited.
> . . . Where the end or object is reasonable and adequate, the act resulting
> in pain is necessary or justifiable, [as where] the act is done to protect
> life or property or to minister to some of the necessities of man.

So human interests always come first. It is also worth noting that the extensive catalogue of prohibitions cited in the act takes no cognizance of behavioral or psychological cruelty. Animal protection laws are typically Cartesian, seeing animals merely as bodies and failing to take account of their psychological needs and interests.

One of the most telling examples of the failure of the anticruelty laws to protect animals in virtue of their flawed conceptual base occurred in 1985 in New York State. A group of animal advocate attorneys, The Animal Legal Defense Fund, brought suit against the New York State Department of Environmental Conservation, the agency in charge of public land use, on the grounds that the Department permitted the use of steel-jawed traps on these lands. The use of these traps resulted in cruelty to animals; for example, the trapped animals were deprived of food and water.

The judge was clearly a compassionate and sensitive individual. In his decision, he asserted that

> If this court could substitute its own personal feelings and emotions in
> place of legal precedent, we could end this opinion here with a decision
> favoring the protection of animals. However, courts must follow legal
> precedent and leave to the other branches of government the decision
> as to which of the competing interests will prevail. The issues here are
> important ones, but the plaintiffs, if they are to prevail, must convince
> the legislative and executive branches of government of the rightness of
> the cause (*Animal Legal Defense Fund* v. *The Department of Environ-
> mental Conservation*).

The judge in essence based his decision on the fact that the way the anticruelty laws are written does not prohibit the use of the steel-jawed trap. The steel-jawed trap is routinely used and has not been legislatively prohibited; therefore its use cannot be seen as falling under the statute that enjoins a person from "unjustifiably" injuring, maiming, or killing an animal.

In other words, the traditional ethic embodied in the anticruelty laws does not suffice to justify legal action against the steel-jawed trap. Any such action, the judge concluded, required the action of the legislature, in short, requires the codification of a new ethic for animals that goes beyond cruelty into new laws by legislative bodies.

The crucial philosophical point that emerges from our discussion thus far must be stressed. For almost two hundred years, the traditional legal category for dealing with animal abuses was "cruelty." This was mirrored by the traditional humane society categorization of the treatment of animals as evidencing either "cruelty" or "kindness," and the related injunction to "love animals." It is for this reason that those concerned with animal welfare tended to describe those who caused any animal suffering as "cruel individuals," and to lump into that class both dog-fighters and biomedical researchers.

A major component of the new ethic we have been developing in this book is the realization that kindness and cruelty are inadequate concepts for discussing our moral obligations to animals. In the first place, most animal suffering is not a result of intentional cruelty. Most researchers are not cruel, most animal agriculturalists are not cruel, most rodeo people are not cruel, even most trappers are not cruel. They are not trying to hurt animals, they are not deriving pleasure from animal suffering; they are trying to advance knowledge, cure diseases, make a profit, keep food prices down, supply fur coats, etc. Nonetheless, their activities produce immeasurably more suffering to animals than the actions of the (thankfully) very small number of sadists who do fit the cruelty rubric.

Second, kindness, good intentions, and love for animals does not assure moral treatment of animals, as we will evidence clearly in our discussion of pet animals. Pet owners may feel much love for their animals, yet cause them much suffering through ignorance or thoughtlessness.

Third, if our theoretical discussion in chapter 1 has been correct, such concepts as "kindness"—and even "humaneness"—do not capture the conceptual basis of our moral obligation to animals; they are far too patronizing and too suggestive of an overflowing of benevolence on the part of special individuals. Just as those who are concerned with fair and moral treatment of women in society would be quick to reject "kindness to women" as a basis for such treatment, so, too, ought animal advocates. The issue of proper treatment of animals, as of women, is a matter of justice and moral obligation to which one is forced by the logic of one's own morality, not something nourished by one's happening to have an overflowing of good will.

Not only can the anticruelty laws easily be set aside for human utilitarian considerations, their very *raison d'être* is often as much a concern for human welfare as for the animals, for the rationale behind such laws often follows the logic of Thomas Aquinas or Kant: that cruelty to animals ought to be prevented because of the potential danger to the human population if any sort of cruelty is not nipped in the bud. In *Waters* v. *The People,* a case testing the Colorado anticruelty law, this point is made clear when it is asserted that:

> The aim of this section is not only to protect these animals, but *to conserve public morals* [Italics mine].

As was the case in nineteenth-century slave protection rulings, the object of moral concern is not the slave or the animal, but the general welfare of the "real" objects of moral concern, humans. Humans may be brutalized by cruelty to nonhumans, be they Negroes or animals; therefore, such cruelty must be prohibited!

The anthropocentric basis of such laws is made manifest in still another way. In twenty-four states, the already weak anticruelty laws are further diluted by stipulations that make the acts of cruelty violations of the law only when they are performed "wilfully," "maliciously," "intentionally," etc. In short, the measure of criminality is not the effect on the health and welfare of the animal, but rather the intentions of the *human perpetrator.* Clearly, the laws are designed to deal not so much with animal suffering as with human sadists, who can presumably represent a grave danger to public welfare. Most of these laws exempt from cruelty by definition *any* activity done in a research establishment in the name of science. Even the most extreme examples of confinement agriculture, such as the raising of crated white veal calves, are exempt from prosecution under these laws, so long as they are commonly practiced. Many of these laws do not include under cruelty deprivation of food, water, shelter, shade, ventilation, space, exercise, or sanitary living conditions.

Not surprisingly in light of the above, cases of cruelty are rarely prosecuted. Witnesses are hard to find, intentionality and malice are hard to prove, police officials are overworked and/or do not care. An attorney recently told me that the district attorney of one of America's largest cities could not remember when the last anticruelty case had been prosecuted and won. In his filing system, there was an entry for cases of "unnatural copulation," but none for "cruelty to animals." In Denver during 1978 not a single case was prosecuted under the state law. But even if a case is prosecuted and a conviction won, the culprit is unlikely to suffer in any significant way. Typical maximum penalties stipulated are "up to $500-$1000 fine and/or up to six months or one year in jail," and these are rarely fully invoked. Often the law says "up to $100 or up to thirty days."

I, unfortunately, experienced this very dramatically in 1987. Two of my veterinary students had acquired a kitten, in violation of their apartment lease which prohibited animals. The landlord found out, let himself into the apartment, and beat the kitten to death with a hammer. He then left a note to the students telling them what he had done and reminding them that they were not to have animals. They filed charges of cruelty against him, and he was eventually convicted and fined $25. As he left the courtroom, he leaned over to the students, who were sitting in the gallery, smiled, and said, "For $25, I'd do it again."

Federal laws promulgated for the welfare of animals are also severely inadequate. Consider the pioneering Animal Welfare Acts of 1966 and 1970. In the first place, a primary purpose of the act was human utility—it licensed dealers in animals sold to research laboratories, in order to allay the fears of pet owners who were concerned that their dogs and cats might be kidnapped and sold to experimenters. In fact, what motivated this act was a rash of highly publicized kidnappings of pet dogs that were stolen and sold to research facilities. Included under provisions of the act are dogs, cats, monkeys, guinea pigs, hamsters, and rabbits. Excluded, amazingly enough, are rats, mice, all nonwarm-blooded animals, poultry, horses, cows, sheep, pigs, goats, donkeys, and all other farm animals. Among other things, the act authorizes the Secretary of the Department of Agriculture "to promulgate standards to govern the humane handling, care, treatment, and transportation of animals by dealers, research facilities and exhibitors." According to the act:

> Such standards shall include minimum requirements with respect to handling, housing, feeding, watering, sanitation, ventilation, shelter from extremes of weather and temperatures, adequate veterinary care, including the appropriate use of anesthetic, analgesic or tranquilizing drugs, when such use would be proper in the opinion of the attending veterinarian of such research facilities, and separation by species when the Secretary finds such separation necessary for the humane handling, care, or treatment of animals. The Secretary shall also promulgate standards to govern the transportation in commerce, and the handling, care, and treatment in connection therewith, by intermediate handlers, air carriers, or other carriers, of animals consigned by any dealer, research facility, exhibitor, operator of an auction sale, or other person, or any department agency, or instrumentality of the United States or of any state or local government, for transportation in commerce. The Secretary shall have authority to promulgate such rules and regulations as he determines necessary to assure the humane treatment of animals in the course of their transportation in commerce including requirements such as those with respect to containers, feed, water, rest, ventilation, temperature, and handling.

Much as this act represented an undeniable step forward in favor of animal welfare, it was greatly deficient, not only in its failure to cover all animals, but in its failure to license individual experimenters (it licenses only research institutions). Even more important is its failure to place any constraints whatsoever on what can be done to research or test animals in the course of actual experimentation and testing. It puts one in mind of a sex manual that deals only with foreplay, leaving the sex act itself undiscussed. The preliminaries are dealt with; the main event untouched:

> Nothing in this Act shall be construed as authorizing the Secretary to promulgate rules, regulations, or orders with regard to design, outlines, guidelines or performance of actual research or experimentation by a research facility as determined by such research facility.

Once again, the experimental animal is hardly being treated as an object of moral concern in this act when it specifically disavows any control over what happens to the animal in the course of experimentation! The only feeble exception to this resounding abrogation of responsibilities for dealing with the essential core of the research process was a requirement that research institutions issue annual reports that

> show that professionally acceptable standards governing the care, treatment, and use of animals, including appropriate use of anesthetic, and analgesic, and tranquilizing drugs during experimentation are being followed by the research facility during actual research experimentation.

Note that this stipulation is essentially vacuous and toothless. It merely requires that research institutions *report* on their appropriate use of anesthetics and analgesics. No definition of appropriate use is provided; institutions can (and did) comply with this provision simply by stating that in the course of their research the use of such drugs was deemed inappropriate!

In the next chapter, we shall discuss what constituted a major step toward meaningful legislation governing animal experimentation. But before we can do this, we must provide a theoretical legal framework for the ideal legal status of animals. We have just seen that animals do not enjoy a legal status commensurate with the fact that they are legitimate objects of moral concern. All extant legislation has primarily been oriented toward protecting human interests and property, preventing human brutalization, and protecting animals only as far as human emotions or sentimentality are stirred by dramatic atrocities. This is clearly inadequate. If animals are moral objects, if they enter into the scope of moral concern, if they enjoy moral rights, then they must be granted legal rights as well to protect that moral status. Our legal gestalt on animals must change, along with our moral gestalt. And in part, changing the legal gestalt will lead to new moral perceptions.

LEGALIZING THE RIGHTS OF ANIMALS

What would it mean to grant legal rights to animals? Very simply, it would mean that the law would recognize animals as enjoying legal standing in themselves, not as property. As such they could institute legal action, or more accurately, have legal action instituted on *their* behalf (rather than on behalf of their owner), have injuries to *them* legally considered (rather than to their owner), and have legal relief directly to their benefit. The relevant legal analogy here is the case of children. Although children cannot press legal claims on their own behalf, they still enjoy legal rights. They are not the property of their parents. Their rights can be pressed by others, by social welfare agencies, police, courts, guardians, etc. Granting rights to entities that cannot themselves speak for those rights is far from unprecedented. It is not difficult to imagine those who might serve to press claims for the animals; the most plausible candidates are members of humane societies and veterinarians.

There are two major ways in which rights could be established for animals. In the first place, we can speak of *extending* existing rights to animals, even as constitutional rights were extended by arguments stressing the absence of relevant moral differences from native-born, white, adult, male, property owners to corporations, naturalized citizens, nonproperty owners, blacks, Orientals, children, and women. A brilliant and accessible analysis of the logic of rights extension has been presented by Professor Christopher Stone in his book, *Should Trees Have Standing?* Although Stone's argument does not deal with animals, the points he makes are directly relevant to our problem. Stone's argument was originally submitted as a brief to the Supreme Court in the *Disney-Mineral King* case. In this case, the U.S. Forest Service had granted a permit to the Walt Disney Corporation to develop the Mineral King Valley Wilderness Area into a "Disneyland." The Sierra Club sought to stop this action. However, both the lower courts and the Supreme Court ruled that the Sierra Club was not a directly injured party and could not sue. As laws are written, one can sue only for injuries one directly sustains. For example, if you pollute a stream running through my property, I can only sue to recover direct damages—loss of income from sale of fishing rights, loss of property value from despoliation of beach, etc. I cannot sue because the stream has been ruined, even if it would cost a good deal to restore the stream to its original state. Thus, if the stream runs through the property of five people who collectively sustain $15,000 in damages, the polluter can only be sued for $15,000, even if it would cost $100,000 to restore the stream. For this reason, Stone argued that natural objects—streams, wilderness areas, forests, etc.— should be granted legal standing, with guardians like the Sierra Club able to press claims on their behalf. As Stone points out, the argument that only human persons can have such rights is easily trumped by the fact that corporations have enjoyed such legal standing since the early nineteenth century, as have ships, trusts, cities, and nation-states. Obviously it is far more difficult to defend legal rights for such nonliving things than for animals, given our earlier argument connecting legal and moral rights. It is hard to defend the notion that a ship or corporation is a direct object of moral concern, yet corporations have legal rights. It is, as we have seen, essentially impossible rationally to deny that animals are direct objects of moral concern, so it is quite easy in this light to demand legal standing for them.

How might such an extension be accomplished? Let us imagine a bold, daring test case that would force these issues to the forefront of legal discussion. Let us recall that we have shown in detail that rationality and capacity for language are strictly irrelevant to something being a direct object of moral concern. Nonetheless, the intuitions of ordinary people and historical precedent both militate against ready acceptance of this position. Most people are still committed to the idea that speech is somehow of pivotal moral significance. One of my colleagues, for example, who has no interest whatever in animal rights, concedes that he would be greatly interested in these questions if we found an animal that could speak. Very well, let us milk this essentially indefensible intuition. Most of the public is at least passingly familiar with recent work done on teaching language (or something seen as language by most people) to higher primates. Though many theoretical linguists, most notably Noam Chomsky, would decline to speak of these animals as linguistic beings for a number of technical reasons, our intuitions push in the other direction. After all, these animals do put signs together in new ways, even to the point of insulting the researchers. Since language is, philosophically speaking, morally irrelevant anyway, what counts is not whether this is or is not language, but that many people who *think* language *is* morally relevant see these animals as having language.

Now consider an ape who has learned to communicate with humans using some system *seen by most people as linguistic*. The experiment is terminated, and the animal is no longer of use. What can be done with it? The animal, as has actually happened, is turned over to a zoo or worse, to a toxicology laboratory. Could we not press the claim that the animal is suffering cruel and unusual punishment and has been denied due process? By current standards, the animal has measurable intelligence; in fact, one such animal scored an 85 on a standard I.Q. test—many humans score a good deal lower. In fact, the animal lies, swears, and equivocates—sure marks of intelligence. In any case, could one not press a plausible case on the grounds that the animal's civil rights had been violated? I am envisioning a new "monkey trial" at least as spectacular in its implications as the Scopes trial, which tested the Tennessee law against the teaching of evolution. Such a trial would be extraordinarily salubrious in just the same sense. The Scopes trial forced a public airing of our scientific, conceptual, and educational commitments as well as a dialectical examination of the roles of science and religion. This trial would force an examination of our moral commitments and illuminate areas too long left in the dark. Eventually, and incrementally, by a process of legal and moral argument stressing the absence of relevant differences, one can envision the judicial extension of some rights to all animals.

The second way of establishing legal rights for animals involves not judicial extension but rather legislative *conferral.* Laws governing the treatment of animals must be written in the language of rights, with animals seen as objects of moral concern, and with human utilitarian interests relegated to the background. This, as we have argued, is the force of all talk of "rights." Probably, in the long run, this route is more plausible than judicial extension. But the question remains as to *what* rights need to be legally established, by whatever means employed. There are innumerable areas in which this question ramifies—animal experimentation, factory or intensive farming, horse and dog racing, pet ownership, zoos, etc. In our next chapter we shall discuss in depth the role of such laws in animal experimentation. In the following chapter, we shall discuss pet animals—perhaps the most psychologically acceptable candidates for legal standing in the minds of most people, who can and do compare these animals to children. Suffice it to say that the basic content of such laws has already been established in our earlier discussion of the moral status of animals and of the rights that accrue to them in virtue of that status. Fundamentally, some version of the right to life, the right to be protected from suffering, and the right to live life according to their *telos* or nature are basic rights that should be legally codified for animals. Indeed, when I ran a full-day seminar for Canadian government officials charged with making decisions relevant to animal use, many felt that a Bill of Rights for animals would be a desirable basis for encapsulating emerging social change.

WHAT CAN WE EXPECT TO ACHIEVE?

Clearly it is utopian to expect these rights to be established immediately in our current socio-economic and cultural context. People are not prepared to give up meat or the benefits that come from biomedical research. And in a real sense, it is absurd to expect them to at this stage. After all, consciousness that animals are moral entities at all is only just beginning to develop. But what one can expect is that as the consciousness does awaken, as the gestalt shift prevails, people will be more and more willing to make sacrifices for moral reasons. The process is, of course, dialectical. Awakening moral awareness leads to codifications of this awareness in law, but, even more importantly, codification in law serves as a spur further to awaken moral awareness. We are, happily, a people who respect the law and, correlatively, to a certain significant extent one can use law to further morality. In the mid-1950s, in the wake of the monumental civil rights decision, one heard plaintive wails from those who argued that one could not "legislate morality." Integration had to evolve, it was declared: it could not be accomplished by laws and regulations; one first had to change hearts and minds. Today, we can see just how wrong these people were. Much remains to be done, but it is demonstrable that integration has worked in the U.S., and most dramatically in the South, politically, economically, educationally, and socially. Slowly but surely attitudes change, and children now grow up with tolerance, not hatred, inculcated and sanctified by laws and institutions. For this reason, we shall shortly be discussing laws that, while falling short of the full rights model, can move society in that direction.

It is not utopian to project laws that provide significant regulation of the use of animals in research, as we shall shortly see. Nor is it utopian to suggest laws governing intensive farming that take as fundamental the animal's right to live its life in accordance with its nature.

Such a law was passed in Sweden in 1989, and the EEC is moving in the same direction. Related laws have been passed in Germany, Switzerland, and Scandinavia, and were recommended as long ago as the 1960s by the Brambell Committee in Britain, based on a philosophy not unlike that we have developed. I am quite certain that, having demanded laws for animals used in research, society will next demand laws providing at least limited rights for farm animals. Unfortunately, the quest for efficiency and productivity in twentieth-century agriculture has not benefited agricultural animals. Whereas traditional agriculture had to fit animal and environment, *telos* and husbandry, else the animals would get sick and die, technology has allowed the development of a confinement agriculture which puts square pegs into round holes, animals into conditions for which they are not suited by their *telos,* and which keeps them alive by use of "technological sanders" like vaccines and antibiotics. This sort of agriculture has also accelerated agribusiness and helped drive out small family farmers, who cannot afford to compete. Ominously, in most universities, departments of animal husbandry are now called "animal science."

Laws assuming some rights for farm animals would go a long way toward eliminating major atrocities, such as the raising of veal calves—

kept in tiny boxes where they cannot turn around, they are fed on diets which keep them anemic and in constant distress from diarrhea—all in order to keep the meat pale. Such laws might plausibly specify, on the basis of ethological knowledge, the form that feed lots would have to take. They might limit the number of egg-laying chickens that are kept in cages or mandate alternative systems. Currently as many as nine chickens are put into 19" × 24" cages. They might require ethologically sound husbandry for swine. Hopefully, laws requiring moral husbandry would not be too economically disruptive. According to Dr. Michael Fox, a good deal of data currently available in animal science research sources indicates that moral husbandry is economically profitable. For example, Quantock veal, a division of the largest veal retailer in Great Britain, in the 1980s abandoned the use of the tiny boxes for raising veal calves, partially in response to public pressure, but also for economic reasons. Writing in the *Veterinary Record* in 1980, a Quantock executive stated that

> The calves are contented and healthier, the culling rate has halved. The system is less costly for the farmer, less capital need be tied up in buildings which need not have been expensively built for a controlled environment. (p. 450)

It turns out that it is actually 50 percent cheaper to raise the calves in this new way, in groups of thirty in straw-filled pens with natural light and ventilation where they can move about, ruminate, and groom themselves. There is also evidence that indicates that milk yield from dairy cows is a function of the care and attention the cows receive from the herdsman. In fact, research indicates that this variable is far more important to productivity than are physical facilities. If proper care is not economically feasible, perhaps we need to turn our attention to breeding food animals that are essentially devoid of interests, incapable of physical or behavioral suffering, which basically enjoy mere protoplasmic existence. We might perhaps breed microcephalic animals, or perhaps even clone sides of beef, or produce meat protein in fermentation vats through biotechnology.

We can also envision laws that regulate adoption of pets as strictly as the adoption of children, and that provide harsh penalties for abandoning animals or letting them run loose. We shall discuss the law in relation to pet animals in a later chapter. Other areas sorely in need of legislation to protect the rights of animals include zoos, animals in entertainment, and wildlife management.

It is important to stress that legislation alone is not enough. As we shall see in the next chapter, for example, it does not suffice simply to pass laws governing what can and cannot be done to experimental animals.

Scientists must be made to understand the rationale behind such laws, must be made aware that such regulations are not simply another set of bureaucratic hoops they must jump through, another set of obstacles to freedom of thought and inquiry. But such awareness can only be accomplished through education, so education and legislation must go hand in hand. And the sort of education that is required would in many ways entail a complete rethinking of science education, an incorporation, as we shall shortly see, of conceptual and moral questions into curricula hitherto conceived of as unsullied by anything other than technical concerns. Wherever one intends to legislate, one must also educate, be it in the field of animal experimentation or in the area of responsible pet ownership.

IS OUR POSITION ABSURD?

It is quite easy to caricature everything we have suggested, to imagine a case for "freedom of bark," or for giving turtles the right to vote. (In this regard, we may cite a cartoon showing an animal control officer with a morose dog in his truck. The officer is reading from a card, "You have the right to remain silent. . . ."). But in the final analysis, we must recall that the notion of extending rights to blacks and to women was similarly vilified and ridiculed. One need only look at newspapers of the period to find these concepts broadly and viciously lampooned. In fact, the Equal Rights Amendment was so treated recently. Even the courts found the notion of slaves having rights an absurdity; witness the Virginia court's opinion in *Bailey* v. *Poindexter* in an 1858 decision.

> So far as civil rights and relations are concerned, the slave is not a person, but a thing. The investiture of chattel with civil rights or legal capacity is indeed a legal absurdity. The attribution of legal personality to a chattel-slave—legal conscience, legal intellect, legal freedom or liberty and power of free choice and action . . . implies a palpable contradiction in terms.

It will not do to ignore a moral argument just because it has always been ignored. Immorality sanctified by tradition is still immorality. Nor can moral arguments be repudiated on the grounds of convenience. Each step in moral progress exacts a cost in convenience and utility. Slavery was economically useful. Seizing Jewish property was quite useful to the German state and indeed to the majority of the German people. Breaking treaties with American Indians was convenient. If animals are objects of moral concern, then they have moral rights and, correlatively, they must have legal rights. To be sure, they cannot be the rights of an adult human being; but neither are the rights of children and corporations. *That* animals have rights can be established *a priori,* by reason, as we have done. But what these rights are—legal and moral—is only partly a matter of reason. As we argued, answering this question requires a clear, empirical understanding of an animal's *telos* or nature. This in turn requires that we carefully study animal behavior and biology to establish clearly the needs and interests of other creatures, though it does not take a Konrad Lorenz to tell us that our treatment of veal calves, for example, is an obscene perversion of the natural.

To grant legal rights to animals is to institutionalize their claim to moral concern, to recognize this status in a way that is writ large, to force us to pause and look at what we take for granted and to confront the inexpedient and bothersome consequences of being moral agents. Certainly the utilitarian costs are enormous, but so too were the opportunity costs of abolishing slavery and child labor.

3

The Use and Abuse of
Animals in Research

INTRODUCTION

Thus far, we have allowed ourselves the luxury of theory, unsullied by
the pressures and constraints of *realpolitik*. We have arrived at the ideal,
the target in Aristotle's phrase, the yardstick against which we can measure
actual practice. Certainly the significance of such an activity cannot be
underestimated; yet humans and society being what they are, we cannot
expect immediate reversal of habits and traditions entrenched by time and
nurtured by expediency. What, then, can be done? Despairing of foreseeable
total success, does one retire to polish and refine one's abstract theoretical
model? Here we may take a clue from David Hume, the great philosophical
skeptic, a thinker whose powerful arguments cast doubt on our grounds
for believing in minds (including our own), physical objects, causality, order
in nature, God, science, reason, and the difference between the subjective
and objective. Having done this, Hume does not reject his arguments but
sets them aside and does practical ethics for, after all, one must live in
the world. "Be a philosopher," he tells us, "but be first a man."

In a similar vein, we must conclude that being a philosopher does
not allow us the luxury of escaping from the world, however attractive
that may be. Philosophers, especially moral philosophers, can no longer

justify disengagement from the mundane on the grounds that they are concerned with what ought to be, not with what is. The crystalline purity of our reasoned arguments must be sullied by an encounter with social reality. This is especially pressing in the case of the moral status of animals. An arsenal of well-wrought arguments proving conclusively that we all ought to be vegetarians or that all animal experimentation is immoral is important, as we have stressed, but will probably in and of itself make little direct difference to the total amount of suffering in the universe. It is equally important to make these arguments count in some real and efficacious way. And to do this requires that we confront in detail the existential facts of our moral situation and realistically assess the ways in which our arguments can meaningfully intersect with practice.

We must not expect our philosophical model to serve as a blueprint for immediate social change, for this expectation is as realistic as Allen Ginsberg's attempt to levitate the Pentagon. There has never been a social revolution in the history of American democracy which did not proceed incrementally. And this is *a fortiori* true in the area of animal treatment, where society is only just beginning to think through our obligations to animals, something which was essentially invisible even to highly morally sensitive individuals throughout history. Our moral model must provide us with a yardstick to measure our moral progress. Most people who consider themselves Christians are not capable of turning the other cheek; that does not make them hypocrites. To some, our willingness to deviate from the ideal we have set up in the face of what is practically possible may appear as hypocrisy, as "selling out," as prostitution of one's ideals. But in the final analysis, the question that must always loom before us is this: Are the animals any better off in virtue of our efforts? We must avoid contenting ourselves with serving as moral *kamikazes,* going down in a blaze of glory, yet making little difference to the outcome of the battle.

So it is to the question of animal experimentation that we now turn, where we shall attempt to adjust our theoretical model to the harsh landscape of reality. It is here that we find a significant amount of animal suffering, and correlatively, the greatest potential for diminution of that suffering. We shall find, in the course of our discussion, that the problem is enormously complex and not amenable to simple solutions. The traditional rhetoric that has characterized the debate between proponents and opponents of research is so simplistic as to be almost meaningless. Yet, tragically, it has served as an insurmountable barrier to genuine dialogue and, even worse, as a barrier to the determination of common ground. In addition to the invective invariably hurled by both sides ("Sadistic vivisectionist"; "Bleeding heart humaniac"; "You would stop us from curing leukemia"; "You torture kittens for fun," etc.), the situation has been characterized by abysmal ignorance on both sides. Typically, opponents of animal experimentation know little about research and often discredit themselves by offering wholly implausible "alternatives" to the use of animals. By the same token, researchers have rarely thought through the moral questions associated with animal experimentation and discredit themselves with absurd claims that animals have no awareness, or really don't suffer, or that might makes right, or that science is value-free. Our problem then is to bridge these gaps of ignorance and to work toward a realistic improvement in the lot of the experimental animals, keeping always in view the ideal model we have constructed, yet not hesitating to deviate from it if the pressures of reality force us to do so. The problem of the research animal serves as a dramatic exemplar and best case for our ultimate purpose—unifying moral philosophy and current reality. Our society is not yet ready to grant full legal and moral rights to animals—we must look to the best approximation of these ideas that can be actualized in our current socio-cultural context.

THE SIX SENSES OF RESEARCH

Few of us realize the extent to which animals are employed in research and testing of all sorts. In fact, the figures stagger the imagination. It is currently estimated that the total number of laboratory animals now used throughout the world annually is 200 to 225 million. The United States accounts for about 100 million of these animals as follows: 50 million mice, 20 million rats, and about 30 million other animals, including 200,000 cats and 450,000 dogs. These statistics, incidentally, indicate the true absurdity of the original Animal Welfare Act, growing out of its failure to provide any protection at all for the vast majority of animals used, as rats and mice alone constitute over 90 percent of the total.*

Most of us tend to think of laboratory animals in terms of cancer research and the cure of disease, major areas of activity that are clearly of enormous significance in potentially bettering all of life, human and animal. As a result, many people are not too terribly concerned with the "plight" of laboratory animals and tend to see whatever suffering they do undergo as major contributions to the common good. Indeed, scientists tend to perpetuate this image of the use of research animals and, where referring to the killing of laboratory animals, even in scientific papers, tend to speak of "sacrificing" the animal. (We shall return to a detailed discussion

---

*In a 1992 decision, a federal judge ruled that exclusion of rats and mice by the USDA, the federal agency charged with interpreting and enforcing the act, violated congressional intent.

of such language shortly.) It is revelatory for most people that most laboratory animals are in fact employed in far less noble pursuits, although no
clear statistics are available to document this in any detailed way. Such
activities include the toxicity and irritation testing of various consumer
products, such as foodstuffs and cosmetics, teaching, extraction of products,
and the development of drugs. Thus, when speaking of the question of
"research on laboratory animals," we must take great care to realize the
variegated activities subsumed under that rubric. We must take care to
distinguish a number of distinct activities. For convenience, we may group
them into the following categories, recognizing that they represent gross
oversimplifications:

1. Basic biological research, that is, the formulation and testing of hypotheses about fundamental theoretical questions, such as the nature of
DNA replication or mitochondrial activity, with little concern for the practical
effect of that research.

2. Applied basic biomedical research—the formulation and testing of
hypotheses about diseases, dysfunctions, genetic defects, etc., that, while
not necessarily having immediate consequences for treatment of disease,
are at least seen as directly related to such consequences. Included in this
category is the testing of new therapies: surgical, gene therapy, radiation
treatment, etc. Clearly the distinction between category one and this category
will constitute a spectrum, rather than a clear-cut cleavage.

3. The development of drugs and therapeutic chemicals and biologicals: this differs from the earlier categories, again in degree (especially
category two), but is primarily distinguished by what might be called a
"shotgun" approach; that is, the research is guided not so much by well-
formulated theories that suggest that a certain compound might have a
certain effect, but rather by hit-and-miss, exploratory, inductive "shooting
in the dark." The primary difference between this category and the others
is that here one is aiming at discovering specific substances for specific
purposes, rather than at knowledge per se.

4. The testing of various consumer goods for safety, toxicity, irritation, and degree of toxicity: such testing includes the testing of cosmetics,
food additives, herbicides, pesticides, industrial chemicals, and so forth, as
well as the testing of drugs for toxicity, carcinogenesis (production of cancer), mutagenesis (production of mutations in living bodies), and teratogenesis (production of monsters and abnormalities in embryo development).
To some extent, obviously, this category will overlap with category three,
but should be distinguished in virtue of the fact that three refers to the
discovery of new drugs, and four to their testing relative to human (and,
in the case of veterinary drugs, animal) safety.

5. The use of animals in educational institutions and elsewhere for

demonstration, dissection, surgery practice, induction of disease for demonstrative purposes, high school science projects, etc.

6. The use of animals for the extraction of products—serum from horses, musk from civet cats, etc. This is not, strictly speaking, research.

It is thus quite important to be clear about which activities one is referring to when discussing "research on animals," since arguments relevant to one area will clearly not fit one or more of the others. A failure to do so on the part of many well-intentioned opponents of "animal experimentation" has traditionally led to a breakdown in communication with those who utilize animals in their activities. It is obviously necessary to discuss each of these categories separately, taking cognizance of the problems unique to each pursuit.

MORAL PRINCIPLES FOR RESEARCH: THE UTILITARIAN AND RIGHTS PRINCIPLES

Before embarking on these discussions, it is worth clarifying some basic moral presuppositions that follow from our previous discussion, and that will underlie our subsequent argument. We have argued that there is no clear-cut line between humans and animals from a moral point of view, and further, that animals have moral rights following from their nature or *telos* if or even as humans do. We have correlatively argued that since law rests on morality and that a key moral notion encoded in the law is the notion of rights possessed by human individuals, animals, too, ought to possess legal rights that protect their fundamental natures. From a strictly philosophical point of view, I think that we must draw a startling conclusion: If a certain sort of research on human beings is considered to be immoral, a *prima facie* case exists for saying that such research is immoral when conducted on animals. Our reasons for saying that various kinds of research on humans is immoral is that it causes pain or infringes on freedom or violates some basic interest or right of man. Clearly then, such reasoning should be carried over to animals as well, unless one can cite a morally relevant difference that characterizes the animal, and we have already argued that such a difference is not likely to be forthcoming. Such a criterion would not eliminate *all* research on animals, even as use of that criterion has not vitiated all research on humans. After all, we still do experiments on people that do not violate their right to dignity, equality, choice, and freedom from suffering. But use of that criterion would effectively curtail the vast majority of research in all of the above categories. Clearly such a position is utopian and socially and psychologically impossible in our culture. And if, as I suggested earlier, morality must deal with what is in some sense at least in part actualizable, we cannot even adopt the abolition of animal experimentation as an achievable moral goal in our socio-psychological milieu. As Kant said in other context, "ought implies can." That is, meaningfully to suggest that we *ought* to abolish our animal experimentation, legislatively or otherwise, is absurd unless this is something that *can* happen in our world—cf. abolishing war. That is not to suggest that it cannot serve as a regulative ideal or yardstick against which to measure our activities, but it is to suggest that it cannot currently be seen as a goal to be achieved.

Why not? Primarily because most of society is not prepared to sacrifice the benefits that research brings, especially in the area of disease control and treatment. Nor is society prepared to give up faith in science as a dominant mode of dealing with reality, and the abolition of animal experimentation would essentially mean an end to much of science as we know it. That is, our rejection of the moral status of animals in this context grows out of *utilitarian considerations,* out of considerations that suggest that more good than suffering comes out of experimentation. We have seen in the previous chapter that such an approach typifies our societal approach to decision making. We are not prepared to give up the chance to cure cancer in order to limit the suffering of mice.

This is not to suggest that the human benefit rationale provides a good, philosophically defensible argument to justify invasive animal use to achieve that benefit, though many researchers assume that it does. Thus, in a statement typical of such arguments, Dr. Theodore Cooper, a medical researcher defending the invasive use of animals in reseach, asserted that:

> The main purpose of . . . research . . . is to improve or protect the health of people. . . . Scientists make a distinction between the value of human life and the value of animal life. . . . Most modern societies (not all) place a higher value on human life than on nonhuman animal life. Therefore, in the absence of the perfect information or the currently needed information, the scientist is willing to make progress.

Most defenses of invasive animal use make a similar argument.

But is this argument cogent? Let us assume without question both that a great deal of human benefit has flowed from animal research and that animal life is valued less than human life. That in itself, of course, would not ipso facto morally justify the invasive use of animals. The last one hundred years have witnessed a great deal of documented exploitation of humans for research—humans who were or are valued less than first-line humans—blacks, primitives, criminal and political prisoners, women, retarded and insane persons, indigents, derelicts, and the elderly. Even if great benefit flowed from these activities, that would not make them right. (If we felt it did, we presumably would do all of our research on humans of this sort, for scientific reasons.) What this argument comes down to, I think, is the assertion that given perceived human need and self-interest, given the benefits that flow from animal research, and given animal impotence, invasive research will continue to be done. (Most scientists I know do not feel comfortable in asserting that they have a *right* to hurt animals for our benefit, but they nonetheless believe it will and should be done for the benefit it brings.)

This point was articulated well to me by members of the Australian biomedical research community at a recent conference on ethics and animal experimentation. Philosophers and others who have articulated the ideal for animals, they explained, have indeed developed cogent and hitherto ignored points. But, they continued, do you really expect us to immediately give up our careers, our research activities and the benefits to humans which flow from them? Such an expectation, they argued, is naive. What they wanted from philosophers, and others concerned with animal rights, is some program for improving the lot of animals, for approximating to the ideal, short of abandoning the entire enterprise. And their response is, it appears, typical of how researchers do react as they begin to understand the moral dimensions we have outlined. (Some researchers do, of course abandon animal research when they understand the moral issues at stake, but these are not a majority.) This then, I think, circumscribes the arena upon which our discussion of animal research must be played out if our arguments are to have any potential effect, or point of contact with the real world, or potential for ameliorating animal suffering. For one to argue and work only for the total abolition of animal experimentation is to act as a moral *kamikaze,* a suicide pilot, though the analogy breaks down insofar as the *kamikaze* had some statistical chance of making a dent in the opposition. Perhaps, as we said earlier, Allen Ginsberg's attempt to levitate the Pentagon during the Vietnam War is a better analogy. This is not, of course, to suggest that one must simply accept the status quo; in fact, much of our subsequent discussion will be directed precisely toward making significant changes in this monumental edifice.

One point emerges quite clearly here: If utilitarian considerations govern our acceptance of animal experimentation, it is reasonable to ask, as Bentham and Mill did, why *all* creatures capable of feeling pleasure and pain are not included in the utilitarian reckoning. It is sometimes said that they are; that research on animals benefits animals as well as humans, so that the net benefit outweighs the net cost. This may be true for certain areas of research, but a moment's reflection on our categories of research makes it quite clear that this is far from usual.

Ignoring this inconsistency, and accepting as currently socially inevitable the idea that human utility will always be paramount, at least in the foreseeable future, one can at least reasonably make the following demand of all our categories: *that the benefit to humans (or to humans and animals) clearly outweighs the pain and suffering experienced by the experimental animals.* Granted that the weighing of pleasure and pain is notoriously difficult, still we all do so daily. I judge that I will cause more total pain than pleasure by having an affair with one of my students. My colleagues judge that we will engender more pleasure than pain by sharing our meager raises equally than by rewarding one or two people at the expense of the others, and so forth. Correlatively, as we shall see, there are many cases of research in which the pain to the animals is clear and extreme, whereas the benefit to humans or animals is questionable and nebulous. Let us call this demand *the utilitarian principle.*

We may reasonably make another demand. If we are socially committed to research on animals and are prepared to embrace the utilitarian principle, we should also reasonably embrace the following dictum: In cases where research is deemed justifiable by the utilitarian principle, *it should be conducted in such a way as to maximize the animal's potential for living its life according to its nature or telos, and certain fundamental rights should be preserved as far as possible, given the logic of the research, regardless of considerations of cost.* We can call this the *rights principle.* It essentially suggests that certain aspects of the animal's nature are sacred and need to be protected against total submersion by utilitarian considerations. This in turn means that we cannot do as we see fit to a research animal, even if we have determined that the animal's use is justified by the utilitarian principle. We must avoid encroaching on the animal's fundamental interests and nature, and this in turn means that it has a right to freedom from pain, to being housed and fed in accordance with its nature, to exercise, to company if it is a social being, etc.; in short, to being treated as an end in itself, regardless of the cost. What this means in practice is this: We weigh a piece of research by the utilitarian principle. If it meets this test, it may be performed. There may be discomfort associated with such an experiment that is unavoidable—e.g., if we are infecting the animal with a disease. The point of the rights principle is that even if the experiment is justified and does involve infringing on some aspects of the animal's nature, we are still obliged to protect the other aspects of its nature and other interests, and to do so regardless of cost. Thus, if the disease is accompanied by pain, the animal should be given analgesics. The animal should be housed so as to respect its *telos,* etc.

Furthermore, I think that it is both morally required and pragmatically feasible to envision these principles incorporated into a meaningful federal

Animal Welfare Act, covering all animals in all categories. This is the point of intersection between our previous chapters and our actual socio-cultural situation. Legislation must be written that insures that research be chosen (and funded) in accordance with the utilitarian principle and conducted in accordance with the rights principle, with animal advocates serving as guardians of the animals' rights, and as reviewers of the adherence of the research to the two principles, empowered to bring legal action to the direct benefit of the animal. Further, meaningful penalties must be provided for violators of this legislation—perhaps researchers ought to be licensed, and violation punished by loss of licensure.

It may be thought that such a suggestion is as utopian as abolishing all research altogether. Scientists will never consent to such a surrender of their freedom, especially when the scientific community has historically tended to resist all control and has tended to minimize the significance of animal suffering. This is a major objection, and we shall return to it in what follows. So now, let us review the various categories of research in greater detail, keeping in mind our previous arguments and the two principles we have distilled from them.

INTRODUCTION TO THE TESTING OF CONSUMABLES

According to regulations promulgated by the Food and Drug Administration, each new chemical or biological substance marketed for consumer use—drugs, food and food additives, herbicides, pesticides—must be subjected to safety evaluation. Cosmetics, shampoos, etc., are also subject to such testing, in part due to additional federal regulations, and in part due to manufacturers' desires to protect themselves from lawsuits, in case a substance should later prove to be detrimental to human health. With increasing numbers of substances being marketed, and more pressure from the consumer lobby, and greater litigiousness in society, more and more testing is required. The primary vehicles for testing these substances are animals (circa twenty million per year), and the methods employed fall into a few major categories.

THE LD50 TEST

The testing of these various substances first of all requires some standard way of judging their *toxicity,* i.e., the extent to which they are poisonous. One standard measure that has been adopted is called the LD50 test, short for Lethal Dose 50 percent. The test was introduced in another context in 1927 by Trevan, who was concerned with providing a statistical solution to the problem of biological variation: that is, given a group of rats exposed to a given substance, not all the rats responded to the same dose in the same way. The LD50 indicates the amount of a substance that, when administered in a single dose to a group of animals, will result in the death of 50 percent of the group within fourteen days. (The LD100 indicates the minimum dosage that would kill *all* of the animals in the time period; the LD0 indicates the maximum dosages that would kill *none* of the animals.)

The LD50 test is thus a measure of acute toxicity, i.e., single dose or fractional doses given over a short period, typically orally, though there are also inhalant and dermal versions of the test. It is by far the most widely used test of toxicity of drugs, chemicals, pesticides, insecticides, food additives, and household substances; it is invariably the first study done in toxicity evaluation and *often the only test done.* A high percentage (no exact figure is available) of the animals used in product and drug testing are used in LD50 tests. By the time the classical LD50 is determined, sixty to one hundred animals have been poisoned. A variety of federal regulations and agencies in the United States militate in favor of the use of the LD50, and procedural methodology for the test has been standardized through the Hazardous Substances Act, the registry of Toxic Effects of Chemical Substances (or Toxic Substances List), and the Federal Insecticide, Fungicide, and Rodenticide Act. For example, the most conspicuous value listed in the Toxic Substances List is the LD50. The LD50 is also effectively required by the Interstate Commerce Commission, since a failure to supply LD50 data forces a manufacturer to treat the substance as belonging to the most toxic category, and shipping requirements become very stringent and expensive.

Given the prevalence of the test, and the number of animals who suffer in virtue of its widespread use, it is worth considering its legitimacy as a scientific device, ignoring moral considerations for the moment. Extraordinarily, one finds a wide variety of stringent criticisms directed against the test, considered as an indicator of safety evaluation for humans. In a 1968 article in *Modern Trends in Toxicology,* "The Purpose and Value of LD50 Determinations," Morrison, Quinton, and Reinert critically reviewed the literature on LD50 testing. These authors, it must be emphasized, were totally unconcerned with the moral problems surrounding the test, or with the moral status of animals—their concern was simply methodological and theoretical. The authors point out, first of all, that LD50 tests tell us only about the gross effect, all or nothing, of a given substance. That is, all we learn is that a certain dosage either kills or does not. Correlatively, LD50 results are totally unextrapolatable to *chronic* (prolonged) exposure to the substance in question. The effect in an animal of massive acute doses tells us nothing about the long-term effects of small doses. This is especially significant in light of the fact that the typical danger to humans from these substances comes from *repeated, low-level* doses. For example, if one is evaluating a new drug, one is typically not concerned with the effects of massive doses, barring suicide attempts and major industrial accidents. Rather, one is worried about the possible long-term effect of a cumulative series of relatively small doses. One is also concerned with the *mechanisms* of toxicity, the sites of toxic action, and the *metabolic processes* affected by the drug, etc., none of which the LD50 deals with at all. In fact, emphasis on the LD50 figures tends to lead to a de-emphasis upon qualitative data, such as clinical signs and autopsy results. Nor do LD50 tests contribute much to design of further toxicity trials, since they are purely quantitative and consider only mortality.

Most dramatically, cross-species variation, coupled with a total failure of the LD50 to come to grips with the metabolic pathways taken by the various toxins, renders the results of animal LD50s all but meaningless *vis-à-vis* a justifiable extrapolation to human beings. Nor is this mitigated by tests across different species. Morrison et al. flatly assert that:

> Neither variations nor uniformity of LD50 figures in a number of laboratory animals species can assist in estimating toxicity in man. (p. 4)

So without knowledge that the metabolic pathways of the substance are identical in man and test animal, we cannot draw inferences to human toxicity from LD50 studies on animals.

Furthermore, there are huge numbers of variables, typically not controlled for, that can radically alter LD50 results on test animals. Among these are species differences, genetic differences even in the same species (LD50 for the substance thiourea was 4mg/kg in Hopkins rats and 1340-1830 mg/kg in Norwegian rats), crowding conditions, sex, age, composition of diet, latent infection, caging conditions (in mice caged alone, an increase of cage size has been shown to reduce toxicity of amphetamine by 50 percent), temperature, humidity, and light. The LD50 for amphetamine in rats increases 700 percent when the rats are caged in groups of twelve, compared to when they are caged singly.

Other articles echo these criticisms. For example, F. Sperling, in a 1976 article in *Advances in Modern Toxicology: New Concepts in Safety Evaluation,* severely criticizes the LD50 test. In Sperling's words,

> It is no longer sufficient to count bodies and from such an account develop an index of toxicity. . . . The LD50 is in fact only marginally informative, toxicologically inadequate, and misleading. (p. 177)

Sperling argues that the LD50 pays no attention to morbidity (sickness) arising out of exposure to toxic substances, nor to chronic exposure. He points out that emphasis on number of animals dead leads to the ignoring of vital factors, such as time to death and rate of recovery of survivors, factors that could provide important information regarding site, mechanisms, and duration of action of the toxic material. In writing up LD50 results, scientists typically ignore important, qualitative, clinical data that may or may not be reported in publications but are essentially irrelevant to the LD50. Sperling concludes that:

> The numerical acute LD50 is not an indicator of toxicity, whatever the route of administration. . . . It is an indicator of the end effect of catastrophe—industrial, suicidal, or accidental as in children. (p. 185)

To be facetious, the LD50 typically tells rats what dose of a chemical they need in order to commit suicide effectively.

We have thus encountered doubts about the value of the LD50 test from a variety of points of view. Most important, it is by no means clear whether a measure of acute toxicity ought to be the fundamental tool of product safety evaluation at all. But even supposing that there continues to be a demand for some standard measure of acute toxicity, there are strong arguments in favor of an alternative to LD50 testing. In a 1943 article, Deichmann and Leblanc described a method for "Determination of the Approximate Lethal Dose with About Six Animals," in the *Journal of Industrial Hygiene and Toxicology*. The method employed involves guessing at the lethal dose, administering it to an animal, then proceeding in approximately 50 percent increments up or down until ascertaining the first dose at which the animal dies. Since we have seen that an exact measure of the lethal dose is not required or even coherent in the uses of the LD50, but rather what is sought is some approximate, relative scale of toxicity, it is hard to see why the Deichmann and Leblanc method does not present a viable alternative to the LD50, with tremendous savings in suffering, lives, and money, and little loss. In the words of Morrison et al.:

> We would like to see more use made of methods such as that of Deichmann and Leblanc, who were able to derive an approximate lethal dose with less than ten animals. This should be adequate for most purposes. (p. 13)

It is interesting to note, as a result of our rather detailed study of the LD50 test, that there is good reason to believe that from a strictly scientific point of view, millions of animals are being wasted, merely to provide an arbitrary measure of toxicity, with little carry-over to real human dangers. From a moral point of view, this is completely intolerable. Thus far, we have encountered a kinship of scientific and moral factors. Unfortunately, this is unlikely to be a full partnership. Those scientists critical of the LD50 test are not concerned with the moral status of animals, but rather with the waste of animals as economic resources, and with the potential danger to human beings. It is not the use of animals for the testing of toxic substances that is being criticized, but the specific methodology entrenched in federal regulations and industrial practice. *It is, by no means clear that whatever might replace the LD50, for example, long-term tests of chronic toxicity, would not result in as much and perhaps more suffering and death to laboratory animals.*

The way to resolve this entire question of toxicity testing lies in demonstrating, and then reflecting in legislation, the thesis that the interests of experimental animals and the interests of human welfare do overlap. *Basically, it is in both our interests to diminish the number of potentially toxic substances being introduced into the market and the environment!* No degree of toxicity testing can reliably predict long-term, chronic effects of the incredible array of chemicals to which we are exposed at all times, especially since we lack any method at all of evaluating the potential for synergistic activity between substances. That is, we have no way at all of knowing the potential toxicity of two or more substances acting in combination in the environment. Enough has been written over the past twenty-five years by ecologists to indicate that we are playing a bizarre Russian roulette with the biosphere; witness the aerosol spray cans and the much discussed destruction of the ozone. Public consciousness of these dangers has unquestionably been elevated, and people are demanding assurances of the safety of products and chemicals.

One possible and easy avenue of response to this pressure is for manufacturers and government to increase the number of animal tests. But to depend on this is to rest on a bent reed, both because of species differences and other methodological problems of the sort we have raised in discussing LD50, and because they cannot detect synergy (substances acting together), nor can they model subtle ecological catastrophes. It is far better, it would seem, to make a social decision, expressed as legislation, to limit the number of products being spewed forth into the environment and into our bodies, at least until we have a purchase upon the possible pernicious consequence of the estimated more than 500,000 toxic substances that are or will shortly be in common use. (The 1978 *Registry of Toxic Effects of Chemical Substances,* which listed only substances upon which research has been done, lists 125,000 substances. Today that has easily doubled.) One clearly needs a calculator even to begin to imagine the magnitude of possible synergistic effects! Even if all possible synergistic reactions were exhausted by *pairs* of chemicals interacting, which is surely not the case, since there is no reason to believe that groups of 5, 10, or 3,000 don't interact, 500,000 substances would give us approximately 125,000,000,000 possible pairwise combinations! Obviously, in a deep sense, "safety testing" is impossible. It would seem plausible, then, to put a curb on the number of chemicals being developed. One might demand that each manufacturer of a new, potentially toxic substance be required to show in great detail why the substance he proposes to introduce represents a marked improvement over preexisting substances already tested and in use. And such claims ought to be assessed with great care before still another food additive, for example, is permitted. Promulgating such a policy, or law, could discourage the development of chemicals that functionally duplicate products already in existence and would reduce the ever-increasing risk of toxicity to humans, as well as reduce markedly the number of animals made to suffer so that we can have yet another food coloring or laxative. Our point is further underscored by the recent tragedies and publicity surrounding toxic waste disposal, a problem we as a society have not yet even begun to deal with.

THE DRAIZE TEST

A similar point can be made about cosmetics, an industry that is primarily associated with another test open to a good deal of serious criticism—the Draize test. Since cosmetics are capable of being highly irritating to skin and eye, various tests have been devised to determine the irritant qualities of different substances. Tests of skin irritancy are also applied to various household substances. The Draize test is most often singled out in sensationalistic tabloid accounts of the abuse of laboratory animals. An irritant substance is put into the eye of rabbits, and the resultant irritation or lesion formation is noted and evaluated according to standards for scoring ocular lesions. This test has been criticized widely for its poor reproducibility and its poor ability to project results in human beings, for example, by Buehler in the *Toxicology Annual* for 1974. It has also been criticized for causing unnecessary suffering. The Draize test has been criticized even by that stalwart defender of animal research, Dr. D. H. Smyth, in his book *Alternatives to Animal Experiments*. Smyth, while not wishing to abolish the Draize test, would severely mitigate its effects on animals. In his words,

> There is a case for testing for eye irritancy, but a mild eye reaction would seem to be sufficient to establish the point. This is particularly so, since in general the rabbit's eye seems to be less sensitive than the human eye,

so that anything causing a mild reaction in the rabbit would appear to be highly undesirable in the human. . . . I cannot see any justification for causing severe eye damage. (p. 68)

It is interesting to note that while Smyth claims that the rabbit eye is "less sensitive" than the human eye, other "experts" claim the opposite and thus argue that the test ends up identifying irritants that would not affect human beings! As many scientists have indicated, the whole notion of greater or lesser sensitivity is obscure, since sensitivity is undefined. Sensitivity to what, and as measured by what? And the fact that a substance does or does not produce an observable lesion in a rabbit eye in a short period of time tells us nothing about long-term effects of the substance in the human eye. Once again, the problems evidenced in the LD50 test arise, for here too we are interested not in acute effects, but in long-term chronic effects. What happens in the person who uses the cosmetic daily for years? How do we know that pernicious, nonobservable biochemical changes are not taking place? Clearly the benefits of the Draize test do not outweigh the suffering. In fact, the test may well give us false confidence where prudence is more rational.

Given the plethora of cosmetics already available to consumers, it is difficult to justify *any* animal suffering merely for the sake of marketing yet another species of nail polish or shampoo. It is difficult to imagine any justification for the claim that the cosmetics industry would suffer by a curb on its ability to develop new products. The demand for cosmetics, after all, is relatively inelastic. Competition could proceed in other ways, say, by utilizing principles already known in new ways. The real competition in any case, as manufacturers have admitted, lies in advertising and packaging. So once again, we need to ask ourselves whether this is not an appropriate area for legislation or regulation.

It is probably utopian to expect such regulation, but it appears to me that a viable alternative to skin and eye tests on animals does exist. Given that these tests are not fatal, and given that courts have sometimes refused to accept animal results as tests of product safety, it would seem plausible that the industry make use of paid human volunteers. This is in fact already done after animal testing. It is difficult to see why it could not replace animal testing in this area altogether. It seems probable that public intuitions would concur with this view, since it seems somehow "fairer" to use paid people; animals can derive no possible benefits from cosmetics, which are a luxury item, and the subjects would be paid.

Over the last two decades, public concern with animal testing has steadily increased. As early as 1974, a British poll showed that the overwhelming majority of repondents objected to cosmetic testing on animals, a view that was later echoed, surprisingly, by the readership of *Glamour* magazine when surveyed by the magazine, and by a 1990 Gallup Poll conducted for *Advertising Age*. Such sentiment has not been lost on the cosmetics companies. In 1980, a coalition of animal activist groups attacked Revlon in newspaper advertisements for using the Draize test. By 1981, Revlon had allocated $750,000 to Rockefeller University for the study of alternatives to the Draize test. Shortly thereafter, the other cosmetics companies, acting through their trade association, chartered a center for alternatives to animal testing at the Johns Hopkins School for Public Health. A number of promising alternatives to the Draize test have been emerging from these research centers, the most promising being the use of a fertilized chicken egg, whose membrane displays an inflammatory reaction similar to what occurs in the conjunctiva of the human eye.

Some limited progress has also been made with regard to the LD50 in the face of mounting public pressure. In 1985 and 1988, the Environmental Protection Agency (EPA) discouraged the use of the classical LD50 and suggested that it be replaced by other approaches, including the approximate lethal dose we discussed above, and the use of the so-called "limit test." In the "limit test," which is used for substances known to be basically nontoxic, a small number of animals are given a single oral dose. If no animals die and no major ill effects occur, no further testing is initiated. The EPA has also urged the extrapolated use of data from structurally related chemicals whose toxicity is known. Also, small numbers of animals can be used to detect toxic effects at doses which are not lethal, and animals can be euthanized before pain and suffering occur. The EPA also said it would only accept classical LD50 data when there is a specific reason alternatives cannot be used. Similarly, in 1985 and again in 1988, the Food and Drug Administration (FDA) announced that it had ceased to require the classical LD50 in the early 1980s. In contradistinction to the EPA, however, it did not refuse to accept classical LD50 data without special justification.

Most heartening, perhaps, has been the decision made in 1989 by the Avon and Mary Kay cosmetics companies to discontinue the use of animals for safety testing. Avon now uses alternative testing, human clinical testing, and an extensive, computerized toxicity data base. Most notable, perhaps, is Avon's endorsement of the EYTEX system, an approach based on a synthetic matrix of proteins which has been used as an alternative to the Draize test. Responses of matrix proteins to irritants show high correlations with eye irritation.

Though all of this bespeaks some progress, in my view it is too little and too slow, given the serious moral and scientific criticisms that we have raised against the LD50 and the Draize tests. Bureaucratic inertia, habit, fear of lawsuits in an ever-increasingly litigious society, and the innate conservatism of standard toxicological laboratories all militate in favor of preserving the status quo. In my view, the only way to cut the Gordian Knot is with a legislative sword. Legal prohibition of the Draize and LD50 tests would accelerate the alternative approaches, to the benefit of science, animals, and consumers. Such legislation has been recommended by an Australian Senate Committee on the welfare of experimental animals, and it has been proposed in various states in the U.S.

CARCINOGEN, MUTAGEN, AND TERATOGEN TESTING

There are numerous other areas in which animals are employed in testing, most noteworthy being tests of cancer-causing substances (carcinogen testing), mutation-causing substances (mutagen testing), and tests of the effects of substances on embryo development and malformation (teratogenesis or, literally, "monster-producing" testing). Historically, most carcinogen testing has been done on animals. While the artificial use of massive doses on animals whose metabolisms may or may not accurately replicate human metabolism (as in the famed saccharine studies on rats) is subject to skeptical doubts about its validity, it is clear that no one is prepared to sacrifice any possible identification of carcinogens. There are major drawbacks to animal tests, however. First of all, as just noted, many scientists express doubts about whether results on animals can be meaningfully extrapolated to humans, given the myriad differences in physiology and metabolism. Tests on rats last two years; tests on dogs last seven, as the animal must be exposed to the chemical for large portions of its life. Thus, in addition to being methodologically suspect, these tests are expensive and time-consuming. It costs at least $8 to $20 million, in fact, fully to test a substance.

Fortunately, there are alternatives to the use of animals, most noteworthy being the Ames test, which is also a test for mutagens. In fact, the Ames test as a test for carcinogens is predicated upon the assumption that many (if not all) carcinogens are mutagens. It is known that carcinogens produce cancer by engendering somatic mutations. The Ames test is ingenious, simple, and inexpensive (it costs about $500 and takes three weeks to test a substance) and utilizes bacteria as the test group. In the test, a suspected carcinogen is added to a nutrient medium (agar) in which a special strain of *salmonella* is growing. This strain, unlike its parent strain, requires that a chemical called histidine be added to the nutrient medium for the bacteria to grow. In the presence of a mutagen or carcinogen, the special strain of *salmonella* reverts to the properties of the parent strain and will grow in the absence of histidine. One then simply observes the growth of these colonies. A quantitative measure of the mutagenic potential of a substance can be constructed by use of different concentrations of the suspected substance. Modifications of the Ames test exist for detecting carcinogens that require metabolic activation. A homogenate of rat or human liver is added to the nutrient, enabling researchers to detect such carcinogens. The validity of the Ames test and its variants seems quite well established. A good many substances that are known to be carcinogens through animal testing have been subjected to the Ames test and 80 percent of them have been shown to be mutagenic. Correlatively, a large number of noncarcinogens have been subjected to the Ames test and under 10 percent have been found to be mutagenic.

Here, clearly, is a happy case where human and animal welfare coincide. It is in the human interest to use tests like the Ames test because they are cheaper, quicker, and probably more reliable. It is obviously in the animals' interest not to be used for cancer testing. In any case, the Ames test ought surely be done at least as a preliminary screening device, prior to large-scale animal testing.

The final special case of toxicity testing is that of teratogens, substances that act on embryonic tissue to produce pernicious changes in the developing organism. Thalidomide is perhaps the best known of such substances and, ironically, it had been extensively tested on animals. Because of our inability to extrapolate across species, most obstetricians today urge pregnant women to avoid drugs and chemicals altogether, even where there is no evidence that the substance is teratogenic in animals. This seems a wise course, especially in virtue of the possibilities of synergy discussed earlier. A textbook of toxicology, Loomis's *Essentials of Toxicology,* cautions that

> In general, tests on one species have limited value in predicting effects on another species. This is seen in regard to the drug cortisone which is teratogenic in mice but only in some strains of rats. (pp. 211–12)

There currently exists no clear-cut, viable alternative to animal testing for teratogenicity. Though enjoining pregnant women to avoid all chemicals serves to alleviate much of the problem, the unenforceability of such exhortations requires that teratogenic properties of substances be known. Claims have been made for the use of developing chick embryos, but this is generally considered unsatisfactory for two reasons. First of all, the developing embryo test is highly sensitive to a wide variety of variables. Second, and more important, concern with teratogenesis in humans requires that it be known if, when, and how the substance in question can pass through the placenta. Since chick embryos are nonplacental, clearly this method can supply no information concerning this crucial question. Another alternative is epidemiological studies—studies of the appearance of terata in human populations, and of the factors common to members of that population. The disadvantage here, of course, is that one must wait for large-scale appearances of the congenital malformations, whereas what is desired is advance knowledge. (Computer-assisted epidemiological studies of carcinogens, searching for common features in the histories of cancer victims, are also being attempted.) Another suggestion that has been advanced is the use of human embryos destined for abortion as test subjects. Though from a strictly scientific point of view this would clearly be preferable to animal studies, and though these fetuses would be killed in any case (cf. the argument for using impounded dogs for experimentation), such an activity would be deemed monstrous and does not seem to be acceptable to the vast majority of society. It thus appears that teratogenicity testing can probably meet the utilitarian principle, and thus current efforts at improving the lot of animals used for these purposes ought to be based upon the rights principle, insuring that, as far as possible, the animals live painless and natural existences while science continues to seek alternatives to the use of animals.

THE CONCEPT OF ALTERNATIVES TO ANIMAL EXPERIMENTATION

In discussing this first category of research, namely testing of substances on animals, we have implicitly and explicitly come up against the much-discussed question of "alternatives" to animal experimentation. An alternative, following the classic discussion of Russell and Burch in their *Principles of Humane Experimental Technique,* is a method that could either (1) *replace* the use of laboratory animals altogether, (2) *reduce* the number of animals used, or (3) *refine* a procedure so as to diminish the amount and degree of pain, suffering, and stress experienced by the animals. The Ames test is a good example of *replacement;* laboratory animals are wholly eliminated in favor of bacteria. The Deichmann and Leblanc method of estimating acute lethal toxicity is a good example of *reduction,* since that method employs six animals, as against the sixty to one hundred employed by the LD50 method. And finally, our whole discussion of the utilitarian and rights principles are injunctions toward *refinement,* especially the rights principle, since the utilitarian principle is in effect a mandate for drastic reduction.

One major thrust of opponents of animal experimentation is the demand for alternatives, though this demand is often not clearly defined. What is usually meant, it seems, are methods like the Ames test that will *replace* animals. However well-intentioned, an extremely heavy emphasis on replacement is misdirected. In the first place, it ignores the very obvious economic fact that the scientific and industrial community welcomes and actively seeks replacements for animals, because many animals are expensive to obtain and expensive to care for, and because the use of animals is increasingly controversial. Tissue and organ culture, for example, in which cells are grown in the laboratory and used in various experiments, has extensively replaced the use of animals in a number of research areas. Second, the demand for replacement tends to impeach the credentials of those who offer utopian replacements for animals. For example, one often hears opponents of animal experimentation demanding that "the computer" be used to replace animals. "After all," it is said, "if a computer can send a man to the moon, can it not model a mouse?" The answer, unfortunately, is "no." Any computer, however complex, is essentially an adding machine, a calculator, a formal system, which can only spit out variations on what is put into it. If we knew enough molecular biology, physiology, and biochemistry to model a mouse on a computer, we probably would not need to! Attempts at modeling even tiny parts of the body have been markedly unsuccessful. Finally, the heavy emphasis on replacement tends to obscure the other two Rs, reduction and refinement, and especially the latter. Those who try to mitigate the lot of the laboratory animal are seen as "sell-outs," whores, acceptors of the status quo. And yet, as we shall see, the most currently viable hope for diminishing the total amount of suffering is by refinement of existing procedures, by the introduction of anesthetics and analgesics, by the mitigation of stress and anxiety, and by improving living conditions and husbandry, all of which attempt to deal with the current realities of research.

THE USE OF ANIMALS IN TEACHING

When one talks of the use of research animals as teaching aids, one finds ample opportunity for all three Rs—reduction, refinement, and replacement. Let us recall that animals are used (and abused) in elementary schools, secondary schools, colleges, universities, medical schools, and veterinary schools. Many of these uses entail extraordinary degrees of suffering for the animals. Consider, for example, high school science fairs and science projects. These are often exercises in sadism and stupidity. I have heard of a high school biology class spaying dogs and a junior high school student surgically implanting cobalt 60 into a guinea pig! As another example, we may cite the case of the dairymen's group that travels from school to school setting up the following absurd "experiments": Three rats are used: one is fed nothing but water, one is fed nothing but glucose, and one is fed nothing but milk. This is designed to show that milk is nutritious, by showing that the other two rats die of malnutrition! One student in junior high won an award for closing up the anus of a shrimp and watching what happened. There is no reason that high school and grade school children need to experiment upon living creatures. We all recall dissecting frogs; we all recall learning nothing. In any case, at the heart of awakening interest in science is not carpentry and butchery—it is learning how to ask questions, how to formulate hypotheses, and how to observe. There is value in youth being exposed to animals, but let these observations be ethological and ecological; let us teach them to see with the eye of the naturalist, for this will enrich their lives in a permanent way that dissecting frogs will not. There is no justification, not even a utilitarian one, for allowing children to inflict pain upon animals, or to violate their bodies. On the contrary, the old Kant-Aquinas brutalization argument we discussed earlier is quite germane here. Harking back to our earlier arguments, it seems plausible to imagine legislation that simply forbids painful or surgical experiments on animals in elementary and secondary schools.

A variation on such legislation currently exists in California, where it was in fact supported by many university scientists who do animal research, and who realize that there is little value in invasive research done at the precollege level and a good deal of potential harm that may be done to the animals and to the psyches of the young students. The California law, adopted in 1973, is generally considered to be the most effective of such laws, and a model for others of its kind. According to the law

> In the public elementary and high schools or in public elementary and high school-sponsored activities and classes held elsewhere than on school premises live vertebrate animals shall not, as part of a scientific experiment or any purpose whatever (a) Be experimentally medicated or drugged in a manner to cause painful reactions or induce painful or lethal pathological conditions. (b) Be injured through any other treatments, including, but not limited to, anesthetization or electric shock.
>
> Live animals on the premises of a public elementary or high school shall be housed and cared for in a humane and safe manner.

Ideally, some version of these principles should be included in a meaningful federal Animal Welfare Act since, as currently constituted, the Animal Welfare Act excludes elementary and secondary schools from its jurisdiction. Unfortunately, this has not occurred, though public sensitivity has unquestionably constrained unbridled animal use on this pedagogical level.

What of higher education? Surely, it might be argued, one cannot train biologists, veterinarians, physicians, etc., without using animals. This is certainly a more difficult case than elementary and secondary education and is endlessly debatable. In Great Britain, veterinarians are trained without ever touching an animal, save for therapeutic purposes. In the United States, it is considered necessary that prospective veterinarians do a good deal of practice work with animals in order to develop technical abilities, for example, surgical skills. Similarly, medical students historically also learned surgical techniques on animals. It is utopian to expect these practices to be abolished in their entirety, but there is a good deal of room for amelioration of suffering.

One of the most flagrant abuses in this regard, only recently abolished, was the widespread practice of multiple recovery surgery. Recovery surgery is practice surgery done on an animal where the animal, most often a dog but sometimes a cat or other animal, is not euthanized while under anesthesia but instead is permitted to recover. What makes this practice abhorrent is the fact that recovery from surgery, as we all know, involves shock, pain, distress, and suffering. Often, however, little care was taken to keep the animal comfortable, and sometimes water, blankets, and adequate heat were denied to these animals, who were seen merely as teaching aids. Analgesics, however inexpensive, were rarely used. (In fact, compared to other areas of knowledge, our knowledge of analgesics in animals is relatively limited.) In some institutions, the animals were used as many as six or eight or more times in different, unrelated surgical procedures, in order to save money for additional animals. Large animals, such as horses and cows, were sometimes used until they literally dropped, and a wide variety of procedures were often performed in the course of one session.

There was no educational justification for this proliferation of suffering. It was often argued that veterinary and medical students needed to recover the animals in order to learn about management of surgical patients, and thus the utilitarian principle was satisfied. This is debatable, but it is a serious argument. Unfortunately, the force of the argument was often lost in schools where the animals were treated with cavalier disregard for their recovery, and emphasis was placed only on the surgical technique. (This, of course, violates the rights principle.) No one to whom I have spoken in either the medical or veterinary profession could provide any pedagogical or moral justification at all for multiple, unrelated recovery surgeries.

Such a practice in fact represented the worst sort of crass economic opportunism. Unfortunately, with ever-increasing budgetary pressure upon academic institutions, one could expect economic considerations to loom large. Therefore, it seemed plausible to incorporate a blanket prohibition on any unrelated multiple surgical procedures in the new amendments to the federal Animal Welfare Act we shall discuss shortly. Such a prohibition in fact already existed in the National Institutes of Health Guidelines for the Care and Use of Laboratory Animals, a set of guidelines that was quite enlightened and that incorporated some of the notions we have been developing. Unfortunately, these guidelines were essentially unenforced. In principle, it was possible for the federal government to freeze all federal research funding to any institution violating these guidelines—in actual practice, this was never done prior to 1982. And since these guidelines were not enforced, they were all too often not observed. Even worse, many research scientists did not even know the details of these guidelines, and were not aware that they were violating them.

It is also currently acknowledged by most medical, veterinary, and other biomedical educators that a significant amount of the work done with live animals can be supplanted by videotape, film, computers, and models. For example, at one time anaphylactic shock was demonstrated each year in veterinary school by inducing it in a rabbit in front of the freshman veterinary class. The symptoms of strychnine poisoning were demonstrated by actually poisoning dogs. It is cheaper, pedagogically sounder, more defensible morally, and less brutalizing to put this on videotape. Once on tape, the student can go over such demonstrations repeatedly, can be alerted as to what to look for, and most important, can see what is taking place much more clearly than in a lecture hall. A similar point holds of witnessing surgical procedures, which are far easier to follow when one is guided by narrative and by the eye of the camera. Furthermore, using audiovisual devices, the student can watch surgery as performed by the top practitioner in each respective area. Computers can be used to teach some physiological information better and more predictably than animals, e.g., the effects of drugs on the cardiovascular system. Suturing, bone fixation, and other surgical skills can be learned on models prior to applying these techniques to live animals. Lives are conserved, suffering is diminished, and money is saved. As we shall see, such changes are taking place, under the impetus of new laws and rising social concern for animals.

RESEARCH ABUSE AND THE TRAINING OF SCIENTISTS

Much of the abuse to which animals are subjected in scientific practice can be traced directly to the nature of scientific education, or perhaps one ought to say, scientific training. Contrary to what the layperson or humanist tends to expect, the training of professional scientists, pure and applied, is not designed to foster Newtons, Einsteins, or Darwins. Although the essence of science in one sense consists of free thought and inquiry, the spirit of wonder harnessed to relentless questioning, the actual molding of a scientific career bears little resemblance to this ideal.

Beginning at the undergraduate level, the student is put through a series of courses that emphasize techniques, manipulation of data, acquisition of facts, and manual dexterity, rather than thought or understanding. The tests given are typically short answer, true or false, or multiple choice, geared to the regurgitation of discrete bits of information. No emphasis is typically placed upon conceptual understanding or upon ability to synthesize. Let me cite two illustrative examples from my own experience. On numerous occasions, I have asked senior physics students the following questions, drawn from the Middle Ages: "If the earth moves, why don't we feel it, and why aren't the clouds left behind?" Many students *cannot answer this question,* though they can plug data into formulae. Again, I often ask senior biology students to indicate what set of beliefs stands at the cornerstone of contemporary biology. Few can tell me that it is, of course, evolutionary theory, and even fewer can discuss the relationship between evolutionary theory and the various parts of modern biology. In fact, few can even discuss evolutionary theory. Even worse, so abysmal is their ignorance that they feel no shame at this state of affairs. After all, any one of them can rattle off the Krebs cycle!

But it is on the level of graduate education that one can really see the pernicious nature of science education assert itself. One can do virtually nothing but wash test tubes or become a lab technician with only a bachelor's degree in science, so typically, students who genuinely wish to pursue a scientific career must proceed to a master's and doctoral level. Perhaps, one would expect, it is here that science as thinking is inculcated into the student. This, unfortunately, is not the case—in fact, the situation is even worse than on the undergraduate level. On the undergraduate level, the option at least sometimes exists for students to take classes in a wide variety of fields, to take humanities and social science classes, to enter into learning experiences that are reflective upon the nature and activities of science. Often, unfortunately, the option does not exist even there as the major requirements are so stringent and restrictive. On the graduate level, anything outside the immediate area of apprenticeship is viewed as frivolity and is frowned upon. Undergraduate school is not serious—no one with a bachelor's degree is really a scientist. Granting someone the doctorate—the "union card," as it is often tellingly called—is quite another matter. To grant someone a doctorate is to acknowledge him or her as a peer, as a fellow guild member, as certified by you or your institution to instruct and conduct research. To grant someone a Ph.D., M.D., or D.V.M. is to certify him or her as a fellow professional, whose behavior reflects on *you* and on *the profession.* As a result, doctoral education (or medical education or veterinary education) involves total immersion of the student in the language, practices, prejudices, procedures, predilections, biases, and concerns of his or her particular field or, more accurately in the case of Ph.D.'s, of that minute part of the field that the student or advisor has chosen as his or her area of expertise.

In a nutshell, graduate education is *nonconceptual*. It is not designed to produce revolutions in a field, to turn out people who will upset the apple cart. Science essentially resists changes in its bases, for such changes are obviously threatening to those currently defining the field, who would find themselves superseded and rendered superfluous by major conceptual upheavals. The sociology of scientific conservatism is admirably defined in Thomas Kuhn's influential book, *The Structure of Scientific Revolutions,* where Kuhn defines the activity of "normal" (i.e., nonrevolutionary) science as puzzle solving, the answering of questions that flow from the field as currently defined, and that are passed on from advisors to students and by the textbooks.

Thus, the graduate student is essentially handed a problem for research by the advisor and even handed the ground rules for possible solutions. This is his or her apprenticeship—if he or she succeeds, or makes headway, he or she is certified as a member of the field and is entitled to pursue these puzzles, seek funding, and replicate himself/herself through his/her graduate students. The same sense of certification holds, in fact even more strongly, in professional schools: medical, veterinary, and dental. There the student is being certified as a clinician, as someone who will carry the principles and practices of the profession before the public, whose behavior can bring honor or discredit to all members of the guild; so these schools often foster conformity and uniformity, not only in medical theory and practice, but in dress (though this has declined in recent years), mode of speech, professional etiquette, carriage, and deportment. Once again, individual thought, ingenuity, and creativity are systematically de-emphasized and pushed to the background. It is not so much that these traits are considered dangerous; rather, they are viewed as irrelevant to the fundamental task of training a uniform and predictable corps of individuals with a dependable set of skills.

How does all this relate to the treatment of animals? In very direct and dramatic ways, which are easily illustrated anecdotally. One of my good friends, an experimental psychologist, recounted to me a telling incident. As a young graduate student, he was running an experiment with rats. The experiment was over, and he was faced with the problem of what to do with the animals. He approached his advisor, who replied, "Sacrifice them." (We shall discuss this locution in a moment.) "How?" asked my friend, assuming that the professor would produce a hypodermic needle and barbiturates. "Like this," replied the instructor, dashing the head of the rat on the side of the workbench, breaking its neck. (While this is not in fact a painful way to kill a rat if done correctly, since cervical dislocation causes instant death, it is not easy to learn and is highly offensive to the uninitiated.) My friend, a kind man, was horrified and said so. The professor fixed him in a cold gaze and said, "What's the matter, Smith, are you soft? Maybe you're not cut out to be a psychologist!"

This is a wonderful story, for it illustrates so many aspects of the problem: the disregard for normal sensibility, the cult of "objectivity," the threat that failure to toe the mark elicits, the cavalier disregard for student concern, the use of a phrase like "sacrifice." Let us examine some of these points. My friend, like countless other embryonic scientists, physicians, and veterinarians, was starting with a sense of moral concern for the animals, with respect for them as ends in themselves, as living creatures. This, however, is seen as sentimentality, squeamishness, lack of professionalism, etc., and so values are transvaluated, as Nietzsche says, and what are ordinarily virtues —compassion and sensitivity—become vices. When I make this point to some of my scientist friends, I am often told that prospective physicians and veterinarians must "get used to the sight of blood and to death and to pain." (One man actually attempted to justify a particularly brutalizing lab exercise by saying that "it underscores to students that they are in vet school now.") Yes, I reply, but must they get used to callously inflicting pain and causing death? Must they be brutalized to be good physicians and veterinarians? Surely sensitivity and good medicine are not mutually exclusive—indeed, are they not complementary? As I travel and lecture around the country, I am often asked the same question by educators involved in human and veterinary medical education: "Why do students come into medical (or veterinary medical) school sensitive, concerned, idealistic, morally aware, and suffused with a desire to promote health and alleviate illness and suffering, yet emerge four years later cynical, hardened, brutalized, and rigid, their ideals and enthusiasm forgotten?" Clearly, the educational system has a pernicious effect not restricted to the problem of animals. But it is not at all clear that it must be that way, as we shall discuss shortly.

Correlatively, it is utter nonsense to suggest that my friend's concern for the animals might be good evidence that he is not cut out to be a psychologist. Perhaps it will be harder for him to be a psychologist, in the sense that he will think long and hard before doing certain things to living creatures, but perhaps he will then be a better psychologist. He will surely be more inclined to study what merits studying, to obey the utilitarian and rights principles, than will be a person to whom the animals are merely expendable laboratory accoutrements, like test tubes. And perhaps with his sensitivity he will notice and see things in the animals' behavior that, to a more callous person, would be invisible.

One of the major sources of educational brutalization harks back to the scientific ideology which we discussed earlier, and which pervades and undergirds scientific education. As mentioned in our discussion, a mainstay of this ideology is the idea that science is value-free, ought to make no valuational commitments, and thus, *a fortiori,* has no truck with ethics. This notion, like many other components of scientific common sense, is rooted in the logical positivism of the early twentieth century, which stressed the need for objectivity, empiricism, and verification in science. Since value claims in general, and ethical claims in particular, are not subject to empirical test and verification, they have no place in science. They are to scientific ideology, at best, emotional predilections and cannot be dealt with objectively. (It is for this reason that otherwise cool and rational scientists are often every bit as emotional on such ethical issues as animal use as their opponents are—their training and ideology has led them to the view that ethical issues are in fact nothing but emotional issues, where rational thought has no place, and they thus believe that battles are won by manipulating emotions and tugging at heartstrings.) The possibility of a rational ethic on anything is instinctively seen as an oxymoron or solecism.

It is not difficult to determine that science education imparts this claim to students. Keeton and Gould, for example, in their widely used freshman biology text, remark that "science cannot make value judgments . . . and cannot make moral judgments." In the same vein, Mader, in her basic biology text, asserts that "science does not make ethical or moral decisions." In 1989 James Wyngaarden, former director of the National Institutes of Health, declared that all the flap about genetic engineering was misdirected, for "science should not be hampered by ethical judgments." In 1988 Richard Marocco, a psychological researcher at the University of Oregon, responded to critics of animal research by asserting that their concern is "not an intellectual concern—it's an emotional, an ethical one, and a moral one," as if ethical concerns were not suited for rational adjudication.

In our earlier discussion, we refuted the pervasive notion that science is value-free. And, as we shall see, social concern and the emerging social ethic for animals have resulted in new legislation which forces scientists to consider ethical questions. But in my view, the incorporation of moral deliberation into science is best achieved by making revolutionary changes in science education, something to which I have devoted almost twenty years, with gratifying results. Before recounting these activities, we must deal with one more component of scientific life which reinforces callousness toward experimental animals.

THE DEBASEMENT OF LANGUAGE IN SCIENCE

Perhaps the callousness is a defense mechanism, an insulator for the experimenter that stands between him or her and guilt and pain. Perhaps it is a matter of convenience. But whatever its source, it is perpetuated by the language scientists employ, in conversation and in formal writing, concerning the animals they utilize. Scientists talk, for example, of the animals being "models." The "model" locution suggests that the nature of the animal, its *telos,* its *raison d'être,* is to serve as a representation of something else. It also deemphasizes the fact that the object in question is alive, possessed of its own needs. Again, consider the phrase "sacrificed," with its exalted religious, sacerdotal connotations. To sacrifice is to make sacred. The animal is *privileged* to die, it ascends to rodent Valhalla, it romps in the Elysian fields. It is privileged, lucky, fortunate to die for SCIENCE. It has advanced the frontiers of knowledge. Oh *felix rodentus!*

The exaggeration is intentional. My comments are silly, but so is the locution. An animal killed in an experiment is not sacrificed. To say that it is is to debase language, to use language to conceal the morally questionable and distasteful, to insulate ourselves and others from the questionable consequences of what we do. In the early twentieth century, Karl Kraus warned of the large-scale moral atrocities presaged by the debasement of the German language. Language, argued Kraus, is a moral barometer, a thesis that George Orwell was later to portray graphically in *1984.* Kraus's prescience was extraordinary, for his predictions were realized in the Nazi state, the quintessence of evil in our time, and perhaps in all of human time: "Work makes one free," emblazoned on the gates of Auschwitz; "Submen," used in reference to Jews, gypsies, and Slavs; "Super-race," "Aryan," "the Jewish question," etc.

Examples of this mentality applied to animals are easily proliferated. In veterinary colleges there were and still are special names for the non-client-owned animals that are used for surgery practice, experimentation, and demonstration. They were called "subanimals." Although etymologically the "sub" is short for substitute, most students hear it as "sub" as in "subhuman." In one school, the dogs employed for these purposes were called "x-dogs"—when spoken, of course, it was heard as "ex-dogs." These locutions are visible examples of the hardening process, the encapsulation and ultimate exorcism of compassion, the "professionalization" of morality and humanity. Fortunately, much of this has changed as socio-ethical concern about animals in science increased.

Such considerations, then, stand as an impediment to improving the lot of animals in higher education. These are deep difficulties, woven into the very fabric of science as it actually exists. As we shall see, the problems that exist in science education ramify throughout research on animals, serving as a major stumbling block to the implementation of moral concern. The scientific gestalt on animals, which sees them as tools to be used, as Cartesian machines, as implements ready at hand for human purposes, is carried in the language of science and perpetuated and reproduced in its educational processes. To improve the situation, then, requires not only legislation and regulation, but even more important, a revolution in science education.

CREATING A REVOLUTION IN SCIENCE EDUCATION— SOME PERSONAL NOTES

Perhaps that phrase sounds a bit too grandiose and is best tethered to earth with some concrete examples. About fifteen years ago, I became seriously concerned with the robotization, lack of thought, callousness, and ignorance of philosophical and ethical questions that seemed to pervade science education. Five years earlier, I had turned my attention to pre-medical education and had developed a course of study in philosophy for premedical students that would counter some of these pernicious trends, and that had enjoyed gratifying results. I now turned my attention to a number of pioneering areas, all of which it is relevant to discuss: veterinary medical ethics, basic biological science, and agricultural science, research, and training.

My interest in animals, coupled with my interest in and knowledge of medicine, made it plausible for me to consider working with the College of Veterinary Medicine at Colorado State University, widely acknowledged to be one of the best veterinary schools in the United States. Rather brashly, I approached the administrators of the school who, much to my surprise, were quite sympathetic to my proposal to teach ethics to the veterinary students. I was informed, however, that such a course was totally unprecedented, that veterinary students had little or no interest or preparation in humanities, that the course of study was quite technical and "applied," that I would probably encounter a fair amount of hostility, suspicion, and opposition from students, faculty, and the veterinary profession at large.

Undaunted, I pressed the course, which was run for the first time in 1978 on an experimental basis. Team teaching it with me was an extraordinary man, Dr. Harry Gorman, past president of the American Veterinary Medical Association, sometime chief veterinarian for NASA, well-known orthopedic surgeon, and inventor of the artificial hip joint. To the astonishment of both of us, we hit it off immediately despite our disparate backgrounds. Both of us were deeply concerned with the same issues: too much emphasis on technique and not enough on thought, the robotization and brutalization of veterinary students, and the emphasis on professional etiquette rather than on morality in discussions of "veterinary ethics." The course was scheduled to run for ten weeks, with both of us in attendance at all sessions, but with my assuming primary responsibility for the lectures and discussions. Eager to develop dialogue with the students, I insisted on teaching them in three groups of forty, so as to make possible discussion and interchange.

As the first lecture drew nearer and nearer, I became more and more nervous. Could I really expect these students, with their totally practical and technical orientation, to have any interest in or sympathy with philosophy? Given their impossibly full schedule, could I really expect them to spend time trying to master Kant and Mill? Could I earn the students' respect? The task seemed impossible, the prospects hopeless; I began to entertain Gauguin-like fantasies of fleeing to Tahiti. Nor was I reassured by the few conversations I had with some members of the veterinary faculty. One man asked me what I expected the students to get out of this class. "My goals are modest," I replied; "I only want to show them that there are moral and philosophical questions associated with veterinary medicine that cannot be answered in a factual way." "Are you going to give them answers?" he said. Guessing at his concern that I might poison the minds of the students with my "radical philosopher" approach, I assured him that I would not give answers, only present options. "You must give them answers," he thundered, to my astonishment. "You must give them the answers of the professional veterinarian!" "But I'm not a professional veterinarian," I protested; "And in any case, I don't think that the answers given by the profession to moral questions are complete or adequate. But since you are a professional veterinarian, perhaps we can debate this before the students." "No way," he said. "Why not?" I asked. "Dialogue is the essence of thought." "Well," he said, "that's your mistake. You think we want them to think. We're not producing thinking men; we're producing professional veterinarians!"

The class began. At first the students saw it as one more hoop they were required to jump through to get a D.V.M. If the vet school demanded Sanskrit, they would learn Sanskrit; if philosophy, so be it. But by the fourth week, the student attitude of suspicion, hostility, and resignation began to change. They began to argue with me, and with each other. They began to stay after class and visit me in the office. They began to appreciate the opportunity to exercise their excellent minds on the sorts of questions we have been dealing with in this book. (They were extremely bright— competition for vet school admission was then more intense than for medical school.) By the eighth week they requested that I run the class for the full semester. They began coming to my office, going out with me for lunch. And by the end of the semester, things began to happen.

At that time, the majority of veterinary students were from ranch backgrounds, and the classes were 80-90 percent male. The macho, cowboy ethos was pervasive, and, not surprisingly, there was a veterinary student rodeo held every spring. This became a fertile topic for class discussion, especially when I began a lecture by asserting that "for veterinary students to participate in rodeo is equivalent to orthopedic surgeons fighting in bars." Needless to say, we had no shortage of lively interaction. Eventually, the students realized that there was tension between their own (previously un-articulated) ethic for animals (don't harm an animal for frivolous reasons) and their cherished cultural tradition. Since students from farm and ranch backgrounds tend to take ethics very seriously, they were disturbed. After a few weeks of discussion among themselves, they informed me that they had reached a compromise, which modified the rodeo to fit their ethic. "Clearly," they told me, "the most abusive part of the rodeo is calf-roping, for the calf is jerked to a stop at twenty or more miles per hour. So we will henceforth use breakaway ropes—ropes tied to a light string which breaks after the calf is lassoed." It was only later that I realized the enor-mous concession these macho cowboys had made; in their culture, break-away ropes are only used for women's events! The Socratic "judo" had worked, even more so than I had ever dreamed. (To fully appreciate just how revolutionary this whole affair was, the reader should recall that, in the West, raising questions about rodeo is as unacceptable as breaking wind in church—perhaps more so!) A year later, one of the students, a professional roper, came to my office. "You son of a bitch," he said, "you made me give up roping." "Care to explain that before you hit the floor?" I responded. "How can I make you do anything?" "You made me think about it," he said quietly.

Even more dramatically, the students became concerned about multi-ple survival surgery in surgery classes. The concern increased until almost half the class presented me with a petition asking for reform in this practice. We began a series of long discussions involving students, surgical faculty, administration, and myself, which lasted through the summer. At the end of the discussions, the school adopted a policy of recovering an animal only once, and of treating each subject animal exactly like a client animal. The students were to be graded not only on carpentry, but also on post-operative care. Despite opposition from some old-line surgeons who felt that this policy was an infringement on their God-given freedom to use animals as they chose, and despite the increase in the cost to the school, the policy was rigidly enforced. A major moral breakthrough in veterinary education had occurred, one which spread to other veterinary schools across the U.S. No longer was the "science is value-free" ideology unchallenged; a wedge was opened which has grown and expanded during the ensuing years. Self-awareness, self-criticism, dialectical moral analysis have become second nature to students and faculty alike, and the reputation of our veterinary school as a pioneer and leader in moral concern for animals has spread world-wide. Some members of the faculty sat in on the class, and participated in discussion. I, in turn, spent time virtually every day with faculty members, in the clinics and in laboratories. I have learned a great deal from the students and faculty; they have been sparked to think by me.

In a sense, I have become a faculty ombudsman for animals. More dramatically, the concept of such a function has been accepted and even welcomed by many of the scientists working with the animals. "We need a conscience," one major researcher on campus told me. And over the past fifteen years, I have been actively involved in many mundane, nuts and bolts sorts of issues that directly affect the well-being of laboratory animals. Through dialogue (sometimes heated, mostly rational), I have worked through solutions with teachers and investigators in areas I had never heard of. We have improved laboratory classes, worked to ensure better use of anesthesia and analgesia, and even worked to increase the number of cows used to teach rectal palpation for determining pregnancy to the veterinary students, so that the cows' rectums would not be damaged through overuse. (I'm particularly proud of that one since I never dreamed, as a philosophy graduate student at Columbia, that I would put my training to work for the benefit of cows' rectums!)

The atmosphere of frank and open discussion of moral issues related to animal use has continued to bear fruit. In 1983, after ongoing self-criticism, the surgery faculty at the veterinary school took the unexpected step of giving up any survival surgery at all. All practice surgery was now terminal—the animals would never recover from anesthesia—and students would learn the management of recovery on real client cases. Despite the increase in cost to the school, this policy was adopted for moral reasons. A spokesman for the faculty, world-renowned surgeon Dr. Donald Piermattei, announced the policy as essentially a moral one, for now students would be taught surgery without causing any pain or suffering! Because we arguably have the best surgery faculty in the world (more Board Certified surgeons than any other school), such a policy again spread to other institutions.

This is not to say that every surgeon initially supported the changes with equal enthusiasm. But rational ethics does work. When multiple survival surgery was first abolished at CSU for moral reasons in 1978, one of the major veterinary surgeons, whom I shall call Dr. X, was irate. As far as he was concerned, what he did with his own animals was his own business. Indeed, he was angry enough to threaten to resign over this issue. Our relations were always strained, since he blamed me for the new policy abolishing multiple survival surgery, and curtailing what he felt was his "right" to do as he saw fit with his animals. Some years later, he moved to another university, and I lost track of him. Then I was invited to lecture at another veterinary college. The student who met me at the airport told me that one of the faculty wished to meet with me. Puzzled, since

I knew no one there, I inquired who the man was. "Dr. X, our new chief of surgery," he replied. "Dr. X wants to see me?" I marvelled. "But he hates me," and I told the student the story of our previous interaction. "Oh no," he said. "It can't be the same guy. Our Dr. X, as his first official act, cut our multiple survival surgery program down to one surgery." Not knowing what to think, I went to see Dr. X; indeed the same gentleman. I thanked him profusely for abolishing multiple surgery at that institution. "Oh no big deal," he said, slapping me on the shoulder. "Same thing we did at CSU!"

Despite the inherent risks to stability that open discussion and questioning poses, the two Deans of the Veterinary College under whom I have worked, first, Dr. Robert Phemister, and currently, Dr. James Voss, have fully supported our efforts. My course was made a required part of the curriculum, and students must pass it as they pass any other class. (The average grade on my very difficult essay final examination is over 90 percent!) I have been invited to speak to clinicians and have become friendly with many of them. We do not, by any means, agree always or even often, but we all respect each other and communicate. And the Veterinary College has been very supportive of my efforts in animal ethics activities. The school, in turn, was acknowledged in the British journal *Nature* as the best in the United States regarding the treatment of animals. The course has attracted international attention, and I have been asked to visit many institutions to lecture on these topics and to help set up similar programs, where I find both students and faculty starved for dialogue on these and other questions. Indeed, I now write a very popular monthly ethics column for the *Canadian Veterinary Journal.*

Veterinary medicine, like human medicine, is beginning to realize that there is more involved in teaching and practicing good medicine than merely knowing how to give lab tests, sew an incision, or treat shock. As I have argued in other papers, and as its history demonstrates, medicine is, by its very nature, fraught with valuational, social, and conceptual questions. Medicine and philosophy have been intimately intertwined since Hippocrates—it is only fairly recently, with the rise of reductionistic medicine, which sees the body simply as a machine (and is itself a highly questionable philosophical position!), that the relevance of these questions to medicine has been ignored or denied. We shall shortly discuss this point in greater detail. In any event, I am now employed on a year-round basis by the university to work on moral problems associated with biomedical science, not only the problems associated with the use of animals, but also the questions involved in human research and in biohazard control.

The lesson to be learned is this: Despite the extreme fragmentation of knowledge, the robotization of science, and the aloofness of the humanities, these obstacles can be surmounted by people of good will with a vision of education as developing the students' minds and awareness, not simply as training. This requires an enormous amount of work. The philosopher or humanist like myself must be prepared to sully his or her mind with facts—to read veterinary books and journals, for example; to ground himself or herself in science in order to have some credibility, and perhaps even to get manure on his or her boots. The scientists must resist the reflex response to see a humanist in their midst as a threat.

Lest it be thought that I am too quick to draw Pollyanna-like conclusions from a single experience, it is worth citing another project that has occupied my attention for fifteen years. Along with a brilliant botanist, Dr. Murray Nabors, in 1978 I began teaching a one-year honors course in basic biology. What was revolutionary about this course is that the relationship of the humanities component to the science component was not that of icing to cake. That is, it is not the case that the students took a traditional science course for eight days in a row, and then on the ninth day the philosopher did a little half-hour song and dance. The philosophical, moral, and social questions connected to the science were viewed as an integral part of the science, discussed along with the science. When the course was initiated, both of us were present at all class meetings, and we constantly interrupted each other, criticized each other, and argued. The net result was that the students learned to see science as full of and subject to questions; they learned to recognize problematic areas, rather than gloss over them; they realized that the essence of the enterprise is free thinking, not memorization. When we discuss DNA, we discuss the moral and social questions surrounding recombinant DNA research. When we discuss evolutionary theory, we raise in detail those difficulties associated with the theory that are ignored by all but specialists in the philosophy of science. We discuss the questions raised in this book about the use of animals in science. We discuss the nature of science, the certainty and uncertainty of scientific theories, the problem of fraud in science, the nature of scientific funding. We even discuss the issues associated with scientific education we have just enumerated, warning the students that they will typically not be encouraged to think for themselves as they proceed through their education. The class has enjoyed remarkable success—the students cover about twice the scientific material dealt with in the standard course, plus all of the conceptual material. The students gladly put in a great deal of extra effort, welcome the challenge, and do far better in terms of grades than do students in standard courses. They also report that in the wake of their experience with us, they are unable to respond to other courses the way their peers do—they feel compelled to ask questions and raise objections. This has not been totally unthreatening to many scientists: when my biologist colleague went on sabbatical, no one was willing to take his place, despite the enormous success and popularity of the course. Enough time has elapsed since the course started that we now receive feedback on the course from former freshmen students who are now physicians, veterinarians, and scientists. Gratifyingly, they report that the course gave them a unique foundation that continued to serve them well into their professional lives.

The success of these courses led to additional experiments. Ten years ago, I began to teach a course for the animal agriculture or animal science students on ethical issues in animal agriculture, the first such course ever done. I anticipated a much greater challenge here as, unlike veterinary medicine, animal science has no "official" commitment to animal welfare, being essentially the application of biological science and economics to maximizing profit and productivity in the food and fiber animal industry. I was delighted to discover that these students are in fact the best students I have ever taught—the ranch background that many of them enjoy has given them both a strong moral commitment to animals living primarily under natural conditions and expressing their *telos,* and also to hard work. Because I travel so much to lecture, I often make up my classes at night, an imposition on the students. Nonetheless, my attendance is excellent, and I consistently turn away more students than I have room for. My hope is to help create a generation of scientists in animal agriculture who have been sensitized to the moral issues inherent therein, who have been reinforced in their tendency to see animals as something other than assembly-line products, and who will carry a moral vector into agriculture. Given that we are not likely to stop using animals for food, it is far better to have a generation of animal scientists for whom concern for animals is part and parcel of their mind-set. In this way, we can perhaps blunt the tragic tendency in twentieth-century animal agriculture and animal science to look only at profit and productivity, and concentrate again on the well-being, happiness, and fulfillment of the animals' *telos,* which technological, "value-free" agriculture has put aside. And increasing numbers of our students are now thinking in terms of animal welfare as an integral part of agriculture. Pursuant to this goal, the animal science department has hired Dr. Temple Grandin, world-famous authority on livestock behavior and husbandry, to help incorporate practical animal welfare considerations into agriculture.

As is the case in my work with the veterinarians and biomedical researchers at CSU, I have established an excellent dialectical rapport with the agricultural scientists—indeed, we are currently working together on ways to eliminate the significant pain and suffering associated with traditional livestock practices such as castrating and hot iron branding.

In conclusion, I certainly argue for regulatory action to constrain the uses of animals in science education; as we have seen, this has already occurred *vis-à-vis* multiple surgery in new federal legislation. Videotaping and the use of other such devices should be made mandatory wherever possible. Correlatively, a real thrust must be inaugurated for liberalizing science education, as I have illustrated. This will ramify not only in immediate attention to animal suffering, but in developing greater sensitivity to the moral and social dimensions of science, both as these dimensions relate to animals and as they relate to humans. Better science, too, is likely to result when students are educated to question, not merely trained to perform.

Unfortunately, it is difficult to inaugurate meaningful changes into science education. Funding is relatively scarce, university budgets are tight, and meaningful interdisciplinary efforts are notoriously difficult to establish, as people are threatened by making themselves vulnerable in an interdisciplinary context. Further, because of the narrowly specialized educational system we have been describing, which is instantiated in the humanities almost as much as in the sciences (a person may know late nineteenth-century British poetry or medieval philosophy and little else), it is extremely difficult to get people to plunge into teaching where they must master material for which they have not been trained. Yet, in the final analysis, such efforts are absolutely essential to both the sciences and the humanities. The sciences require it, as we have seen, so as not to degenerate into a mere set of technical skills, and so that we produce socially responsible scientists, who are morally concerned. The humanities and social sciences require it, quite frankly, to survive in an era of increasing vocationalism. It is well known that the supply of Ph.D.s in the humanities and social sciences typically far exceeds the demand. Further, students seem to be more and more oriented toward "practical" courses of study that will ensure the possibility of their earning a living. Fewer students will be majoring in English, philosophy, history, etc., as the possibilities of academic employment vanish. Such disciplines must thus insinuate themselves into the very fabric of the more "marketable" disciplines—medicine, veterinary medicine, engineering, law. As I have tried to show the members of my profession, philosophy is especially well suited for such activity, partly because it has served since Plato to keep people thinking clearly, and partly because the moral questions associated with science are of such major social import. Unfortunately, as I saw demonstrated at an international conference on animal rights, philosophers are all too often unwilling to speak to anyone but other philosophers and jealously guard the technical jargon that, in their minds, makes them part of an abstruse and technical discipline in which not just anyone can share.

INTRODUCTION TO THE USE OF
ANIMALS IN BASIC RESEARCH

Basic research is, quite simply, what most of us think of when we think of science at its best and at its worst. Unsullied by pressures of practicality, the basic researcher is the person who worries about the age of the universe, or about the strange properties of micro-particles, or about the nature of gravity, or black holes, or pulsars. The basic researcher is also the person who worries about things that strike the average person as absurd or a waste of money—the sort of person to whom Senator Proxmire regularly granted the Golden Fleece Award for wasting federal money in trying to answer questions about the songs of birds, the sex life of fleas, the conditions under which people fall in love, the nature of planes in ten-dimensional space. What typically characterizes the basic researcher is a remarkable lack of concern for the practical effects or usable consequences of his or her research. If the results do find real and pragmatic applications, all to the good. If they do not, equally good. The concern is with the problem, the puzzle, the joy of the chase. Researchers attack the question because it is there or, as some researchers will admit if pressed, to advance the frontiers of human knowledge. More cynically, in many cases the basic researcher finds himself or herself having inherited some problems simply in virtue of what he did his doctorate on, or who his advisor was, or what is likely to get funded in her area of expertise. In any case, what is important for our purposes is that such research in biology, physiology, anatomy, psychology, etc., sometimes involves the use of animals in ways that cause pain and suffering.

FREEDOM OF THOUGHT VS.
THE MORAL STATUS OF ANIMALS

The extreme positions regarding this sort of research are easily identified and may serve to orient us toward the complexities inherent in this question. On the one hand, it is argued by defenders of research that basic research is the essence of human thought, the root of science, nothing less than the quest for knowledge. Our entire civilization and all progress, it is argued, rest upon allowing people to pursue those questions which ignite their curiosity. As to the utilitarian principle, we may grant that basic research does not always have built into it any clear-cut advances in human happiness or welfare. On the other hand, one never knows what applications a piece of research may have, however far removed from reality it may seem to be. Crick and Watson surely did not think in terms of their work providing a basis for altering human genetic patterns. My wife was quite surprised when she was informed that her abstract mathematical research into strange geometries that we cannot even visualize had direct application to communicating with and controlling satellites. Any piece of knowledge may have unprecedented potential for good, and consequences undreamt of by its discoverer. This, in fact, is the rationale behind the activities of research facilities like Bell Laboratories, which essentially turn bright scientists loose to follow their curiosity, without regard for immediate, practical implications. It is immoral to close the door to the advancement of knowledge; it is a rejection of our very humanity. We as a civilization have fought long and hard to free ourselves from political, theological, and superstitious constraints on rational inquiry; we should not sell that freedom cheaply.

These arguments are powerful, and as a person who values intellectual freedom and activity above all else, I can feel their appeal. But there are compelling arguments on the other side as well. It is true that free inquiry is integral to our humanity, but so too is morality. Few of us put knowledge over right and wrong. If the quest for knowledge were our ultimate concern, we would applaud those who callously experiment upon humans, instead of vilifying and loathing them. We could learn much by experimenting upon unwanted children, upon the retarded, the brain-damaged, the terminally ill. Yet we shudder at the thought; we see the Nazi "experimenters" not as free inquirers, but as perverted monsters. Knowledge must yield to compassion, and decency, and morality. In the more than forty-five years since the Nazi horrors were revealed, societies have labored long and hard to develop strict ethical codes dealing with research on human subjects, often, unfortunately, to the opposition of scientists. In major universities like mine, all such research is rigidly scrutinized by watchdog groups, fully backed by federal mandate and regulations. Even benign experiments on innocuous items like learning word lists must be submitted for approval and certification. (Having served for over fifteen years on such a committee, I can attest to the zeal with which its members protect all rights of the human subject.) Illicit experimentation does, of course, go on, most notably in university hospitals on the poor and ignorant, on derelicts, on those who cannot protect themselves. But the point is that this is not socially condoned or supported, and is clearly seen by most people as wrong.

So the quest for knowledge must be tempered by moral concern. And we have seen throughout this book that animals have profound and legitimate claim to moral concern, even as we do. For this reason alone, animals must be protected from those whose thirst for knowledge outstrips their moral sensibility. It is thoroughly utopian to expect basic research on animals to cease altogether; as I have said before, society is not prepared to give up the possible benefits that such research might bring. If there were suddenly no animals, I strongly suspect that we would quietly begin experimenting upon the defenseless humans mentioned earlier. Peter Singer, in his excellent book *Animal Liberation,* suggests that we ask ourselves, in thinking about a given piece of animal research, whether we would be prepared to do that research on retarded humans. Unfortunately, I think the answer for too many researchers would be "certainly!" (Recall the hepatitis experiments done at Willowbrook on retarded children.) And if there were no animals, I think that many researchers would not be inclined to restrict themselves to the retarded if they were allowed free reign.

But it is not utopian to expect researchers to accept constraints on what can be done to animals for moral reasons, even as they have accepted constraints on what can be done to humans. The right to inquire, like all rights, is not absolute. Furthermore, only the most naïve researcher would think that he or she currently enjoys unrestricted freedom of inquiry. All sorts of powerful forces currently serve as constraints upon that freedom. Certain research, for example, is socially unacceptable, a clear example being that of scientists like Shockley whose thesis is that certain racial groups are intellectually inferior. Such research is eschewed by major universities and by funding agencies. Similarly, certain hypotheses and theories have been ruled out *a priori* by the research community, often for no good reason at all, simply because the hypothesis is "preposterous" and "clearly absurd." This harks directly back to the points we made about the insularity and unthinking nature of scientific education and, correlatively, of the scientific "establishment." (One is uncomfortably reminded of Galileo's bishops, who refused to look through the telescope because they already knew that the moon was perfect and unflawed!) Twenty years ago, one would have been thrown or laughed out of a medical school if one even suggested studying acupuncture. More dramatic is the case of Velikovsky, whose radical ideas concerning the solar system were viciously and hysterically attacked by prominent scientists *who had not even read his books and admitted it!* Another powerful force puncturing the myth of free inquiry is research funding. Given the incredible costs of research, salaries, overhead, physical plant, equipment, supplies, etc., virtually no one can do research on their own without major sources of funding. The funding agencies are capricious, often subject to vagaries of research fashion, social pressure, "old-buddyism," and political influence. Any scientist will tell you as a matter of course that the best scientists aren't necessarily the ones funded. In fact, a physicist I know makes an eloquent and strong case that Einstein would not be funded today—his work was too esoteric, abstract, and counter to the mainstream of thought.

All of this shows that freedom of research is essentially in a deep sense simply a slogan—one cannot simply choose to investigate whatever strikes one's fancy. A complex nexus of social, cultural, and political factors forms the arena on which research is played out. Why not, then, simply add one more rational, moral vector to these constraints? Why not require that the interests and nature of animals be considered by funding agencies and by researchers.

THE USE OF "ALTERNATIVES" IN BASIC RESEARCH

One of the recent thrusts by those interested in the welfare of laboratory animals has been a heavy emphasis upon alternatives to animals in experimentation. Various pieces of legislation have been introduced, designed to press the use of alternatives: one such bill would have established a center for the study of alternatives, the other would have allocated up to 50 percent of the current federal biomedical research budget to the study of alternatives to the use of animals. To some extent, basic biological research already utilizes replacement for live animals, for example, tissue and organ culture, which involve growing living cells in the laboratory and using these cells for various experiments that might in the past have utilized animals. On the other hand, as Smyth has pointed out, the development of these methods often spurs *additional* research on animals, to extrapolate or test the results gained from the *in vitro* (literally, in glass, i.e., test tube) methods. In any case, the development of possible viable alternatives to animals often requires a knowledge of biology and physiology far in excess of what we currently have and would itself be unable to proceed without research on animals! Certainly, a meaningful Animal Welfare Act would require the use of alternatives to animals where this is possible and ought to further require justifications in each case where alternatives are not used. But it is currently unrealistic to expect replacement to be the major vehicle for ameliorating animal suffering in basic research.

There is, however, a good deal of room for refinement and reduction in basic biological research. One of the simplest methods of reduction involves tightening up of experimental and statistical design in biological research. It is notorious that biologists are rather poorly trained in statistics. As a result, they often do not prove what they think they are proving and also fail to extract the maximum amount of information from a body of data. Increased attention by funding agencies to the design of experiments and ruthless criticism of experimental methodology would benefit both science and animals by eliminating waste and unnecessary suffering. There is no point in doing experiments if the experiments have no sound theoretical grounding. This point, of course, applies across all of our research and testing categories. A case that dramatically illustrates this point was reported in *Science,* in June of 1979. It was revealed that the National Cancer Institute's program of testing possible carcinogens, long represented as one of the best in the world, was extraordinarily deficient. Fifty-one long-term programs were so deficient that they could not even be written up as technical reports. At one laboratory under contract to NCI, 89,394 animals had to be killed because of preventable infections, at a cost of $320,000. At another laboratory, 53,000 animals were wasted.

THEORY-BASED SCIENCE VS. EMPIRICAL DABBLING

So one simple source of reduction is, paradoxically, a demand for better science, science in which animals are not wasted, in which experiments are well-reasoned and well-designed. And this harks back to our earlier point about science education. Given the manner in which scientists are trained, it is no surprise that there is so little theoretical, methodological, and conceptual self-awareness and self-criticism in research. So long as scientists are instructed to do rather than to think, to work within set theoretical patterns rather than to criticize them, to get funded rather than to reflect on the significance of the tasks before them, we will have sloppy science. Surveying the contemporary research situation, I am often put in mind of the reaction of the British Royal Society to Newton's revolutionary works. Betraying a marked lack of understanding of Newton's achievement, some members of the society became convinced that what distinguished Newton from other thinkers was his empiricism, and that if they, too, became more empirical, they could do Newton-like things. One can find in their commonplace books (or intellectual diaries) accounts of experiments that they performed in the hope of shaking out another revolutionary discovery ("Today I mixed horse manure and Coca-Cola and nothing happened!"). They had no theoretical basis or imaginative insight to spark hypotheses; in fact, they had few hypotheses. They equated science with *trying things and seeing what happens,* much as children do. Unfortunately for science and for the animals, there are still scientists who proceed in precisely this manner, totally atheoretically.

Does this really happen? Unfortunately, yes. There are numerous experiments conducted that have as little scientific value and credibility as the high school demonstration involving feeding rats milk, water, and glucose mentioned earlier. Take, for example, the experiment conducted that involved starving a coyote for a couple of weeks, throwing a sheep in with it, and concluding that a hungry coyote will eat a sheep. Following this, the coyote was again starved, only this time two sheep were thrown in with him, one ordinary sheep and one covered with hot pepper. Conclusion? A hungry coyote would rather eat the plain sheep but, in a pinch, will eat the seasoned one!

One can chronicle endless numbers of this sort of experiment, where it is difficult to understand how any adult human being can devote serious time and money (usually federal) to such a study. Oftentimes experiments involve telling us what we already know from common sense. Other times one has little idea what the significance of the results are, as the experiment does not stem from any theoretical vision that will better help us understand the world.

Ten years ago, I debated the head of the National Society for Medical Research, then the chief lobby group for the biomedical establishment, before an audience of seven hundred people. In the course of the debate, he remarked that any attempt to constrain what can be done to animals would stifle science, since science is, after all, nothing but "the gathering of facts," and a process of "trial and error." The fact that such a major figure could blatantly espouse such a simplistic view of science is shocking but illustrative of our thesis. As I pointed out to him, science is not just or even basically the gathering of facts. Scientific theories do not typically emerge from random data collection. The main importance of data is in the *verification* of hypotheses, not in their discovery. After all, when one considers any major scientific theory, be it the theory of gravitation, relativity, quantum mechanics, the gene, etc., one makes reference to entities and processes that are unobservable, and whose discovery required imaginative leaps. Newton was certainly not the first man to be hit by a falling apple; yet it took Newton's theoretical vision to postulate gravitation!

The most superficial look at the history of science reveals that virtually no major advances were made simply by gathering data. The great scientists were guided by theory and vision, indeed, sometimes by erroneous vision, as in the case of Kepler, who sought to prove that the orbits of the planets could be related mathematically as the notes of the musical scale, thereby establishing the music of the spheres postulated by the Pythagoreans. Or let us recall Galileo, who is often said to have shown that the acceleration of falling bodies is independent of their mass and is uniform by dropping a heavy and a light object from the Leaning Tower of Pisa. In actual fact, as seen in his *Dialogues Concerning the Two Great Systems of the World,* Galileo was a good deal more ingenious than that and employed reason to establish his point. Take two five-pound weights, said Galileo, and drop them from the same height. Surely they will hit the ground at the same time. Join them by a weightless rod—surely they will still hit the ground at the same time when dropped. Shrink the rod until the two weights are stuck together. Surely they will still hit the ground at the same time. But now we have a ten-pound weight, showing that rate of fall is independent of mass.

As another example of where theory precedes data and predominates over it, consider Einstein. His world-shattering critique of Newton was not based on data or experiment unavailable to others, but rather on a conceptual analysis of the concept of simultaneity. Correlatively, when asked what he would have said if some astronomical predictions generated by the general theory of relativity had not been supported by the data gathered by Eddington, Einstein said in essence, "So much the worse for the data—the theory is correct!"

A similar account can be given about the father of genetics, Gregor Mendel. Every schoolboy knows of Mendel's famous experiments with the pea plants, which allegedly led him to the discovery of genetics. In fact, statistical analysis of Mendel's studies indicate that the probability of Mendel actually obtaining the experimental results he claimed was only .00007, or one in 14,000! In short, Mendel knew that the theory was correct and chose the data which met his expectations.

We know too from the history of science that in the face of theoretical commitment, recalcitrant data is easily dismissed or explained away, and that theory determines what we see. Consider Galileo's bishops, who refused to look through the telescope because they knew the moon was perfect. Suppose they would have been forced to look—would they then have been forced to admit that it was not perfect? Not at all—they simply would have said that Galileo had created an instrument that made the perfect moon look flawed. An even more dramatic example is told of Franz Anton Mesmer, the discoverer of "animal magnetism" or hypnotism. In order to illustrate the anesthetic effects of hypnotism, Mesmer hypnotized a patient who was to undergo amputation, and the limb was removed with no visible discomfort. "Have I not proved my point?" asked Mesmer triumphantly. "Not at all," replied the physicians. "The man felt pain, he just failed to show it."

The point, then, is this: Contrary to the way science is often taught and contrary to the way many researchers proceed, science is not merely fact gathering. To paraphrase the great philosopher Immanuel Kant, "theories without data are empty, data without theories is blind." Certainly we shall make no progress without accumulating data and facts. But those facts must not be gathered at random. They must be gathered in order to test hypotheses and theories arrived at via the creative power of thought, reason, and imagination, as the members of the Royal Society after Newton we discussed earlier ruefully discovered.

BEHAVIORAL PSYCHOLOGY: SOME PARADIGM CASES OF BAD SCIENCE AND UNNECESSARY SUFFERING

Rather than chronicle random cases that illustrate the pernicious nature of atheoretical research from a variety of scientific fields, it is perhaps better to focus upon the field most consistently guilty of mindless activity that results in great suffering. This is the field of experimental, behavioral, comparative, and sometimes physiological psychology. Nowhere are researchers further removed from theory, nowhere are researchers less engaged in trying to develop a picture of some aspect of the world, nowhere are researchers less able to discuss intelligently the significance of their experiments, nowhere are researchers less concerned with the morality of what they do. Robert Paul Wolff once remarked that what is most wrong with contemporary science is that scientists totally lack perspective—each individual researcher sees himself as throwing a little piece of dung onto the giant dung heap, and somehow, eventually, there will stand a cathedral! I recall one of my students who was a psychology graduate student being particularly shocked by a nasty piece of animal research and asking the researcher what the significance of that experiment was. Without blinking an eye, the psychologist replied, "That is for future researchers to decide."

Since I have become interested in animal rights, I often argue with psychologists about the morality of what they are doing. When they are not too defensive to engage in dialogue, I pose the following dilemma to them: "A good deal of your research is on mice and rats, studying behavior and learning, utilizing pleasure and pain to condition the animals. Clearly, you are not interested in the mind of the rat for its own sake. You study these animals because they are relevantly analogous to human beings, because rat behavior is a good model for human behavior. The dilemma is this: Either the rats are relevantly analogous to human beings in terms of their ability to learn by positive and negative reinforcement (i.e., pleasure and pain), in which case it is difficult to see what right you have to do things to rats that you would not do to human beings, or the rats are not relevantly analogous to human beings in these morally relevant ways, in which case it is difficult to see the value in studying them!" I have never received an adequate response to this question; in fact, I have rarely received any response at all. The only semblance of an answer is something like "Well, we're stronger than rats," or "We're not allowed to do it to people," both of which are obviously morally irrelevant, as we saw in earlier discussions.

On one occasion, when a psychologist justified his behavior on the grounds that he was "stronger" than the rats, I must confess to responding with a most unphilosophical counterargument. Being a weightlifter, I picked him up by his lapels and snarled, "Well, I'm stronger than you are—how

about I run you through a maze?" (I don't know whether he got the point,
· but I certainly enjoyed it!)

Obviously, then, there is a clear moral problem associated with psychological research. But there are also deep conceptual problems associated with parts of the field, one of which is implicit in the dilemma, namely, what is the value of studying animal learning and responses? What theory connects rats and humans? Does psychology have a theory at all? Consider the work of B. F. Skinner, certainly the most revered of contemporary behavioral psychologists, who operated in the behaviorist tradition, a tradition which dominated American psychology for many years and is still very influential. Does Skinner's lifetime of research give us a clearer understanding of the human mind? No! Skinner, like other behaviorists, loathes even talking about the mind, which for them is an imprecise, unmeasurable, mystical notion. Does it give us an understanding of the processes underlying human or animal behavior? Again, it does not. In a brilliant and readable article entitled "B. F. Skinner—the Butcher, the Baker, the Behavior-Shaper," my friend and colleague Dr. Richard Kitchener has demonstrated, I think conclusively, that Skinner was not doing pure science or basic research at all. Nothing in what Skinner does, Kitchener points out, helps us to understand the workings of nature. He discovers no laws and generates no theories. Behavioral psychology, says Kitchener, is "cookbook knowledge"; it is "generalizations from practice and trial and error experimentation . . . very similar to the kind of knowledge one finds in certain trades or crafts." Skinner himself, Kitchener points out, admits that psychology "is not concerned with testing theories, but with directly modifying behavior." In *Beyond Freedom and Dignity*, Skinner talks constantly of "behavioral technology."

This development of techniques for molding the behavior of animals and men is therefore not science. It tells us nothing new about the world, it does not help us to understand either ourselves or animals. It is no more science than a book on how to play tennis, or a guide to improving one's golf swing, or a book on how to raise and train a goldfish! True, these all count as knowledge, but not as scientific knowledge—rather as skills, or manipulatory techniques. In Skinner's case, as in his predecessor Watson's case, the goal is developing the technique of manipulating and controlling human behavior, as Skinner amply demonstrates in works like *Beyond Freedom and Dignity* and *Walden Two*. The point is that this is not basic research helping us to understand the universe, advancing the frontiers of knowledge in a "value-free" way. Since no theoretical understanding of the world is gained, this research amounts to looking for ways of molding human beings, surely a value question of the first magnitude. And surely this does not count as pure science, protected by the value of free inquiry. There are grave social dangers in developing such methods under government aegis, as military abuse of psychedelic drugs has demonstrated, and this surely ought not be done without a good deal of social discussion and control.

Besides the potential pernicious consequences for human beings, the lack of theory, the empirical dabblings, and the trial-and-error approach that characterizes behavioristic psychology are extremely mischievous from the point of view of animal suffering. Suffering is essential to psychological research in a way that is unparalleled in all other research, except research on pain, anesthetics, and analgesics. A basic feature of much behavioral psychological research is the use of negative reinforcement (i.e., pain, anxiety, stress, etc.) to condition animal behavior in various ways. It is for this reason that I am so strongly critical of such psychological research. Not only does it not advance our understanding of the world or, for that matter, of the mind (behavioral psychologists hate the word "mind"; they see it as mystical), not only is its *raison d'être* the manipulation of human beings, but it causes incalculable amounts of pain on all sorts of creatures for no apparent benefit. It is extremely revealing and interesting that other scientists who work with animals, even strong defenders of the researcher's right to use animals, often have great contempt for behavioral psychology and point out that by far the most "cruel and useless" experiments are done by psychologists, and that these experiments give *all* researchers a bad name!

There is, furthermore, a good deal of reason to believe that the entire behaviorist enterprise may be misdirected, since some thinkers have argued that human beings (and very likely animals, too), do not learn important things by stimulus-response conditioning. Noam Chomsky, in a series of books and articles, most notably *Rules and Representations,* has argued that the most important cognitive "organs" we possess—like language—are innately programmed and are triggered by experience, not derived from it. If Chomsky is correct, all the conditioning experiments in the world will tell us nothing about the features of the human mind we are most interested in understanding. As we saw earlier, researchers like Donald Griffin and many cognitive psychologists see no reason to be hamstrung in their researches into the minds of animals by the archaic straitjacket imposed by behaviorism. It is indeed ironic that although behaviorists have run countless experiments on dogs, cats, and rats in bizarre situations, no attempt has been made to publish work giving any insight at all into the mind of any of these creatures.

Lest it be thought that we cannot buttress our claims, it is worth citing some salient cases of stupid and useless psychological research, though any reader could make his or her own list today simply by leafing through the journals. These examples were taken from the excellent survey of the *Physical and Mental Suffering of Experimental Animals,* prepared by Jeff Diner at the Animal Welfare Institute, a study that surveys the scientific literature from 1975-1978. A similar list could be constructed today.

- At the Department of Psychology at MIT, hamsters were blinded in a study showing that "blinding increases territorial aggression in male Syrian golden hamsters."

- At UCLA, monkeys were blinded to study the effects of hallucinogens on them.

- At Harvard, experimenters used squirrel monkeys trained to press a lever under fixed-interval schedules of food or electric shock presentation. The purpose of the experiment was to compare hose biting induced by these two schedules.

- At the University of Maryland, experimenters studied the effect alcohol had on punished behavior in monkeys, i.e., on lever-pressing behavior conditioned by electrical shock.

- At the University of Texas, psychologists studied the effect of foot-shocks in rabbits on brain responsiveness to tone stimuli.

- A particularly bizarre experiment on "learned helplessness" induced by electric shock is worth quoting at length:

When placed in a shuttle box an experimentally naive dog, at the onset of the first electric shock, runs frantically about, until it accidentally scrambles over the barrier and escapes the shock. On the next trial, the dog running frantically, crosses the barrier more quickly than on the preceding trial. Within a few trials the animal becomes very efficient at escaping and soon learns to avoid shock altogether. After about 50 trials the dog becomes nonchalant and stands in front of the barrier. At the onset of the signal for shock, he leaps gracefully across and rarely gets shocked again. But dogs first given inescapable shock in a Pavlovian hammock show a strikingly different pattern. Such a dog's first reaction to shock in the shuttle box are much the same as those of a naive dog. He runs around frantically for about 30 seconds, but then stops moving, lies down, and quietly whines. After 1 minute of this, shock terminates automatically. The dog fails to cross the barrier and escape from shock. On the next trial, the dog again fails to escape. At first he struggles a bit and then, after a few seconds, seems to give up and passively accepts the shock. On all succeeding trials, the dog continues to fail to escape.

Learned helplessness is supposedly justified as a model of human depression, which of course puts us foursquare back into the dilemma we raised earlier. Between the years 1965 and 1969 the behavior of about 150 dogs that received prior inescapable shock was studied. Such research continues to flourish.

- Diner cites six 1977 and 1978 experiments that illustrate the use of electroshock to study "learned fear." He also cites numerous studies of the effect of electroshock on the sexual behavior of rats.

- The National Science Foundation funded researchers at Brooklyn College to study methods of tail shock in rats, in order to avoid the following difficulty with footshock:

Footshock, even when scrambled, can be drastically altered in effective duration or intensity by rearing, hopping, or jumping, and some experimentally sophisticated rats have been observed to balance on single grid bars, lean against nonconductive walls, or even roll over onto their fur-insulated backs.

- An extremely popular area for research is induced aggression in which animals are conditioned to aggressive and fighting behavior by use of electric shock.

- Since 1962, Dr. Roger Ulrich had been inducing aggression in animals by causing them pain. Dr. Ulrich has repudiated his work in a poignant letter to the American Psychological Association Monitor, March 1978, which illustrates some of the points we are trying to make:

When I finished my dissertation on pain-produced aggression, my Mennonite mother asked me what it was about. When I told her she replied, "Well, we knew that. Dad always warned us to stay away from animals in pain because they are more likely to attack." Today I look back with love and respect on all my animal friends from rats to monkeys who submitted to years of torture so that like my mother I can say, "Well, we knew that."

Ulrich is not the first psychological researcher to draw back from earlier activities. Richard Ryder, once an experimental psychologist, is now one of the most eloquent spokesmen for laboratory animals in Britain. Curiously, some years ago, Professor Harry Harlow stated in the *Journal of Comparative and Physiological Psychology* that "most experiments are not worth doing and the data obtained are not worth publishing." Harlow should know; it will be recalled that he is the man who forcibly removed baby monkeys from their mothers and substituted wire surrogate mothers, or other surrogate mothers that spike, chill, eject, or otherwise harm the infant. Harlow then concludes that the monkeys do not develop normally! It is a pity that he did not read his own statement with greater care. A scientist friend of mine who worked with Harlow, and has recently experienced

a gestalt shift, can no longer understand how he was able to do that sort
of work.

• Investigators at the Department of Psychology at Rutgers studied
the effects of induced brain lesion on mouse killing in rats.

• Another researcher at Rutgers introduced single "intruder" male rats
into an established rat colony with female rats nursing young. After
twenty-one hours the intruder was removed. It was found that on
the average the intruder sustained 509 small wounds, 126 medium
wounds, and 46 large wounds, and also developed ulcers.

• Diner cites numerous cases of stress and fear-induction experiments
by various means, including electroshock, drugs, social isolation in
primates, etc. One particularly vicious and useless experiment is worth
citing:

Arthritis was induced by injecting rats with [a substance, FCA] which
has been found to produce a syndrome similar to rheumatoid arthritis.
Three days after injection of FCA into the right rear foot pad, a localized
inflammatory response occurred which was followed after ten days to
two weeks by a generalized arthritic syndrome of pain, heat, and joint
swelling. Stress consisted of a forced swim in cold water (16 degrees C).
Extensive literature describes the stressful effects of cold water immersion.

Geophagia, the eating of non-nutritive substances, was measured in
response to the arthritis and stress. It was reported that

there is no difference in the amount of geophagia shown by stressed or
unstressed animals injected with FCA, [and that] "the stressed rats squealed
loudly while being placed in the swim tank."

In a particularly vicious piece of irony, until forbidden to do so by
the new federal legislation we shall shortly describe, psychological researchers (who were agnostic about animal consciousness) were wont to do brain
surgery on animals using paralytic drugs (which are not anesthetics) because
they wanted the animal "conscious."

There is little point in continuing to chronicle atrocities—this has been
done well by others: Diner, Dallas Pratt, M.D., in his *Painful Experiments
on Animals,* Richard Ryder in *Victims of Science,* Peter Singer in *Animal
Liberation.* We are interested only in pointing out that not all basic research
ought to be sanctified by the "right to know." There are certain things
studied in the name of research that we already know; there are others

we do not need to know, most notably in the field of psychology. Projects such as the ones described above should not be funded; public pressure should be brought to bear on government to achieve this result. This sort of research makes all research look bad, is methodologically suspect, cannot be extrapolated to humans, belabors the obvious, and can result in no conceivable benefit to human beings. Lest the reader think that this is the radical statement of an unsympathetic outsider, it is valuable to point out that Dr. Alice Heim, chairperson of the psychological section of the British Association for the Advancement of Science, and a scientist who has been described by the London Times as "one of Britain's most distinguished psychologists," said the same thing in an address in which she discussed animal experimentation. Diner quotes the speech, where she raised the question as follows:

> With respect to animal experimentation, two issues arise: First, how important and informative are the ends? Secondly . . . to what extent is it permissible to use means which are intrinsically objectionable. . . . [By that I mean] those experiments which demand the infliction of severe deprivation, or abject terror, or inescapable pain—either mental or physical—on the animals being experimented upon. . . . It is abundantly clear that such experiments involve the subjects in prolonged and intense suffering—but "suffering" is not of course a behavioral concept. One can read endless accounts of such work and very rarely come across the word "suffering" or "disappointment" and, literally, never meet the word "torture." Yet surely torture may be defined as the infliction of severe pain, often as means to an ulterior end. (p. 178)

Dr. Heim concludes that "some knowledge is too trivial to be valuable in any sense, [and] the acquisition of some items of knowledge is to be deprecated because they are acquired at such cost" (p. 178). She believes that psychology can proceed without torture and infliction of such pain. Further, she cites addiction research, tumors, and neurosis as areas that ought to be studied in humans and not induced in animals, both for moral reasons and because of the lack of analogy between humans and experimental animals.

IMPROVING THE LOT OF RESEARCH ANIMALS

How is one to effect this sort of change in the work of psychologists in particular and basic researchers in general? A fruitful approach has been adopted by the Friends of Animals organization. This group has approached a number of qualified scientists and physicians and has asked that they review projects currently funded by the National Institute of Mental Health (NIMH), which funds most psychological research in this country, for scientific validity, value of the research, and treatment of animals. Although, in theory, the papers describing the projects are public knowledge and ought to be made available upon request to any interested citizen, in point of fact the agency consistently failed to turn over the documents and was sued by Friends of Animals before they released them. The point is to look at these projects in the cold light of day, to have them reviewed by people outside the circle of mutual masturbation that sometimes tends to characterize "peer review" for federal funding. The public, and the legislators, must be made aware of the incredible amounts of public money being spent on psychological research of questionable validity and significant animal abuse. The psychological researchers must be forced to justify their research according to the utilitarian principle, i.e., according to what possible benefits could accrue to humans from such research, which balances the animal suffering, and justify their investigations with animals according to the basic canons of scientific methodology and logic. If they cannot do so (as I suspect in many cases they cannot), if they cannot answer questions about what light this work sheds, what theory is being tested, what aspect of the world is being illuminated, what truths are being unearthed, then they ought not be funded, both for moral and for economic reasons. Ideally, federal legislation governing appropriations should require that projects be assessed in this way. If such a procedure were followed, a good deal of mindless activity masquerading as research and responsible for incalculable amounts of suffering would vanish.

But what of basic research that passes such tests, that does enjoy scientific legitimacy and does carry great potential benefit in its wake? Here we found some very simple and plausible solutions. The more I studied animal research, beginning more than fifteen years ago, the more I realized that the laissez-faire situation regarding research animals that researchers had traditionally enjoyed was both morally *and* scientifically unacceptable. (As we saw, the Animal Welfare Act of 1966 had barely any effect on how animals could be used.) And, despite researcher claims that they could police their own house, they were not doing the right thing by animals either in terms of science or proper treatment of animals. For one thing, many researchers, especially human medical researchers, know virtually nothing about the animals they use, save that the animals model a particular disease syndrome. One could get an M.D.-Ph.D. degree in an animal-using area of biomedicine and never learn anything about the animals one uses in terms of their needs and natures, physical and psychological. Such ignorance alone assured that a significant amount of animal abuse would attend the reseach process. Buttressed by scientific ideology's denial of concern with ethics and with mental states in animals, one had a situation that made such abuse inevitable (for example, by absolving the research community of any knowledge of laboratory animal analgesia).

Furthermore, such ignorance led to bad science, not only to bad animal care. Much scientific research has been put in peril by a failure to see how various forms of pain, suffering, disease, and unhappiness can skew relevant physiological and metabolic variables. All of us are aware of the metabolic and physiological changes that stress, tension, pain, fear, and anxiety can cause in our bodies. The same is true of animals. Vernon Riley showed that, not surprisingly, animals living under unpleasant conditions experienced higher incidence of tumors; the implications of this for cancer research are obvious, especially in light of numerous scandals mentioned earlier that have come to light regarding the husbandry of laboratory animals used in such research. And far too few researchers do appreciate fully just how vulnerable animals are to all sorts of variables that do arise. Interestingly enough, cavalier disregard of animals as anything other than (in most cases) cheap tools, leads to compromised or even meaningless research results. Researchers who would never dream of dragging a microtome to work behind a pick-up truck will treat animals in ways which bespeak ignorance of or disregard for the extraordinary sensitivity of animals to noxious experiences. Unimaginable amounts of data are jeopardized by a failure to acknowledge, let alone control for, widely overlooked variables. Few researchers worry about such things as noise levels, technician personality and handling of the animals, restraint, housing congenial to the animals' natures, opportunities for play and social interaction for the animals, yet all of these have demonstrable physiological and metabolic effects. To cite some eloquent examples: Barnett et al. studied the effects on pigs of being gently stroked versus slapped or shocked. The pigs that were handled unpleasantly showed significantly lower growth performance, feed conversion, and reproductive success. Boars unpleasantly handled developed smaller testicles at 160 days of age and showed later attainment of behavioral puberty. Seabrook has shown what successful dairymen always knew, namely that how herdsmen treat cows is a major factor in milk production. Ingram has shown that variation in environmental conditions during the neonatal period can change brain chemistry in piglets. Isaac has discussed the incredible range of experiences which can serve as stressors for laboratory rats. In fact, he tells us, any stimulus can serve as a stressor.

Few scientists control for anything like this range of variables—in the case of research on swine, an up and coming research animal, there aren't even standards for housing, care, and husbandry—one can easily imagine the incommensurability of data across laboratories. When I spoke before the Shock Society, an international group of circulatory shock researchers, they were bitterly divided on the legitimacy of using anesthetized animals in traumatic or burn or other shock research. Many wished to use anesthesia for ethical reasons, yet others declared that anesthesia would skew results. Interestingly enough, not a single researcher had heard of Gärtner's monumental results, which showed that having a familiar technician simply move rats in a cage three feet was enough, 100 seconds later, to produce major changes in 25 plasma variables, all of which changes demonstrated a microcirculatory shock profile, and which persisted for a considerable period of time. I pointed out that until they controlled for such morally neutral stress variables, they could hardly piously withhold anesthesia on scientific grounds.

An excellent example of researcher ignorance and its effect both on research and on animal suffering may be found in an experiment conducted some years ago. A researcher was studying the effect of starvation on the digestive system of mule deer. (Many mule deer starve to death each winter in the mountains.) To do so, the researcher starved the animals systematically, withholding food until the animals died and could be necropsied. Aside from the fact that deer in the wild do not starve systematically with all food withheld, the experiment was ironically rendered totally meaningless by the researcher's use of a basic scientific tool, the control group, that is, a group of deer that was not starved, for purposes of comparison. Amazingly, the experimenter kept the two groups separated only by a wire mesh, so that the starving deer were treated to the spectacle of watching the control group eat! Aside from the extraordinary insensitivity displayed here, the stupidity is obvious. The experiment is totally skewed by the metabolic changes and correlative changes in the rumen, which may be and very likely are wrought in the starving deer by the visual and olfactory stimuli occasioned by the proximity of the food.

So proper treatment of animals and good research often go hand in hand, but of course not always. And as illustrated, not all experimenters are smart enough to see the connections even when they are there. Furthermore, it was clear from my own experience that researchers did not typically do everything they could, or indeed do anything, to mitigate pain and suffering in experimental animals, even when it would not interfere with their experiment to do so. Laziness, ignorance, habit, ideological disregard of animal suffering and of the morality of animal use all combined to assure that animals did not receive the best treatment possible in research. The Animal Welfare Act did not require this; and, though the National Institutes of Health (NIH) did promulgate, since 1962, excellent guidelines for laboratory animal care, which every researcher and institution receiving federal funding through NIH theoretically had to adhere to, this was never enforced and thus, given human nature, was cavalierly ignored. (One dean of a veterinary school told me he had never heard of the NIH *Guide for the Care and Use of Laboratory Animals,* the publication containing the rules; another said he had helped write the rules, but didn't mean them to apply to knowledgeable people like himself!) When I phoned NIH in the late 1970s to complain about flagrant violations freely acknowledged at institutions I visited, I was informed that they were not in the enforcement business. Indeed, NIH did not sieze any grants until forced to do so in 1982 in the wake of the infamous Taub case, where the grossly immoral treatment of some experimental monkeys became an international scandal.

It thus became clear to me in the mid-1970s that animal research was desperately in need of meaningful legislative regulation, something traditionally anathema to researchers. (Indeed, it was only in the face of the threat of Congressional action in the mid-1960s that the research community, through NIH, grudgingly accepted self-regulation of research on *human* subjects!) Researchers tend to believe that science—free inquiry— should not be tainted by legislative regulation. The simple response to this is that scientists are as human as everyone else. In society, we simply do not trust others to do the right thing where objects of moral concern can be harmed by a failure to do the right thing. We ensure that people will do the right thing by formalizing the requirements. For example, we have laws against driving on the wrong side of the road even though, presumably, only a lunatic would do such a thing, since it is in one's serious interest not to risk death. Scientists are indeed human and cut corners like everyone else, under pressures of career advancement, budgets, time pressure, and so on, as increasing numbers of reports of data falsification eloquently document. The fact that the U.S. Government felt compelled to pass the Good Laboratory Practices Act of 1978, an act which mandates practices like record-keeping and disease control, which are essential to science anyway, yet which were found to be flagrantly ignored, eloquently demonstrates that researchers, like everyone else, need to be nudged to do what their calling naturally demands. And it is well known that animal care and treatment did historically suffer from being unregulated, as the case of laboratory animal analgesia alluded to earlier demonstrates.

THE EMERGENCE OF VIABLE LEGISLATION

In 1977, a group of people in Colorado joined together to draft model legislation for the care and treatment of laboratory animals. The group was headed by Robert Welborn, a prominent Denver attorney and longtime animal advocate, and included myself (a philosopher), three veterinarians, including two with extensive research and laboratory animal experience, a physician, and two attorneys. After extensive discussion, we emerged with some key concepts. First of all, we realized that research animals were simply not protected and that the best step toward protection was legislation. Second, we felt that laboratory animals were at least morally entitled to having pain and suffering controlled during research, and also to proper care, housing, and husbandry, ideally such as to accommodate their natures. We also felt that multiple surgery (as described earlier) ought to be banned and that all animals used in research, not just the cute and cuddly, should be protected. At the same time, we did not wish to see "a cop in every lab." Rather, we wanted the law to be an educational device as much as a regulatory one, one which would force researchers to think about the moral issues in animal use; to think about pain and suffering and to become knowledgeable in their control and elimination; to think about the animals' natures; and, in general, to break the conceptual shackles which tradition, habit, and scientific ideology imposed on researchers by asserting that animal research was value-free, and that animal thought and feeling was unknowable.

Two of us had enjoyed significant experience with institutional human subjects committees, federally chartered in the 1970s to protect human subjects in research, and we knew that they worked beautifully. These committees, consisting of human researchers, other academics, and lay people from the community—ministers, physicians, attorneys—were created in the wake of well-publicized examples in the 1960s of researchers taking unfair advantage of subjects without informed consent, to the detriment of the subject. Although suspicion immediately arose that such "enforced self-regulation" was tantamount to setting the fox to watch the chickens, from our own experience we knew this was not the case. Once researchers were appointed to the committee, they took their charge very seriously, and, instead of, as it were, wearing their researcher's hat, they wore their subject protector's hat. Although researchers initially joined such committees quite sure that all other researchers were wise and honorable, and not really in need of oversight, it did not take long for them to be shocked out of their dogmatic slumber.

This, we felt, was to be the backbone of feasible legislation—general moral principles, legislatively encoded, enforced self-regulation at the local level, and auditing of that self-regulation by a central authority. Our hope was to educate researchers so as to make concern for the animals second nature. We did not wish to create bureaucratic hoops and hurdles for researchers to jump through and over, yet not take seriously—we wanted them to internalize and appropriate moral concern for the animals.

Initially, we naïvely intended the law to govern research in Colorado. Although we had the backing of leaders of the academic community in Colorado, the bill was defeated in the state legislature. Shortly thereafter, Representative Pat Schroeder of Colorado contacted us and, after extensive discussion, offered to introduce the bill on the federal level as an amendment to the Animal Welfare Act. Though the bill was defeated by pressure from the medical research community, it did not die but was reintroduced again and again, and it was supported by increasing numbers of legislators. By 1982, when I testified on behalf of the Walgren version of the bill before Congress, public concern for experimental animals had clearly increased, and certain elements of the research community had begun to state publicly that they could live with the law. Indeed, in my testimony, I carried the endorsement of the American Physiological Society, the traditional opponent of any intrusion into research. By 1985, public concern was so intense that *two* related pieces of legislation were passed based on our model, one an amendment to the Animal Welfare Act known as the Dole-Brown Bill, the other a bill essentially turning NIH Policy into law, known as the Health Research Extension Act.

Before discussing the strengths and limitations of each of these pieces of legislation, it is essential that we summarize them. The major statutory provisions of the 1985 Amendment to the Animal Welfare Act (P.L.99-198) are as follows:

1. Establishment of an institutional animal care committee to monitor animal care and use and to inspect facilities. Members must include a veterinarian and a person not affiliated with the research facility.

2. Standards for exercise of dogs are to be promulgated by the Secretary of Agriculture.

3. Standards for a physical environment which promotes "the psychological well-being of primates" are to be promulgated. (Provisions 2 and 3 show the influence of what I have called the Rights Principle, but also show that the public still favors certain animals.)

4. Standards for adequate veterinary care, including use of anesthetics, analgesics, and tranquilizers, are to be promulgated. The control and minimization of pain and suffering is emphasized.

5. No paralytics are to be used without anesthetics.

6. Alternatives to painful procedures must be considered by the investigator.

7. Multiple surgery is prohibited except for "scientific necessity."

8. The Animal Care Committee must inspect all facilities semi-annually, review practices involving pain, review the conditions of animals, and file an inspection report detailing violations and deficiencies. Minority reports must also be filed.

9. The Secretary is directed to establish an information service at the National Agricultural Library which provides information aimed at eliminating duplication of animal experiments, reducing or replacing animal

use, minimizing animal pain and suffering, and at aiding in training of animal users.

10. The facility must provide for training for all animal users and care-takers on humane practice and experimentation, research methods that limit pain, use of the information service of the National Agricultural Library, and methods of reporting deficiencies in animal care and treatment.

11. A significant penalty is established for any animal care committee member who reveals trade secrets discovered in the course of research protocol review.

12. The Secretary is directed to consult with the Department of Health and Human Services (under which falls biomedical research funding re-sponsibility through the National Institutes of Health) in establishing the standards described.

13. New civil penalties are provided for violation of the Act.

Along with the statutory provisions of the Amendment came the need for detailed regulations interpreting these provisions. And since the new law significantly broke with the tradition of laissez-faire in research and now did propose to regulate certain aspects of the design and conduct of research, most notably that relevant to the control of pain and suffering, the drafting of these regulations involved considerable controversy. Although the law passed in 1985, Parts 1 and 2 of the regulations were not finalized until late 1989, and the USDA received over 7000 comments concerning the proposed regulations. The controversy over Part 3, that defining the requirement of exercise for dogs and environments for primates which enhance their psychological well-being, continues to rage (as of 1991), with major portions of the research community arguing that psychological well-being is scientifically meaningless. As a result, the regulations interpreting these provisions were not released until 1991!

One major focus of the regulations is an attempt to harmonize the requirements of the Animal Welfare Act with those of the NIH policy that, as we mentioned, was made into law by the Health Research Extension Act (P.L.99-158). This Act essentially puts the power of law behind the NIH Guide and applies to any institution receiving NIH money as well as to NIH's own intramural laboratories. Each grantee must submit an assurance statement to NIH that they will comply with NIH policy. Violation of such policy entails seizure of funding. In addition, grantees must have an Institutional Animal Care and Use Committee (IACUC) that must meet regularly and review research and teaching protocols involving animals before they are funded; inspect facilities at least semi-annually, and assure that all researchers, technicians, and other personnel involved with animals are properly trained; and which may suspend any activity involving animals not in compliance with policy. The committee must consist of at least five members; one a veterinarian with laboratory animal medicine background, one a scientist experienced in animal research, one member whose primary expertise is in a nonscientific area, and one public member not affiliated with the institution. In September of 1986, the Office of Protection from Research Risks of NIH issued a detailed account of its regulations interpreting the new law, entitled the *Public Health Service Policy on Humane Care and Use of Laboratory Animals.* Among other provisions, the new rules require that institutions designate clear lines of authority and responsibility in animal care and use. Record-keeping requirements have also been strengthened. In addition, the new Guide strengthens the requirements for adequate veterinary care, makes reference to the social environment for laboratory animals, requires aseptic surgery for rodents, and strengthens euthanasia requirements. Animals that experience pain that cannot be alleviated must be euthanized at the end of or during an experimental procedure, in accordance with the recommendations for the American Veterinary Medical Association Panel.

POSITIVE FEATURES OF THE NEW LAWS

One can see immediately that the new federal laws entail a significant and frontal attack on the aspect of scientific ideology which claims that science is value-free and thus has no truck with ethics. For both laws make quite clear that animals enjoy a moral status beyond that of mere tools for research and one which ensures greater protection than that encoded in traditional prohibitions against cruelty. One can indeed argue that the new laws encode some limited rights for animals in the sense we have discussed earlier— research animals are now entitled to the alleviation of pain and suffering not essential to the research in question, even if such alleviation is expensive or burdensome to the researcher. In other words, in a limited way, the moral status of animals supersedes human utility. And insofar as the Amendment to the Animal Welfare Act requires exercise for dogs and enriched environments for primates, it again codifies some rights for a limited set of animals.

A second way in which the new laws erode science's distancing of ethics is the requirement for review of protocols. One can hardly discuss and evaluate protocols for animal use without coming up against a whole host of moral and morally-tinged questions: Can and ought the same ends be achieved without inflicting pain and suffering? Has everything been done to assure the animals' comfort? Does the knowledge gained always (or ever) justify the animals' suffering? Should painless euthanasia be construed as harming an animal? Does the fact that animals suffer in the wild have any moral relevance to the fact that we inflict suffering on them for research? Do we have a right to hurt animals for our benefit? For their benefit? Even though some of these questions are legally mandated and others are not, all of the above, and more, inevitably arise in open discussions. And even though, theoretically, animal care committees are not mandated to look at and weigh cost-benefit (i.e., suffering of the animals versus benefit to humans, science, or other animals) the way human subjects committees do, or look at scientific merit of proposals, but only at animal care and alleviation of suffering, in practice the distinction is impossible to maintain. Many times members of committees will feel that a procedure, though state-of-the-art scientifically, should give way to something less invasive. Other times, especially when looking at projects that are not funded by NIH or other agencies and thus are not peer-reviewed, committees may indeed use a cost-benefit standard. This is in fact almost impossible to avoid when looking at teaching uses of animals. Furthermore, insofar as the laws expect committees to look at whether the researcher is using the proper species and number of animals, the distinction between scientific and welfare considerations is further eroded.

Thus a major benefit of the new laws is to generate among scientists dialogue on morally problematic aspects of animal research, thereby eroding the indefensible ideology that in the past served to allow animal research to be seen as a value-free activity. The way in which this operates is fascinating. As one might expect, when scientists are initially asked to serve on an animal care committee, many are suspicious and resentful about looking over their colleagues' shoulders and perceive the whole enterprise as yet another bureaucratic impediment. Almost invariably, in my experience, this changes when they see that their colleagues aren't perfect; that there are researchers whose protocols are stupid, or badly reasoned, or who are antiquated in their methodology; and that the result of such stupidity or laziness is indeed unnecessary animal suffering. I recall one scientist, who had tended to say very little at animal care committee meetings, coming in one day quite agitated. "It's really interesting," he exclaimed, "that all research projects using mice specify hundreds or thousands of mice. Yet if a project asking exactly the same sort of question is using horses, all of a sudden five animals is deemed an adequate number. That doesn't reckon." Other members of the committee agreed, and the committee now pays greater attention to numbers of animals. Such "breakthrough experiences" occur regularly on committees, and each one changes the gestalt of the committee away from the prejudice that suggests "all scientists do the right thing and we are just wasting our time." This, I suggest, is the real payoff attending review committees: leading researchers to think in new ways about animal research and to see the animals as more than tools.

Yet another pernicious aspect of scientific ideology is eroded by the new laws. As we have discussed earlier, one component of scientific ideology has been the claim that one cannot assert, legitimately, that animals are conscious, in the sense of enjoying subjective experiences, feeling pain, fear, anxiety, loneliness, boredom, joy, happiness, pleasure, and the other noxious or positive mental states that figure so significantly in our moral concern for humans. We also saw that this philosophy had untoward moral consequences, leading to the outright denial of pain in animals or to skepticism about its knowability. This in turn led to the ignoring of the management of pain and suffering in laboratory animals.

As soon as the laws passed, scientists were forced to shed their ideological skepticism about animal consciousness and "reappropriate common sense." Not surprisingly, more papers on the recognition, control, and alleviation of animal pain have been published since the passage of the new laws than were published during the previous hundred years! Whereas, prior to the laws, one could distance oneself from animal pain and suffering behind ideological barriers, one must now meet it—and deal with it—head-on. In sum, then, the new laws have begun to erode the entrenched scientific ideology which asserts that science has no truck with ethics (and with the ethical issues raised by animal research), and that one cannot (and therefore need not) deal with or even acknowledge the existence of animal pain, suffering, and other modalities of consciousness (such as "psychological well-being") in science. Thus, genuine and major efforts to control pain and suffering and to develop less invasive alternatives to traditional practices have been directly occasioned by the new laws, as has greater attention to animal experimentation in general. This is discussed in great detail in my recent book, *The Unheeded Cry.*

Another positive feature of the new laws is the emphasis placed on training of researchers and other personnel in proper care and use of animals and in such invasive techniques as surgery. As mentioned earlier, such ignorance led not only to bad science resulting from failure to control for relevant metabolic and physiological variables, but very obviously to animal pain and suffering growing not out of malice, but ignorance.

Another area in which the laws have had a very positive effect is their insistence on clear systems of authority, responsibility, and accountability in animal care. In the past, all too often care was left in the hands of investigators and graduate students, and assumed a very low priority in the face of weekends, holidays, deadlines, and money shortages. The centralization of animal care, or at least of responsibility for animal care, goes a long way toward eliminating suffering arising from neglect.

Finally, built into the Animal Welfare Act amendments is the seed of the idea that animals need more than just food, water, bedding, and painkillers to live morally acceptable lives. Other aspects of their *telos* must also be respected. Indeed, one NIH official confided to me the opinion that more animal suffering results from our housing and husbandry of animals under conditions convenient to us and not congenial to their natures than arises out of invasive manipulations. Whether this is the case or not, it is plain that research animals would be better off if we acknowledged their *telos* in our husbandry systems. The new law, in its requirement of exercise for dogs and psychological well-being of primates, blazes a small but significant trail into this hitherto uncharted area. There is, in sum, no question that the new laws have given rise to greater researcher sensitivity to animal pain, suffering and needs, as well as flagged the need for implementation of the classical three Rs of alternatives to animal use: reduction in the numbers of animals used, refinement in manipulative techniques, and replacement of animals in research by other techniques. They have also focused emphasis on much-needed training, and have spurred conferences and papers on animal analgesia, stress, pain, etc. They have also forced scientists to start thinking about ethical issues associated with animal use. Hopefully, they will breed a generation of scientists to whom these concerns are second nature, and who have transcended the ideology we discussed earlier. I believe they have already effected changes in scientists' thinking.

LIMITATIONS AND INADEQUACIES IN THE NEW LAWS

Despite these salubrious developments, the new laws are by no means ideal or even totally adequate. In the first place, not all animals used in research are covered. Neither of the new laws applies to rats, mice, or birds used in industry, or farm animals used in agricultural research, since the Animal Welfare Act, as interpreted by the USDA, still doesn't consider these creatures to be animals, and the NIH law only applies to federal grant recipients or NIH's own labs. Clearly, an ideal Animal Welfare Act must be extended to cover *all animals;* the exclusion of rats, mice, birds, and farm animals used in biomedicine by the Secretary of Agriculture actually seems to go against the legislative intent of the law. (There is, fortunately, some indication that the USDA may extend coverage of the act to hitherto excluded animals; we have already mentioned the federal judge's decision.)

In addition, these laws are currently restricted in their application either to warm-blooded animals (Animal Welfare Act) or to vertebrates (NIH law). These cut-off points are clearly arbitrary, and many committees have, to their credit, extended their application to such higher invertebrates as squids, where there are good scientific reasons to suspect the presence of thought and feeling. The scope of these laws should be statutorily expanded to include all animals where there are good reasons to infer the presence of pain and/or consciousness.

Another marked inadequacy in these laws pertains to animals used in agricultural research. The Animal Welfare Act specifically excludes from its purview farm animals used in agricultural research; NIH policy, too, does not apply to farm animals used in agricultural research. Yet millions of farm animals are used in such research in ways which may be as invasive and occasion as much pain and suffering as biomedical research. Such agricultural projects may include surgery, deficient diets, food and water deprivation, total confinement, and induced disease, yet these animals enjoy no legal protection. Thus suppose one has twin male lambs, one of which goes to an NIH-funded biomedical research project, the second to an agricultural research project. Both are to be castrated. The NIH lamb will get anesthesia, post-surgical analgesia, and will be castrated under aseptic conditions. The agricultural lamb may have the testicles removed under field conditions in standard ways—which include having them bitten off! To their credit, many committees now apply NIH standards to all surgical procedures done on their campuses—even for agricultural research. Nonetheless, agricultural research animals clearly need to be included under standards as rigorous as those governing the treatment of biomedical animals. The agricultural research community has recently adopted voluntary guidelines for their research animals; not surprisingly, these are far too weak and have no enforcement structure to back them.

The major criticisms of these laws, however, can be made in terms of the utilitarian and rights principles, which we earlier presented as viable moral principles for constraining research. It will be recalled that the utilitarian principle asserts that *the only invasive research that ought to be permitted is research where the benefit to humans and/or animals likely to emerge from the research outweighs the cost in suffering to the animals.* Recall, too, that this principle follows from the researchers' own justification of invasive research in terms of cost-benefit. To be sure, researchers sometimes respond by invoking the *serendipity* argument. In this claim, it is argued that though it may not appear that a particular piece of research will produce foreseeable benefit, one never knows what will arise adventitiously. The response to that is simple: By definition, one cannot plan for serendipity. Society does not fund a great deal of research for a wide variety of reasons. Much research is turned down by the granting agencies because it is perceived as poorly designed, less important than other things, and so on. If the serendipity argument were valid, one could not make such discriminations, and one would be logically compelled to fund everything. In sum, the utilitarian principle decrees that only patently beneficial invasive research ought to be done. Admittedly such cost-benefit calculation as we suggest is fraught with difficulties: How does one weigh one parameter against a disparate one? But the crucial point to remember is that we do currently make such cost-benefit decisions in a variety of areas, including research on humans. All that need be done is that such calculations be exported to the area of animal use. Certainly there will be hard cases, but at least extreme cases will be clear. Invasive research aimed at developing a new weapon, a new nail-polish, or at discovering knowledge of no clear benefit to humans and/or animals—for example, territorial aggression studies—would clearly not be permitted.

Obviously then, some mechanism needs to be developed that will exclude invasive research which produces no benefit, but simply advances knowledge or careers. As we saw, some types of psychological research, for example, are very vulnerable to this criticism. The current mechanism of peer review, whereby experts in the field judge the value and fundability of research, plainly does not address these concerns. Inevitably, this mechanism leads to mutual back-scratching and perpetuation of old approaches to problems. Researchers who throughout their whole careers have taken a particular sort of invasive animal use for granted in their field are not the best source for eliminating such a use from the field. A better alternative, perhaps, which should be encoded in law, would be to allow local committees with greater representation from the citizenry at large to pass on the value of a piece of animal research. Society pays for animal research; researchers ought to be able to successfully defend their need to spend public money to hurt animals to a set of citizens. Such an approach works for our justice system; perhaps researchers need to convince something comparable to a jury of their need to hurt animals for the sake of research.

Thus I would argue that local committees should also be charged with deciding whether a piece of research ought to be done; that such committees be made up of a majority of nonscientists representing the public in general, and that this should be legislatively mandated. I would thus increase the number of nonscientists on animal care committees considerably and require regular meetings of the whole to discuss research proposals. It will be objected that nonscientists "can't understand" what the scientists are doing. This is nonsense, if only because outside of their own field, *scientists* often do not understand what other scientists are doing, until it is explained in terms that an intelligent layperson can understand. I served for three years on a committee that awards biological research grants and have repeatedly observed the ignorance that scientists display toward work outside their own small area. Any decent researcher can outline his or her research to the intelligent layperson in such a way as to justify the significance and methodology, except perhaps in mathematics and physics—areas that don't use animals. Such an exercise in translation is in fact quite salubrious, since it forces the researcher to see his or her research as others who are nonspecialists might. This, in turn, may well necessitate his or her use of a new vocabulary and new patterns of thought, especially if he or she is compelled to provide *moral* justification for the use of animals. Such thinking would be a salubrious counterforce to the myth that science is value-neutral, or value-free, and might ultimately lead to more awareness on the part of researchers of the social and moral dimensions of their work. (In dealing with scientists in my work on animals, I find that significant dialogue on the moral status of animals often leads to additional discussions of such topics as biohazard, recombinant DNA, genetic engineering, and so forth.)

What of the *rights principle,* which, it will be recalled, is pivotal to our ethic and asserts that *in the context of research, all research should be conducted in such a way as to maximize the animal's potential for living its life according to its nature or telos, and certain fundamental rights should be preserved regardless of considerations of cost?* In other words, if we are embarking on a piece of research which meets the utilitarian principle, we by no means have *carte blanche;* we must attend to the animal's rights following from its nature: the right to be free from pain, to be housed and fed in accordance with its nature, to exercise, to companionship if it is a social animal, etc. The animal used in research should thus be treated, in Kant's terminology, as an end in itself, not merely as a means or tool.

Plainly the new laws do move in this direction when they mandate control of pain and suffering, exercise for dogs, and enriched environments for primates. However, they are only a beginning. I would therefore argue that the laws must be augmented to mandate the creation of husbandry and housing systems that allow all animals used in research to live lives approximating that dictated by their *telos,* so as to assure as much as possible their positive well-being, as well as the mitigation of their pain and suffering. Precedent for this already exists in the work done by people like Hal Markowitz on enriched environment for zoo animals. Laboratory animals have traditionally been kept in husbandry conditions that are convenient to researchers in terms of ease of cleaning, maintenance, etc. The standard stainless steel or polycarbonate rodent cage was developed for human convenience and efficiency, not out of regard for the animals' natures. Sophisticated laboratory animal scientists are increasingly coming to realize that life under conditions that do not accommodate the animal's *telos* is a major source of suffering for animals. We have already mentioned the suggestion that being forced to live under conditions for which they are not suited is a far greater source of suffering for laboratory animals than are the experimental manipulations performed on them that have elicited the bulk of social concern thus far.

In my own thinking, I have found it useful to employ the theoretical notion of "happiness" as a basis for designing husbandry systems for animals. An ideal for design of such systems ought to be the satisfaction of the complex set of mental and physical interests that make up the animals' natures or *telos*. It is reasonable to call such a state of satisfaction *happiness* for animals, just as Aristotle long ago pointed out that the meaning of human happiness was the satisfaction of the human rational *telos*. Fortunately, there is a growing body of ethological literature that points the way toward scientifically based design of such systems. The implementation of such an approach to the husbandry of laboratory animals is a plausible and practicable step forward that must also be encoded in law.

THE ROLE OF HUMANISTS IN SCIENCE

Among the most important members of animal care committees, it seems to me, as far as bringing the moral gestalt to consciousness, are moral philosophers and other humanists with some interest in science.* In a pioneering effort, the late Dr. Bernard Schoenberg, Associate Dean of Medicine at Columbia University, instituted a program whereby humanists accompanied physicians on clinical rounds and later engaged in extensive dialogue with the physicians on these cases. Both physicians and humanists benefited from this interchange, and ultimately patients benefited most. Such officially supported interchanges are absolutely vital if there is to be any hope of breaking down the conventionally created but eminently real barriers between the different areas of knowledge. This is not merely an artificial concern; we have already discussed the pernicious effects of the insularity of science education. Unfortunately, the same sort of difficulty obtains regarding humanities. Few humanists are grounded in the sciences, and even fewer seek meaningful dialogue with scientists. The result has been a devolution of the humanities, so that they have often become, in effect, another narrow field of specialization, sometimes, ironically, consciously seeking to emulate the sciences in insularity, isolation, and technical aloofness. Most culpable have been the philosophers, who all too often have forsaken their Socratic mission in the service of neo-scholastic logic chopping. Until very recently, philosophers felt little responsibility *qua* philosophers to deal with social and existentially relevant issues, being content to dispute among themselves and to replicate themselves like DNA molecules through their

---

*"Humanist" is used here in its first sense, i.e., "a person who pursues the study of the humanities."

graduate students. As of a few years ago, however, economic forces began to shake philosophers out of their dogmatic slumbers. Suddenly there were no jobs for philosophers and student enrollment in philosophy classes declined as students became more vocationally oriented; graduate programs dried up as potential philosophers became aware that professional training represented a dead end. Philosophers panicked and began to throw sops to "relevance": they began to write on medical ethics, violence, reverse discrimination, animals, and the like. Some of this was valuable, much was characterized by the same rarefied pedantry endemic to more technical writing. I recently lectured at a significant international and multidisciplinary conference on animal rights where both poles were well illustrated. Some philosophers adapted beautifully, engaging in superb dialogue with scientists and audiences. Others read, word for word, technical papers that almost caused them to be lynched by the nonphilosophers in the audience.

In any case, the major point is that there is a place for nonscientists to pass judgment on the morality of science, and animal experimentation is an excellent place to begin this rapprochement—both for the sake of the animals and for the sake of our culture! A system of the sort that we envision, where funding of research is guided by legislative constraints governing the morality of the research, according to the utilitarian and rights principles, and where research is judged and preliminarily screened and monitored primarily by local committees that represent a broad range of opinion, seems to me eminently rational for a variety of reasons. Not only will the animals benefit, not only will the barriers between disciplines begin to crumble with incalculable fringe benefits arising, but the dangers of federal, bureaucratic overcentralization will be blunted. If it is feared that such committees would be too inbred and in-house, members could easily be chosen from neighboring institutions.

The pattern of argumentation we have followed in the discussion of basic research is long and intricate, but that is because the question of basic research is complex and intricate. We have tried to indicate that there is a drastic need for radical changes in science education, as well as for regulatory action in this area, and that the two approaches are in fact complementary as far as improving the lot of research animals is concerned.

INTRODUCTION TO THE USE OF ANIMALS
IN APPLIED MEDICAL RESEARCH

As we indicated earlier in this chapter, applied medical research differs only in degree from basic research. The most significant difference is that such research seems to have more direct implications for curing or preventing disease. But the patterns of argument we developed while discussing basic research hold equally well here, *mutatis mutandis*. Such research ought first of all to be evaluated according to the Utilitarian Principle and conducted in accordance with the Rights Principle. These requirements ought to be codified by law and applied by funding agencies. If anything, applied research may well be easier to evaluate than basic research because the possible benefits are more easily calculated. Once again, such research ought to be evaluated, both by funding agencies and by the sort of review system just discussed, in terms of experimental design, logical coherence, and theoretical groundedness. Atheoretical, "scatter-gun" empiricism of the "let's see what happens if we try this" sort, without any reason to believe that something will happen, is not defensible when the suffering of objects of moral concern is the inevitable result. The one controversial exception to this statement is drug research, which we shall be discussing shortly.

There is no question that a great number of slipshod and morally questionable experiments and projects occur under the rubric of medical research, as the cancer research scandals, scandals involving falsification of data, and the perennial reports of subrosa, illicit experimentation done on humans in medical centers indicate. It is not difficult to understand the rationale behind this, both from the point of view of researchers and from the point of view of public tolerance. All of us need to believe that a large army of dedicated, brilliant scientists are in a daily battle with the malevolent and incomprehensible forces that for us have assumed almost mythic proportions, that have replaced ghosts, demons, and werewolves as loci of fear: heart disease, multiple sclerosis, and especially cancer in all of its protean, exquisitely horrible forms. Just as we overlook behavior in the frontline soldier that we would consider inexcusable in a bank teller, we are prepared to tolerate much from medical research (as indeed, from physicians, but that is another story). We need our dragon killers, actually and psychologically, so we overlook their peccadilloes and defeats and continue to support them. "They may not be perfect, but they are all we have."

Given this mentality, and given the unquestionable importance of a great deal of medical research, it becomes all the more exigent that we force ourselves to look more carefully at the logic of the medical research we fund. How much of it is simply legitimized by the myth, with little theoretical coherence or defensibility? Because of our tendency to accept medical research uncritically, we should look with an even more critical eye on what we fund. Could the money be better spent in other ways? Are we supporting research that can really lead to curing disease, or are we simply perpetuating an industry that has assumed a life of its own? D. H. Smyth, in his defense of animal experimentation, remarks that "for the amount of money and effort spent, cancer research is probably the field of medical endeavor with least to show" (p. 114).

In the case of medical research, the discrepancy between human interests and animal interests is most dramatically evidenced. But in another sense, often overlooked, the interests coincide. Both benefit from eliminating unnecessary and wasteful research, both benefit from ensuring quality research. And insofar as good research is predicated upon good treatment of experimental animals, if only to control stress and anxiety variables that can and do make physiological differences and that, when ignored, can vitiate a piece of research or render it nonduplicable, it behooves experimenters to treat animals well. It is for these reasons as well as for moral reasons that many biomedical researchers support our legislation. The higher the quality of research, the more secure the researchers can be against the vagaries of fashion that could, in a time of economic difficulty, turn the public against its dragon slayers.

There is no question that money should be spent on studying "alternatives" to the use of animals in medical research. The Ames test discussed earlier is a shining example of such *in vitro* techniques, but as Smyth points out in his book, *Alternatives to Animal Experiments,* one can never be certain that something that, in the short run, may seem to reduce or replace animals may not, in the long run, lead to increased uses of animals in procedures branching out of the new avenues opened up by the *in vitro* advances. On the other hand, there are many places where the development of alternatives would seem to be unequivocally beneficial, for example, replacement of animals in disease diagnosis by tissue culture techniques. As in most cases of alternatives, there is an economic imperative militating in favor of the development of alternatives to animals, so happily there is no conflict here between those concerned with the welfare of animals on the one hand and researchers on the other.

The most viable hope for animals in applied medical research comes from legislation and regulation that would respect the utilitarian and rights principles, that would require the sort of review we indicated, and that would make funding of research responsible to animal welfare concerns. It is here that one is likeliest to encounter the greatest opposition from the biomedical establishment. For this reason it is incumbent upon those who would better the lot of animals to adopt a responsible dialectical position, which eschews the traditional *kamikaze* antivivisectionism of the past, and which involves regular exchange of ideas with working research scientists. It is also incumbent upon those who would better the lot of animals to work toward better education of scientists. The animal welfare movement achieves little by depicting all scientists as kitten-torturing madmen. It merely diminishes its own credibility and effectiveness.

THE FOCUS OF MEDICAL RESEARCH AND PRACTICE— SOME PHILOSOPHICAL REFLECTIONS

There are a number of points bearing on medical research and, correlatively, on medical practice that are relevant here, even though they do not *prima facie* pertain to the use of animals. It is obvious that medical research is designed to provide methods for preventing, curing, and managing illness. Yet few physicians, and even fewer philosophers, have bothered to ask the deep question "What is illness?" One reason the question has not been raised is that all of us, laymen and scientists, have internalized an implicit answer to it. If pressed, most people would probably describe illness as some sort of foul-up in the complex machine that is the body, some structural, functional, metabolic breakdown. As biochemistry and molecular biology have become more sophisticated, an increasing amount of medical attention in theory, practice, and research has shifted to the molecular level. In the jargon of philosophers, medicine has become increasingly *mechanistic* and *reductionistic;* more and more of its concern has shifted from the person, or even the whole body, to its components.

Much of this shift has been extremely valuable, since it has provided us with a way of approaching the physical conditions for illness and treatment in an extraordinarily precise way. But the price of this precision has been a high one: a narrowing of the concept of illness to include only those things that can be dealt with by the tools and language of physicochemistry. The valuational and social dimensions of illness have been neglected, ignored, and reduced to the status of inconsequential and peripheral shadows, unworthy of attention by the serious scientist. There is no room for values and social forces in a universe whose real essence is captured in physicochemistry.

What has been forgotten, in essence, is this: "Illness" and "health" are obviously correlative concepts, and both of these concepts rest upon complex valuational notions. This is easy to see when we focus upon health and attempt to define it. The World Health Organization, which presumably should know whereof it speaks, defines health as "a state of complete physical, mental, and social well-being and not merely an absence of disease." Obviously, this definition is fraught with value notions—what, for example, is "complete well-being"? We cannot simply look at a person as a mechanical body and decide if he enjoys "complete well-being." I am not suggesting that the above definition is a good one, but I do believe it points us in the right direction, the direction of realizing that one cannot simply decide if a person is ill or well simply by looking at the functioning of his or her body-machine. The point is that a set of physical symptoms or biochemical facts about a person does not tell us that the person is ill or healthy, for what counts as ill or healthy will vary from culture to culture, subculture to subculture, and age to age. Mere variability, of course, does not itself determine that all differing opinions are equally legitimate. Some cultures, for example, believe that the sun is a small object, others believe that it is alive, others that it is only a few thousand years old. Clearly, they are wrong and can be shown to be wrong empirically. On the other hand, when one culture says that obesity is an illness and another says that it is something to be prized aesthetically, how do we decide between them in an empirical way? The difference is not a factual difference, but a statement of cultural values. (Current medical textbooks actually speak of obesity as an illness, rather than as a state that can lead to illness.) Again, alcoholism has been considered at different times to be both a moral weakness and a physical illness. If one believes that it is a moral weakness or character failing, one is not dissuaded by empirical data showing the pernicious effects of alcoholism on the liver and brain. One may well respond by saying that promiscuity often leads to syphilis; that does not mean that promiscuity is an illness. On the other hand, alcoholism is currently viewed as a physical illness. Once again, the issue cannot be decided empirically. What counts as illness is a matter of social, valuational choice.

We thus discover that there are alternatives to the biochemical machine view of illness and health. (In fact, there are even alternatives within that view. It is obviously a matter of valuational choice to call this particular body-state healthy or ill as opposed to this one. Think of a machine such as an automobile: what will count as running well or needing repair will obviously vary with the values and attitudes of the car owner, depending on whether the car is viewed as an aesthetic object, a status symbol, a way of getting from place to place, etc.). And once we realize this, we are in a position to criticize the valuational presuppositions of contemporary medicine's view of illness. A nice example concerns hypoglycemia, or low blood sugar. Many people have been diagnosed as hypoglycemic, and thus ill, simply on the basis of a highly artificial blood test called the glucose tolerance test. These people may have no symptoms, feel perfectly fine, function beautifully, yet on the basis of this test are declared hypoglycemic. If they listen to their physician, they must significantly alter their lives in terms of what they eat, how often they eat, etc. Before the diagnosis, the *worst* that happened to them was to realize that if they went too long without eating they became nauseated and dizzy. Many such people never experienced even this. Yet after the diagnosis, they were people whose whole personhood was affected; they were now hypoglycemic, entitled to assume what sociologists call the sick role, licensed to enjoy special and preferential treatment, etc. (I once saw a woman go into a restaurant and ask the hostess how long a wait there was to be seated for lunch. "About an hour," replied the hostess. "Impossible," thundered the woman. "I cannot wait. I am hypoglycemic and *must be fed!*") A life has been changed, almost certainly to the person's detriment, on the basis of an uncritical acceptance of a mechanical model of illness.

The proper response to such a diagnosis is this: "What does the reading on a glucose tolerance test have to do with me as a person? I feel fine and function beautifully. I am not sick." When I first began to develop the theory of illness sketched above, a theory that I discussed in detail in an article called "On the Nature of Illness" in *Man and Medicine* (1979), I encountered a good deal of criticism from many physicians. Ironically, in April of 1980 *Time* magazine reported that the medical community itself had become greatly concerned about the excessive diagnosis of hypoglycemia by physicians in people devoid of symptoms!

In essence, the current medical emphasis on reductionism leads to a large scale emphasis upon illness as a biological fact, rather than as a biological state with socio-valuational components. This, in turn, tends to minimize the acceptability of criticisms of current views of illness, health, and treatment. (If we are dealing with scientific *facts,* how can we criticize them?) But our views of illness, health, and treatment are subject to criticism, as we have just indicated. Perhaps the reductionistic model "works" in its own terms—keeps the body alive—but perhaps those terms are undesirable. Is the person who lives as a hypoglycemic healthier than the one who refuses to recognize such a state? Does the cancer victim whose biological life is prolonged by 1.2 years at the expense of familial strain, financial ruin, and nightmarish life as a cancer patient poisoned by chemotherapy enjoy a higher state of well-being than the person whose cancer took him swiftly? These questions must be addressed, yet are eclipsed when we see illness as concrete scientific fact.

The relevance of all this to animals is clear. Medical research is currently founded on a wholly reductionistic approach to health and illness. Alternative views exist and ought to be explored. The movement toward holism in medicine is a good public protest against excessive mechanism. Medical research that concentrates on the physicochemical will tend to ignore those factors that are not easily reduced, yet that play an important role in what most of us—and even most reductionists—see as health. Such factors are, for example, love, touch, and companionship. Recent studies, for example, indicate that having a pet may be a major factor in preventing recurrence of heart attacks.

I am not of course suggesting an abolition of medical research. I am suggesting a turning away from excessive emphasis on the reductionistic, performed on the basis of the simple idea that the body is a machine and that the animal body models human health and illness. I am also suggesting that understanding the nature of illness and health can lead to less emphasis on drug therapy, which can in turn lead to less iatrogenic illness, that is, less illness caused by treatment, a major problem in contemporary medicine. In the course of understanding ourselves as bodies, we have moved away from understanding ourselves as persons. Many of the important aspects of health and illness can be studied in ways other than through the use of animals, and the reliance on animal models in fact deflects our attention away from the social, cultural, and valuational factors that are of inestimable importance in health and illness. These factors may well be as important as purely biological ones and cannot be studied in laboratory animals. If we became clearer in our own minds about health; if we stop seeing health as something we must worry about only when something goes wrong; if we stop calling everything that affects the body, alcoholism, for example, an illness, and stop studying it reductionistically; if we stop poisoning our bodies through air, water, and chemical pollutants, and then trying to find medicines and treatments that reverse those poisonings; if we stop pouring cortisone into "allergics" and treating the resulting ulcers with Cimetidine, which then lowers the sperm count . . . etc., etc., we benefit not only countless number of laboratory animals, but also ourselves.

The key point is that we have become convinced that medical research as currently constituted is the only way to understand illness and health. I have tried to show that illness and health are far more complicated, since they involve social and valuational factors. The more we look for mechanistic explanations of illness, the more we will find, which is both good and bad. It is good because our knowledge is increased; it is bad because we ignore the fact that other things enter into illness: that our biological problems are often a result of industrial and economic decisions; that we are more than physiological processes; that we are not necessarily caught in a vicious cycle of illness, treatment, iatrogenic illness; that "side effects" are major effects to a patient; that each living, diseased individual is unique, biologically as well as valuationally. In this sense, then, the cheap and plentiful supply of overly simplistic "animal models" for the study of illness, which has been a major factor in medical research, may also be a source of the blinders that the medical community wears and that stops it from seeing the more holistic and subtle factors involved in health and illness. Worse, the over-emphasis upon animal research may well be a major source of a stunted and dwarfed concept of illness and health, which results in profound suffering for those who live in its shadow. In this sense, then, concern for the welfare of laboratory animals can force us to reexamine our approach to health and illness, with great benefit to society as a whole.

INTRODUCTION TO THE USE OF ANIMALS
IN DRUG RESEARCH

The use of animals in the development of pharmaceuticals represents one of the most interesting problems for the animal welfare theorist. As Smyth indicates, "probably by far the largest use of animals in medical research is by the pharmaceutical industry" (p. 40). In the course of development of new drugs, animals are used in a variety of ways—for screening of substances for possible therapeutic value, for toxicity testing, and for efficacy testing.

In the first place, it is worth noting that it is impossible to speak accurately in general terms of "the use of animals in drug development," for the uses will vary considerably depending on the sort of therapeutic agent being sought. The substance being developed may be an antibiotic, an antiprotozoal agent, an antiviral drug, a psychoactive drug, an antihelminthic, a vasodilator, an antacid, an antihypertensive, an analgesic, a cough medicine, etc. As we shall shortly indicate, the development of different sorts of drugs requires use of living animals in varying degrees. There are, however, certain basic steps that are typically followed, and that may provide us with guidelines for our discussion.

The first stage in the development of any therapeutic agent involves preliminary screening of some substance for its possible effects. The candidate substance is decided upon in a variety of ways. Traditionally, for example, in antibiotic development, the basic method has been to take a substance with known therapeutic effects and to effect slight modifications in its chemical structure. The other method for coming up with a putative candidate is the use of natural substances, for example, taking soil samples, extracting chemicals from them, and seeing if they have any effect on microorganisms. Anticancer drugs are sought in this way, for example, by grinding up plants and seeing if they have any effect on tumors in animals. Most of the major drug advances have been made using this "shotgun" approach. This sort of research is clearly "let's see what happens" empiricism. It cannot be criticized in terms of theory or even in terms of experimental logic because it is strictly nontheoretical.

What implications does this have for the use of animals? In some cases, the preliminary screening of these substances does not involve animals; test tube or *in vitro* methods are used. For example, the screening of potential antibiotics is done almost exclusively in terms of bacterial cultures. Such screening is not of course definitive—some substances will work as antibiotics in a living body but not in a test tube, for example, Prontosil, the sulfanomide—but for economic reasons alone, most screening of antibiotics is done *in vitro*. Very sophisticated methods for *in vitro* testing of antivirals, antiprotozoals, and antihelminthics currently exist. And, again, for economic reasons, drug researchers have a vested interest in developing as many *in vitro* screening methods as possible. On the other hand, not all drugs can be screened in this way. One clearly can not screen a psychoactive drug or a painkiller by *in vitro* methods, so typically rats and mice are used. Obviously, this involves a good many wasted lives, as well as a good deal of wasted money. Here is a case in which animal and human interests coincide; it is in the interest of both drug companies and animals to find alternative methods.

Recently, some positive advances have been made in this area. As biochemistry and molecular biology have become more sophisticated, it has become possible to make drug research more theoretical and less a matter of blind empiricism. If, for example, we know in detail what biochemical activity is causally responsible for excess stomach acid secretion in ulcers, it becomes possible actually to *design* a drug, to design its chemical structure, so as to interfere with that activity. This sophisticated approach clearly decreases the number of animals used not only for screening, but also for toxicity testing. The reason is this: Once one. has abandoned the shotgun approach and has designed the drug to work at a specific site in a specific way, one has considerably reduced the risk of systemic, unknown toxicity, and one can imagine more sophisticated tests of toxicity coming in the wake of the development of substances whose structure and function is understood.

This point leads directly into the next stage in the development of a drug. Once the substance has been screened for possible effectiveness, it is typically subjected to various forms of toxicity and carcinogenicity testing, including the Ames test and the LD50. The federal requirements for toxicity testing are very demanding, and are subject to all of the criticisms we leveled against toxicity testing earlier in this chapter. Strangely enough, there is a natural alliance possible here between the drug companies and those concerned with the welfare of animals, at least as far as abolishing LD50 determination and replacing it with determinations of approximate lethal dose is concerned. (The drug companies, of course, are interested in cutting expenses and requirements, not in animal welfare.) Another way to mitigate animal suffering in this area naturally suggests itself here. Currently, federal requirements for drug safety do not accept safety evaluation as performed in other countries. Thus, for example, drugs exhaustively tested in Great Britain must still undergo all tests in this country that an untested drug is subjected to. The result is a huge waste of money, animal lives and suffering, and time. American patients must often suffer for six to ten years before a drug in common use in Great Britain is put on the market in the U.S. One such case is cromyl sodium, or disodium cromoglycate, a drug that prevents asthma attacks in 80 percent of patients. It was ten years from its appearance in Britain before this very effective drug was allowed in the U.S. Thus it would seem plausible to suggest that the U.S. regulations governing toxicity testing of drugs be changed so as to allow results achieved in other countries to count here. Certain branches of the federal government, most notably the veterinary division of the Food and Drug Administration, have begun to move in that direction.

Once a drug has been screened and tested for toxicity, it must be tested for efficacy in a living body. The drugs are tested on all sorts of animals, including primates. Here is where a real problem for the animal welfare theorists arises. There is currently and foreseeably no substitute for drug tests on animals. On the other hand, the overwhelming majority of substances tested turn out to be nonmarketable for one reason or another. No precise figures exist for this, but I have heard estimates from a variety of quarters as to how many beneficial compounds are found relative to the substances tested. A medical school toxicologist informed me that one in every ten thousand substances screened turns out to be valuable; a major pharmaceutical company executive said that the ratio was closer to one out of one hundred thousand. At any rate, even if we very conservatively allow for a considerable number of substances being rejected purely by *in vitro* means and suggest that only one out of every five thousand substances tested on animals turns out to be useful, we are clearly confronting a good deal of wasted lives and useless suffering. But it is difficult to know what to suggest. It is impossible to use our utilitarian principle here, for we have no way at all of knowing when a given chemical is likely or unikely to prove to be of therapeutic value. And it is correlatively hard to rule out a drug as "unnecessary" as we did with chemicals, with the obvious exception of still another new laxative. Any drug could prove to be a major therapeutic breakthrough. Consider, for example, antibiotics, which have been developed in just this way. Given the indiscriminate social use of antibiotics both in human medicine and in animal agriculture, we are in effect breeding strains of microorganisms that are resistant to the antibiotics in our arsenal, so we are in constant need of new antibiotics.

It is thus extraordinarily difficult to assess meaningfully the extent of animal suffering against the possible benefits growing out of drug research. Few people would advocate that we curtail the search for new drugs. It has been asserted, in fact, that what most differentiates modern medicine from earlier medicine is precisely the drugs available to the modern physician (though we have argued that perhaps iatrogenic problems would be lessened if drugs were used with greater circumspection). But the amount of wasted suffering and lives of research animals is enormous. It is true, as has been suggested, that a point of diminishing returns is rapidly being reached in this sort of research. Fewer and fewer drugs are resulting from greater and greater expenditure of animals and money. But again, failing some other method of finding beneficial drugs, there seems to be no alternative. At best, one can make sure that the animals are well cared for, but one cannot always expect to diminish significantly the suffering growing out of drug research by using analgesics and anesthetics, because of the possibility of skewing metabolic variables, and thus jeopardizing the drug research. Clearly, the best hope for animals in this area comes from increasing sophistication in *in vitro* methods and in theory-based drug design, which would hopefully cut down on the number of animals used, and in refining the toxicity testing of drugs, for example, by eliminating the LD50 test. It is extremely doubtful that we are socially prepared to sacrifice any drug benefits for the sake of animal welfare.

INTRODUCTION TO THE USE OF ANIMALS
FOR PRODUCT EXTRACTION

The final category of laboratory use of animals we shall consider does not, strictly speaking, involve research. It concerns the use of animals for the extraction of various substances that are then used in research or in human or animal medicine. Examples of this sort of activity are readily apparent. Most people are aware that animals are used for extraction of vaccines and antisera. Vaccines are substances that are used to stimulate a person or animal to produce its own antibodies. Antisera, most commonly antitoxins, are antibodies produced in an animal and used to help an animal or person fight infection. Vaccines work by infecting a person or animal with the organisms that cause a disease and then allowing its immune system to produce antibodies. The infective agents administered may be dead or weakened, resulting respectively in dead or attenuated (live) vaccines. In the past few decades, however, vaccines have regularly been prepared in tissue culture. This, of course, greatly decreases the use of animals. The Salk (dead) polio vaccine was extracted from primary tissue culture derived from the kidneys of rhesus monkeys. (Primary tissue culture involves growing the original cells taken from a living body.) This, however, involved using many monkeys. The Sabin (live) polio vaccine was developed using what is called cell-line tissue culture, i.e., cells grown and cultured from primary cells. This significantly reduced the use of animals. Most vaccines against viruses are in fact developed using tissue culture, not so much out of concern for animal interests as for economy and quality control. Bacterial vaccines also are produced *in vitro*.

The situation with antitoxins is rather different. Some microorganisms produce illness by virtue of the toxins that they secrete and that circulate in the blood of the infected animal or person. Among the diseases so caused are tetanus, botulism, and gas gangrene. Because of the extremely virulent nature of these toxins, the immunological system of an infected person or animal may, by itself, be too slow to produce sufficient antitoxins to neutralize the toxin. In order to aid the immunological system, antitoxins that have been prepared in another animal are administered. The animal is injected with a weakened version of the toxin, called a toxoid, which stimulates its immunological system to produce antitoxin. Blood serum is then collected from the animal, and from this the antitoxin is extracted to be used in fighting disease. Most of us have had antitetanus injections of this sort. The animals most widely used for extracting this antisera are horses, and it is not possible to use *in vitro* techniques to replace the animals.

Application of the utilitarian principle would seem to justify the extraction of antitoxins. The procedure, if properly done, causes virtually no pain to the animal and does not kill it or make it ill or suffer. The advantages to humans and other animals are clear and direct. On the other hand, there are few legal constraints on the manner in which such activities are conducted. While veterinary medicine dictates certain basic procedures that should be followed, for example, frequency of bleeding horses and amount bled, unscrupulous serum companies, motivated solely by profit, bleed animals excessively and with outrageous frequency. Furthermore—and this is a problem endemic to virtually all facilities using animals—many of the people employed in menial capacities lack sensitivity, education, concern for animals, or even basic training in the tasks they are expected to perform. The result is invariably unfortunate for the animals, and sometimes tragic, as when sadistic individuals vent their frustration on the creatures in their charge. During the hearings pertaining to the first version of our bill, the Colorado legislature heard testimony from an employee at a Denver serum company concerning the atrocities allegedly perpetrated on animals at the facility, not only by individual employees, but as policy for maximizing profit. The only possible protection for these animals is provided by the Animal Welfare Act but, as we saw, horses are excluded from its provisions, and horses are the major source of blood for these companies. Once again we see the need for adequate legislation, for an Animal Welfare Act embodying the utilitarian principle and the rights principle. Such an act should also include provisions requiring education and certification of all employees who perform any potentially painful activities on animals. Even if, as a society, we are not prepared to give up the benefits of products extracted from animals, we ought at least be prepared to ensure that such extraction is done with respect for these animals as ends in themselves. And, with profit at stake, we cannot expect morality and decency to triumph on their own.

It is important to realize that many other "biologicals" are extracted from animals, products of which the average person is not aware, yet which form important components of current biomedical activity. In addition to serum extracted from horses for use in antitoxins, serum extracted from the blood of sheep, goats, and rabbits is widely used for diagnostic purposes. Rabbit brain thromboplastin is used in testing blood coagulation. Hormones are extracted from the urine of pregnant horses. Rabbits are used to produce monoclonal antibodies, which are in turn used in research and diagnostics. Various animal cells are used in order to start primary tissue cultures. Gammaglobulin-free horse, calf, and pig serum is used for tissue culture. Sheep blood is used as a bacterial culture medium. Once again, it is totally unconscionable that virtually no laws exist to protect many of these animals. If these practices are judged to meet the utilitarian principle, specific protocols for these procedures should be written and enforced as conditions for licensure of the individuals and firms involved in these activities.

CONCLUSION

We have surveyed a wide variety of uses to which animals are put in research, testing, safety evaluation, pedagogy, and product extraction and have seen that in each area major improvements to ameliorate the lot of these animals obviously suggest themselves. In many cases, these improvements lead to benefits to humans as well as animals, as in substitution of the Ames test for animal studies. Whereas animal studies of carcinogens take six years and cost $1.5 to $2 million for each substance tested, the Ames test can be done in a few weeks for $500. We have also seen that the LD50 test is a bent reed, being essentially valueless and easily replaced, the only barrier being bureaucratic inertia. Elimination of funding for absurd psychological experiments would not only stop immeasurable suffering, but would also save millions of dollars in tax money.

In other cases, we have seen that the amelioration of animal suffering requires greater effort—new legislation, sacrifice of new products, major changes in science education. Nothing we have delineated, however, is unreasonable, pie-in-the-sky, or utopian. The use of the utilitarian and rights principles as guidelines for regulatory legislation governing the use of animals seems to be a minimal step consonant with our earlier argument demonstrating the status of animals as objects of moral concern. And even the use of these principles, it must be stressed, fall far short of a genuine total recognition of the full moral status of animals. Nonetheless, given our contemporary social context, these notions seem to be a likely and reasonable meeting place for those who have hitherto shown little concern for the moral status of animals, and those who have been too tied to utopian ideals to make any meaningful differences. In our next chapter, we turn to the question of pet animals, a question of more direct relevance to most people than the problem of research animals.

4

Morality and Pet Animals

MORALITY, EMPATHY, AND INDIVIDUALITY

We have examined in detail the intersection of moral theory and actual practice in an area that to most people represents foreign territory. Since the vast majority of us enjoy little direct familiarity with the activities of biomedical research beyond the occasional frog that we may have hacked up in a biology class, the problem of the research animal, as well as the suggested solutions, may yet lack gut-level relevance. David Hume pointed out long ago that reason is and ought to be a slave of the passions. By this he did not mean that we should simply follow our irrational emotions in some bizarre Dionysian way, but rather, he was pointing up the fact that arguments alone do not move people; one must have an emotional pull toward actualizing the results of one's reasoning. For Hume, the ultimate basis of morality was feeling: we act on our moral positions because we are born with a psychological predisposition toward empathy or fellow feeling with other persons, because we are made uncomfortable by their suffering. When a feeling of concern is absent, moral theorizing becomes an abstract calculation, an intellectual game, something that one can turn on and off, analogous to mastering theology in the absence of religious feeling.

We read of the suffering of three million starving people, or five hundred thousand people left homeless in the aftermath of an earthquake, or a tribe of people subjected to genocidal persecution. We know intellectually that this is intolerable. We know that we are morally obligated to help, yet we are at the same time strangely unmoved. The numbers are too large. The event is unconnected with our experience. The situation is beyond comprehension, beyond empathy, save for saints. But let us run across a single starving child, or see the story of one homeless family on local television and we are moved to tears and action. Here is something we can grasp, empathize with, understand, ameliorate. Here is something we can relate to as an individual case, one to one, not as an abstraction; something we can grasp and call by a proper name. We cannot live sanely in a world where millions of children starve, for such is a world in which we are impotent. We can deal with individuals and, as Aristotle said in another context, only through direct awareness of individuals ascend to an empathetic grasp of generalities.

It is for these reasons that our task is not complete until we have tied our theoretical machinery not only to an actual situation, as we did with laboratory animals, but to an actual situation with which virtually everyone can find a point of existential and empathetic contact. Here we stand the best chance of engendering the moral gestalt shift with regard to animals that we spoke of in earlier chapters.

THE TRIGGERING OF EMPATHY

Sometimes, as in the case of laboratory animals, moral blindness stems from lack of familiarity. But other times, as in the case of pet animals, it stems from excessive familiarity. Those of us who grow up in cities are not aware of their noise, not, that is, until we move to the country and can't sleep because it is too quiet. In antiquity, the Pythagoreans argued that we could not hear the music of the heavenly spheres because we had heard it from birth. By the same token, most of us have become excessively familiar with the atrocities perpetrated on pet animals, so much so that we take them to be not only necessary, but desirable. One amusing anecdote illustrates this beautifully. Some years ago, I was exercising my Great Dane in New York's Riverside Park when an elderly woman with a very strong German accent accosted me. "That dog is a Great Dane," she snapped, pointing her umbrella at me. I agreed. "You did not crop her ears," she said accusingly. "That's right," I said, a bit smugly. "I don't believe in performing unnecessary mutilation on an animal." "Ridiculous!" she shouted. "It belongs to the nature of the Great Dane that it be cropped!"

Less amusingly, most of us are dimly aware that millions of animals—some twenty million, in fact—primarily dogs and cats, are killed annually in pounds. Most of us, for many years myself included, take this to be inevitable, albeit sad. Yet we rationalize, hiding behind abstractions like "the pet problem" or using anesthetic language like "animal shelters," "putting to sleep," "homeless," "strays." So if we are to try to effect our gestalt shift, if we are to see animals in the moral light that we have argued is their due, this is an excellent place to begin for we have here all the additional ingredients for moral awakening. All of us have or have known pets and probably loved them. Unlike the case of laboratory animals, all of us have the relevant information and experience as part of our life's progress—it needs only to be called to our attention and moved from background to figure. When we have examined the problem, we shall have provided all the ingredients we can for promoting recognition of the moral status of animals. In chapters 1 and 2 of this book we provided a moral theory. In chapter 3 we attempted to find the point at which this theory as an ideal can intersect with actual practice in our social context to effect real moral progress. Now, we combine theory and practice with empathy and individuality of the moral object. Perhaps few of us can easily empathize with the laboratory rat, primarily because we have not known any (but recall the story related earlier of my friend the parasitologist). On the other hand, few of us can fail to empathize with the dogs and cats who are the actual cast of characters in this humanly created tragedy. Again, the intended result is the creation of an intellectual, emotional, and moral gestalt shift on animals.

To provide an existential basis for our preceding and subsequent discussion, and to drive home our points about individuality and empathy, the reader is invited to consider the following story told to me by my former colleague, Dr. David Neil. Dr. Neil is the man from whom I have learned much about laboratory animals, and who taught me to ask the question that has been most important to me in my work on animal welfare: "When all is said and done, are the animals any better off in virtue of your efforts?" In addition, he is a sensitive man, greatly concerned about animal welfare. He is a laboratory animal veterinarian who was a principal architect of the federal legislation described earlier. In addition to being a scientist, he was president of the local humane society. I have described him in detail to stress that he is a man for whom the welfare of animals is the central part of his daily life. Yet even he had accepted the inevitability of euthanasia until one day when he impulsively adopted a little black bitch slated for euthanasia at the humane society, whom he named "Maggie" and who thus became an individual for him. The important point to emphasize is that he was not looking for a black bitch; he was not looking for a dog at all. He just happened on a whim to take this dog home, more or less at random. In any event, he found himself extolling the virtues of this dog to all who would listen: she is bright, she adjusted immediately to his children and other animals, she is a good watchdog, she is loving.

Suddenly, he was overcome with a realization: but for his whim, she would have been dead. Each dog being killed in the decompression chamber was not just an unfortunate statistic, but an individual in its own right, with its own personality, potential, and life arbitrarily choked off. From that moment on, the abstract "dog problem" had become concretized for him, and never again could he accept the inevitability of killing. The abstract concept of the animals' right to life had become for him the question of killing innocent dogs like Maggie. His moral gestalt shift was complete.

Based upon this experience, I should like to propose an experiment for the reader. Set aside a couple of hours and visit the pound in your community. Choose a dog from among those scheduled for euthanasia. Don't choose a puppy, or a particularly cute or affectionate or vivacious animal. In fact, choose a homely, scruffy, nondescript creature. Remove the animal from the cage, and spend half an hour with it. Play with it, pet it, talk to it. Let the animal respond to you. Watch the communication begin to flow back and forth, the affection, the rapport, the bonding that has an evolutionary history of thousands of years. At the end of the half hour, return the animal to its cage, if you have the heart to do so. Whether you do or not, the related concepts of an animal's right to life and the moral question of our responsibility for pet animals will never again be mere abstractions for you. And once the problem has assumed existential relevance for you, return to an examination of the theoretical and practical questions involved in what has come to be called "the pet problem."

PET ANIMALS AND THE SOCIAL CONTRACT

In actuality, talking about the "pet problem" is another piece of verbal lubrication, legerdemain that serves to suggest that there is something intrinsically problematic about these creatures, as when the Germans spoke of the "Jewish question." The problem is not with the dogs and cats, of course; it is with human beings. Earlier in this book we discussed the social contract theory. If one chooses to talk in these terms, it is difficult to find a more clear example of this sort of "contract" than that of man's relationship to the dog. Yet, as we shall see, we are systematically violating the contract and the fundamental rights of the animals who are party to it—the right to life of the animals and the actualization of their *telos*.

Let us elaborate upon this claim. One may choose to see the human relationship to the dog as involving something like a social contract, in which the animals gave up their free, wild, pack nature to live in human society in return for care, leadership, and food, which people "agreed" to provide in return for the dog's role as a sentinel, guardian, hunting companion, and friend. Alternatively, one may simply talk of the natural, evolutionary development of the man-dog relationship. As one who does not put much stock in the nature-convention dichotomy, I do not see much difference in how we put it. It is clear that the dog has played a unique and important role in the development of humans, having been with us since the birth of humanity. (Recent evidence in China indicates that tame wolves were associated with Peking Man society about five hundred thousand years ago.) The dog evidences in countless ways its fulfillment of the contract with humans. The dog has been, and still is, a guardian of the home, a warrior and messenger, a sentry, a playmate for and protector of children, a guardian of sheep and cattle, a beast of burden, a rescuer of lost people, a puller of carts and sleds, a friend, a hunter, a companion, a constant assistant to the deaf and blind and other handicapped persons, an exercise mate, a contact with nature for urban people, an invaluable source of friendship and company and solace for the old and the lonely, a vehicle for penetrating the frightful shell surrounding the disturbed child, a creature that can provide the comfort of touch even to the most asocial person, and an inexhaustible source of pure, unqualified, and total love. And humans have shaped the dog into all sorts of physical and personality forms that are literally incapable of survival outside of human society. (Consider the bulldog, or the chihuahua.) According to some ethologists, notably Konrad Lorenz, humans have actually developed the dog into a creature whose natural pack structure has been integrated into human society, with the human master playing the traditional role of pack leader. It is hard to imagine a more vivid and pervasive example of a social contract, an agreement in nature and action, than that obtaining between humans and dogs. (Similar arguments hold, though not as neatly, for other pet animals, *mutatis mutandis*.)

The dog in its current form is essentially dependent upon humans for its physical existence, behavioral needs, and for fulfillment of its social nature. Man, in turn, is dependent on the dog and on other pets in the ways described above and more, some only recently discovered or rediscovered and that are quite remarkable. This has long been recognized in many cultures. One of the most eloquent statements of this awareness may be found in ancient Eskimo practice. These Eskimos would lay the head of a deceased dog in a child's grave so that the soul of the dog, which is everywhere at home, would guide the helpless infant to the land of souls. Let us look for a moment at some of the more surprising ways that the pet animal, especially the dog, is integral to human life.

Quite recently, psychiatrists and other mental health professionals have begun to study the psychological role of pets in society. It has been found that children who are severely disturbed, autistic children, and adults who are unresponsive to other forms of therapy can be reached by giving them an animal, especially a dog. Children who will not speak will express themselves to animals. Evidence indicates that the loneliness, despair, and descent into senescence endemic to inhabitants of geriatric institutions and nursing homes can be dramatically alleviated by allowing these people to keep pets. There is all sorts of anecdotal evidence indicating that lonely and sick people can enjoy immeasurable improvement in the quality of life when they have a living creature for which to live; something that needs them, something to give and receive love. When something needs you, you don't allow yourself to be sick. In a tragic case, an old woman in a public housing project was forced by authorities to give up her dog and, according to her friends, died shortly thereafter from a "broken heart." There is reason to believe that the presence of an animal can speed healing and catalyze recovery. Aaron Katcher, a psychiatrist at the University of Pennsylvania, has shown that people who suffer heart attacks and who have pets suffer significantly fewer recurrences than people who don't have pets. Pets can be invaluable in easing the pain of separation from home or the trauma of sudden divorce. There is also good evidence that human beings require physical touch with other living things in order to function properly. Once again, animals provide this. Michael Fox has suggested that the purring of a cat can serve as a tranquilizer, a benign relaxant for alleviating tension. People are beginning to realize that the loss of a pet can be as traumatic as the loss of a beloved relative.

Animals, primarily cats, serve to keep down the population of animals that are injurious to human health and welfare—rats and mice, for example, and other disease-carrying rodents. Where pet animals are banned, or where animal control programs are overly effective, or where human beings for one reason or another have fewer cats, such as the inner city, rats run out of control. (Such a situation was covered on national television, describing a luxury island where pets are banned.)

Each reader can supplement this list from his or her own experiences. As soon as we reflect on this question, we realize the countless ways in which pet animals are profoundly involved in our lives, ways that are invisible because taken for granted. My son's first intelligible sound was a meow of greeting to our cat, a cat who had been with us for twelve years and who had consistently ignored or attacked every friend and visitor we ever had, and yet who instantly adopted the baby and tolerated abuse at his hands with infinite patience. I cannot forget the silent commiseration I received from my Great Dane during periods of depression, and the shared exuberance during periods of elation. I shall remain always grateful for the companionship and protection she gave me during the years when I was working on my doctorate at Columbia and was anxious and sick and living in a jungle of a neighborhood, my only release the nightly walks we took together. It was through her that I became part of the strange subculture of "dog people" in New York's parks: the only strangers in New York who talk to one another are people with dogs or children. It was through her that I met some of the city's lost souls, who were attracted by her great size and great gentleness and who stayed to talk to me. And it was through her that I became aware of the mystical bond that can unite humans and animals and came to know intuitively what it has taken me years to put into words.

I recall receiving a phone call one night in the fall of 1968 from my brother, who was a first-year graduate student at Cornell, beginning his first semester. He was uncharacteristically lonely, depressed, alienated from his new environment. It was his first time living away from New York, and he had not yet had time to make friends. In his depression, he talked of dropping out, of transferring to a school in New York City. As soon as we got off the phone, I went immediately to the animal shelter, found a kitten, and drove six hours to Cornell, presenting him with the animal. That was a Friday. By Sunday, he was back to his usual feisty and ebullient self. The depression never returned, and the cat shared his life for sixteen years.

HUMAN BREACH OF CONTRACT

Thus we can see from our own experiences that humans profit immensely from dogs and cats. The animals do not fare nearly as well at our hands, even though billions of dollars are spent—and misspent—each year on these animals, to be exact, $17 billion each year. Much of this money is expended on useless luxury items that appeal to the animal owner rather than the animal—pet food that is appetizing or aesthetically appealing to us, pet food that has been promoted by giant advertising budgets (well over $100 million a year), dog biscuits in the shape of people, Christmas stockings for cats, jeweled collars, nail polish, etc. Although I cannot support this speculation with any hard evidence, I am morally certain that much of this money is spent to assuage the guilty consciences of animal owners who deny the animals something far more precious: time, love, and personal interaction. (This is, of course, one standard explanation for the enormous amount of money that people spend on toys for children. As a culture, we find it far easier to expend money than time, and for this we pay a price in terms of the mental health of our children and our animals.)

In any event, let us examine the ways in which humans do not live up to the "social contract" with pet animals. We saw earlier in the theoretical portion of our argument that the basic rights of animals involve a *prima facie* right to life and the right to live their lives in accordance with their nature or *telos*. In the case of pet animals, both of these are systematically violated in obvious and enormously widespread ways. Let us focus on the dog for the moment. As indicated earlier, humans are responsible for the shape the dog has taken: physically, psychologically, and behaviorally. The dog is our creation. And just as God is alleged in the Catholic tradition to be not only the initial creator of the universe, but also its sustaining cause at each moment of time, so too are humans to the dog. If dogs were suddenly turned loose into a world devoid of people, they would be decimated. Aside from the obvious case of chihuahuas, bulldogs, and others who could simply not withstand the elements or who are too small, slow, or clumsy to be successful predators, the vast majority of dogs of any sort would not do well. We know from cases of dogs who have gone feral that they still live primarily on the periphery of human society, existing on handouts, garbage, and vulnerable livestock such as poultry and lambs. Without vaccination, overwhelming numbers would succumb to disease. The dog, in short, has been developed to be dependent on us; that is at the basis of our social contract metaphor.

VIOLATING THE RIGHT TO LIFE

Yet in one year we kill millions (about 10 million, other estimates range from 6 to 14 million) of perfectly healthy dogs and close to that many cats. About 12 percent of the total number of dogs born in the United States are killed by animal control people: by shooting, carbon monoxide, injection, anesthetic overdose, and even electrocution. Millions more die in automobile accidents or by starvation after they have been turned loose by owners. And the overwhelming majority of the animals killed are not purely feral animals who have never had a home—this population would be reduced to insignificance after a few years of efficient animal control— but animals who have at one point been owned by a person.

For many years, I have enjoyed a good relationship with the people who run the humane society in my home city. Highly conscientious people, they have attempted to catalogue the reasons why people bring animals in to be euthanized. (Bringing an animal into a humane society or pound is tantamount to bringing them in to be killed; very few will in fact be adopted.) Their results are echoed by veterinarians, who are also asked to "put animals to sleep" for extramedical reasons. People bring animals in to be killed because they are moving and do not want the trouble of traveling with a pet. People kill animals because they are moving to a place where it will be difficult to keep an animal or where animals are not allowed. People kill animals because they are going on vacation and do not want to pay for boarding and, anyway, can always get another one. People kill animals because their son or daughter is going away to college and can't take care of it. People kill animals because they are getting divorced or separated and cannot agree on who will keep the animal. People kill animals, rather than attempt to place them in other homes, because "the animal could not bear to live without me." People kill animals because they cannot housebreak them, or train them not to jump up on the furniture, or not to chew on it, or not to bark. People kill animals because they have moved or redecorated and the animals no longer match the color scheme. People kill animals because the animals are not mean enough or are too mean. People kill animals because they bark at strangers, or don't bark at strangers. People kill animals because the animal is getting old and can no longer jog with them. People kill animals because they feel themselves getting old and are afraid of dying before the animal. People kill animals because the semester is over and Mom and Dad would not appreciate a new dog. People kill animals because they only wanted their children to witness the "miracle of birth" and have no use for the puppies or kittens. People kill animals because they have heard that when Doberman pinschers get old, their brain gets too big for their skulls and they go crazy. People kill animals because they have heard that when Great Danes get old, they get mean. People kill animals because they are tired of them or because they want a new one. People kill animals because they are no longer puppies and kittens and are no longer cute, or are too big. People kill animals because they cannot run fast enough to win a race, or because their color is wrong for winning a dog show.

The foregoing catalogue sounds grossly exaggerated and overly dramatic. Once again, let the reader visit a pound or a veterinarian and find out for himself or herself. And the animals who are killed represent pets of people who are at least willing to handle the matter forthrightly, or who delude themselves into thinking that the animal will be adopted. Countless others simply abandon the animal, leaving the animals in an apartment or turning them loose on public roads. A favorite place to abandon them is on country roads. I know this personally because I live on one. I have ended up with three dogs and twelve cats who were abandoned at my place. Any farmer will confirm this. On one occasion, I saw a car stop, throw out a German shepherd, and speed away. I will always remember watching the dog chase the car down the road until it could run no more.

THE HUMAN TRAGEDY

As a result of all these senseless animal tragedies, an ironic human tragedy unfolds. Too often, the animal welfare workers, the volunteers, the people who care most for the animals, find themselves in the grotesque, macabre position of doing the dirty work, of killing these creatures in a humane fashion so that they do not starve to death or die in car accidents. Not only is this tragic in that those who care the most must do society's dirty work, but also because the enormous amount of moral commitment and empathy and energy that these people have and want to put into the service of animals is channeled nonproductively into killing, and into battles about ensuring proper methods of euthanasia. Thus, for example, humane groups around the country have fought and won fierce battles in state legislatures to allow them to use barbiturates for euthanasia, rather than the barbaric hypobaric decompression chamber, which can cause incredible suffering to the animals.

Let me stress that I applauded and supported these battles and urged the abolition of the chamber. My point is that these dedicated people are forced by society into the bitter job of making sure that society's mess, the unwanted animals, are not made to suffer along with being deprived of their right to life. And since doing this is such a herculean task, that energy which could be deployed toward other ends, much more beneficial to the animals, is diffused. Furthermore, these people quite literally pay with their lives. It is well known that many people who are involved with euthanasia of animals for nonmedical reasons end up divorced, alcoholic, drug-dependent, alienated from friends, and afflicted with a variety of stress-related illnesses.

I have given major or keynote addresses to almost every national humane organization in the United States and Canada and have made the same point. Though I expected to encounter defensive hostility, the opposite was the case. Shelter workers and directors, humane workers, animal control people all endorsed my remarks, often with tears in their eyes. To be forced to kill something you love in order to ensure that it not suffer is an awesome burden—a burden society has no right to expect dedicated people to shoulder. Those of us who have been forced to have an animal euthanized because it was suffering or paralyzed or unable to take nutrition know that this experience is one that one never forgets. Many people are so traumatized by it that they never again acquire a pet. Only when we as a society have taken our proper responsibility for eliminating the problem of unwanted animals can the animal welfare workers be free to pursue their fundamental *raison d'être*, working to improve the lot of animals in less tragic ways, by serving as educators of society and guardians of animal rights. We shall shortly return to this point.

VIOLATION OF *TELOS*

While the mass extermination of pet animals is the most obvious problem illustrating our abrogation of the social contract with these creatures, there is another area that is less spectacular but just as reprehensible: the wholesale violation of the pet animals' nature in innumerable ways by those who own pet animals and even attempt to care for them. Earlier in the book, we argued that animals had a right to live their lives in accordance with the physical, behavioral, and psychological interests that have been programmed into them in the course of their evolutionary development and that constitute their *telos*. This is, of course, *a fortiori* true in the case of those animals whose *telos* we have shaped. We also argued that to be responsible guardians of animals, we must look to biology and ethology to help us arrive at an understanding of these needs. Much is known about the behavior and biology of dogs and cats, especially the latter, from a physiological and anatomical point of view. (In fact, if behavioristic psychology were not the intellectual sham we have indicated, much more would be known about the behavior of dogs, cats, rats, and mice, the favorite subjects of psychological experimentation. Unfortunately, as we have said earlier, psychologists are too busy studying these creatures in artificial situations under restraint or with implanted electrodes, or under bizarre conditions of blinding or learned helplessness, to bother to understand the animal. In any event, through the work of more responsible scientists, we do know a great deal.) Yet the average person who buys or adopts a dog or cat is worse than ignorant—I say worse because they are invariably infused with outrageously false information.

Consider some of the "common knowledge" about the natures of dogs and cats: Doberman pinschers' brains get too big for their skulls and they go crazy. Cats suffocate babies. Dogs of the same sex will always fight if put together. A cat will always survive a fall. Big dogs should not be kept in city apartments. Purebred dogs are "better" than mongrels. The way to make a dog mean is to feed him gunpowder. Cats can't swim. Dogs and cats can't get along. The way to housebreak a dog is to hit him when he defecates in the house or to rub his nose in the excrement. When a dog wags his tail, he is friendly and won't bite. Slapping a dog on the nose is a good method of correction. Slapping a rolled up newspaper and startling the dog is a good method of correction. Cats cannot be trained. Castrating or spaying an animal removes aggression. And, of course, that time-honored piece of folk wisdom, "You can't teach an old dog new tricks." The above truisms are, of course, false. To put it bluntly, the average person is either ignorant or misinformed about dog and cat behavior, training, biology, nutrition, in short, about the animal's nature.

In some contexts, this ignorance or misinformation is laughable, as when one man informed me that his dog is part bear, or a student informed me that Dobermans were mean because we had cropped their ears for generations, and that this resulted in hereditary ill temper. "After all, how would you feel if someone cropped your ears? *Pretty mean.*" But most often, the net result of this ignorance is a life for the animal where its basic nature is mocked, thwarted, or ignored. Walk into a parking lot on a hot summer day and attend to the number of dogs left in closed cars without water or ventilation. ("He's just a small dog; there's plenty of air.") In point of fact, if the temperature inside the car reaches 105° F, not at all unlikely given the greenhouse effect, the dog will suffer permanent brain damage within fifteen minutes.

Or consider the claim mentioned above that one ought not keep a large dog in a city apartment, one of the few things that "everyone knows" when they go out to get a dog. Cognizant of that "fact," a family may decide to purchase a small poodle, with unfortunate consequences. The poodle, typically a frenetic, high-strung creature, will be miserable without constant exercise. They would very likely have been better off with a Great Dane, a phlegmatic dog that, despite its size or perhaps because of it, tends to spend most of its time in a semicataleptic state. (In the case of my Dane, my wife and I would call her periodically just to make sure she was still breathing. Generally, we were lucky to exact one tail-thump in response.)

Veterinarians are an excellent source of information about the animal suffering that is engendered by human ignorance. All too often, a veterinarian is asked to kill a dog, sometimes a puppy, but more often an older dog, that is tearing up the house or urinating on the bed. The owners have tried beating, yelling, caging; nothing has worked. They are shocked to learn that the dog, as a social animal, is lonely. Often the older dog has been played with every day for years by children who have now gone to college. Often the dog has been accustomed to extraordinary attention from his mistress, a divorcee, who suddenly has a new boyfriend and has forgotten the dog's needs. Often the dog has been a child substitute for a young couple who now have a new baby, and the dog is being ignored and is jealous.

Veterinarians are called upon almost daily to modify an animal's nature to suit an owner. Consider the case of the house-proud woman who bought a cute kitten on a whim, oblivious to the fact that kittens climb, scratch things, exercise, or "sharpen" their claws on furniture. The "solution": declaw the animal and throw it outside. Unfortunately, the declawed animal is now devoid of natural defenses and is likely to come home maimed, if at all. The animal cannot fight and cannot climb trees to escape. Or consider the case of the suburban couple who buys a dog, leaves him outside at night, and then fields complaints from neighbors that the dog barks. The solution: surgically remove the vocal chords—a mutilation called "debarking" that generally won't work, only serving to leave the animal with a very audible and grotesque honking noise. The American Kennel Club and similar organizations of dog and cat breed fanciers are the major culprits in perpetuating mutilations and distortions of the animals' *telos* through the "breed standards" they promulgate and perpetuate in dog and cat shows. If one wishes to win in these shows, one must have a Doberman with cropped ears and docked tail; a Great Dane, boxer, Boston bull terrier with cropped ears; a cocker spaniel, old English sheepdog, poodle, with docked tails.

In a related area, mindless concern with standards that are purely aesthetic or morphological results in perpetuation of genetic defects that cause suffering in the dog. Concern with a certain shaped face and eye in the collie and Shetland sheepdog has led to a disease called "collie eye" or "sheltie eye," which can result in blindness. The breathing difficulties and heart problems of bulldogs are genetically and physiologically linked to the selection for foreshortened faces. There is some evidence that German shepherd aggressiveness, much prized by trainers and the military, is genetically linked to hip dysplasia. The Irish setter has been bred with an exclusive concern for aesthetics to the point of imbecility. (It is sometimes said of these dogs that "they cannot find themselves at the end of a leash.") Manx cats, bred for taillessness, suffer from severe spinal defects. Dachshunds suffer from genetically based spinal diseases that result in paralysis and tend to have diabetes and Cushing's syndrome. Dalmatians get bladder stones, apparently as a result of genetic linkage with coat color. In Dalmatians and Australian shepherds, coat and eye color is linked with hereditary deafness. Siamese cats are bred for cross-eyes. Silver-colored collies suffer from Grey Collie syndrome, a situation in which their white blood cell count cyclically falls, and they are susceptible to infection. They are also susceptible to digestive, reproductive, skeletal, and ocular problems. Boxers have by far the greatest incidence of every sort of cancer of all dog breeds. Congenital cardiovascular defects are three times more common in purebred dogs. Large breeds are subject to osteosarcoma and heart problems. In fact, more than five hundred diseases of dogs are of genetic origin and have been perpetuated by irresponsible breeding. In short, not only do we *ignore* relevant aspects of our animals' natures, we also systematically *destroy* these natures through breeding for traits that appeal to us, without regard for the effect of these traits on the animals' lives.

Other examples of how we violate the animals' nature are manifest. Through our own failure to understand and respect the dog, train him properly and understand his psychology, we tranquilize our pets, cage them in tiny cages for hours, chain them, muzzle them, beat them, use shock collars. Instead of using the dog's natural protectiveness for home and master, we create instant attack dogs through brutal training methods, dogs that bite anything that moves, including the owner. Many of these dogs are hair trigger weapons, primed by stimulus and response and sold to people who know nothing about dogs and who think that by spending two thousand dollars they have bought respect and loyalty. Many of these dogs, especially those male dogs trained by men and sold to women, are subsequently destroyed for being "uncontrollable." (Then we direct mass hysteria and pogroms at these animals, most recently pit bulls, in a frenzy of what my friend Frank Loew calls "canine racism.") Our failure to know anything at all about the dog's biology or behavior results in people buying any dog as long as it is "cute," which, in turn, results in unscrupulous puppy mills that turn out inferior animals under appalling conditions for profit. Pet stores often neglect and abuse their animals, and misinform customers. Our lack of understanding of the animals' nutritional and biological needs results in myriad medical problems that arise out of bad diet, overfeeding, and lack of exercise. Our use of animals as extensions of ourselves rather than ends in themselves results in the encouragement of behavior that is unnatural or neurotic—begging, limping for sympathy, chronic whining for attention. Our inability to understand the animal results in an inability to train it, which in turn leads to dogs who chase cars and are killed or maimed in traffic accidents (or engender accidents that harm humans), dogs who chase joggers and are maced, and dogs who are euthanized because they nip children. Our failure to confine our animals results in dogs being shot by farmers, run over, becoming pregnant indiscriminately or at an age that stunts their development, overproduction of unwanted animals, problems of damage to lawns and gardens, danger of disease through wholesale deposit of excrement, and worst of all, pack formation.

All evidence indicates that it is packs of owned dogs rather than feral animals that are most dangerous to people and, most tragically, to children, who are most often severely maimed and even killed in unprovoked dog attacks. (Seventy-five percent of those bitten are under age twenty, 41 percent under age ten.) These packs of owned dogs are often responsible for savage attacks on livestock in which the dogs pathologically, and unlike any wild canids, kill for no reason. I have seen dozens of baby lambs left piteously mutilated by such packs. I have seen a kitten killed by a pack of nice family dogs, each of which was totally benign on its own. A pack of pet dogs can be very much like a mob of ordinary citizens: totally benign when taken singly, but literally possessed by mindless destructiveness when formed into a group. In domesticating the dog, man has assumed the role of pack leader; to allow the formation of random packs is an abdication of biological as well as moral responsibility.

We have already mentioned the abuses that arise out of ignorance or false information. One version of the latter is worthy of being singled out for special attention. This is what we might call the "Easy Rider" view of the dog, popularized in the 1960s by many countercultural types. In this view, the dog is indeed seen as having a *telos:* free, wild, roaming, untrammelled. In some circles, it was considered a political act to let the dog live "naturally"; to fornicate, wander, fight, raid garbage cans as it saw fit, the owner living out his or her fantasies through the dog. In that such people have at least gotten to the point of realizing that the animal has a nature that should be respected, this view is an improvement over apathetic inattention. And it is further valuable in that it urges the maximization of the pleasures growing out of the animal's nature. (Thus, for example, we should not forget that animals probably enjoy sexual congress as much as we do, and it is for this reason that I support vasectomies for male pet animals, rather than castration, and the development of effective contraceptives.) Where this view goes wrong is, first, in its failure to recall the major modifications that the forces of artificial selection have imposed on the dog in the course of its socialization for human society. Secondly, and perhaps more basically, the ideal life envisioned for the dog has never been part of its nature. No wild canids live this picaresque existence. And among wild canids, there is little indiscriminate fighting and breeding. Wolves rarely fight among themselves and mate for life.

SOCIAL INSTITUTIONS AS A MIRROR
OF INDIVIDUAL IRRESPONSIBILITY

The individual insensitivity to the social contract with pet animals chronicled in the previous sections is both mirrored in and buttressed by a number of social institutions. Most notable among these, perhaps, are the laws concerning pet animals. As indicated earlier, pet animals are property, the personal property of the people who own them. Given the special place of these animals in our society, one would expect that they would enjoy some different status or greater legal protection than food animals, laboratory animals, or "wild" animals. In fact, this is not the case. The major laws protecting these animals are the ineffectual anticruelty laws we have already discussed. Pets are property. In essence, a dog is like an automobile, even down to the licensing fee, except that one needs to pass a test to drive an automobile. Just as one may junk an automobile for whatever reason one chooses, so one may destroy one's own pets, provided one does not do it at high noon in the public square by whipping the animal to death. Often, local or state ordinances are promulgated that make the lot of pet animals even worse. In Colorado, for example, any person who owns livestock may shoot any dog as soon as the dog sets foot on his property. In many places, unreasonable noise ordinances lead people to either debark or destroy barking animals. At various times, ordinances have been passed to prevent cats from roaming. In a number of states, any cat killing a bird or mammal protected by law, or in some places, any game bird or mammal, is to be destroyed. One such law that has become famous was promulgated in Illinois and was passed by the General Assembly. Entitled "An Act to Provide Protection to Insectivorous Birds by Restraining Cats," the bill would have permitted any citizen to trap a free-roaming cat and would have required impounding and destruction of such an animal. The bill was vetoed by then governor Adlai Stevenson who made the following points in his message to the assembly:

> To escort a cat abroad on a leash is against the nature of the cat. . . . Moreover, cats perform useful service, particularly in rural areas, in combatting rodents—work they necessarily perform alone and without regard for property lines.
>
> We are all interested in protecting certain varieties of birds. That cats destroy some birds, I well know, but I believe this legislation would further but little (this) worthy cause. . . . The problem of cat versus bird is as old as time. If we attempt to resolve it by legislation who knows but what we may be called upon to take sides as well in the age-old problems of dog versus cat, bird versus bird, or even bird versus worm. In my opinion, the State of Illinois and its local governing bodies already have enough to do without trying to control feline delinquency.

Finally, we may cite a recent attempt by a small town to pass a law allowing any police officer to shoot any "vicious dog." In the law, a "vicious dog" was defined as one that was "vicious"!

Recently, some interesting steps have been taken that attempt to utilize the existing laws to the benefit of pet animals and to take some legal cognizance of their value to human beings. As we shall see, these efforts fall far short of granting legal rights or legal standing to the animal, or even of providing significant protection for them. What they do achieve is a recognition that their value cannot be measured simply in terms of replacement value. For example, until very recently, if your dog was killed by someone, you could sue only for the animal's market value. As a result of some recent cases, notably in Florida, courts have declared that the animal has significant sentimental value, much like a family heirloom, in which the value far transcends the replacement cost. In a very interesting case, the court cited the love and affection that the animal provides as justification for placing a high monetary value on a pet. In another case, the director of the San Francisco humane society sued successfully to contest the will of a dog owner that decreed that his dog be killed after he, the owner, had died. The humane society director made brilliant and successful use of a little-known area of the law that prevents people from destroying valuable property, for example, a priceless painting. And in an extremely interesting case, the Michigan Humane Society obtained a court order to prevent an owner from putting an injured pet to sleep because he did not wish to pay for surgery on the dog's diaphragm, surgery that was needed not to save the dog's life but to allow the animal to live a "healthy and happy life."

Such cases are clearly a step in the right direction. They might, for example, serve to make someone think twice before they shoot a dog, since the owner could well sue for great sums of money. They obviously recognize that the death of an animal means something more than the denting of a fender. But such cases still approach the animal primarily as property and are still primarily concerned with the human animal owner, or with the value of the animal for people, rather than with any intrinsic value of the animal itself. To date, no court has been prepared to extend legal rights to pet animals. And no legislative body has been prepared to confer them. It does not seem that such rights will be forthcoming in the immediate future, at least until more people have shifted their gestalts on animals. This will only take place with increasing educational, legislative, and judicial efforts on the part of those who are the natural guardians of animal rights—the humane societies and the veterinarians. These groups, whom we shall be discussing shortly, must aggressively work toward education of the public on the welfare of animals, especially pet animals, which are obviously the natural target for arousing public concern and empathy. Furthermore, aggressive use must be made of existing laws on behalf of pet animals, as the shelter manager did in San Francisco, and the inadequacy of these laws relentlessly pointed out. Finally, new legislative efforts must be forthcoming that address themselves to the complex issues termed the "pet problem."

VIABLE LEGISLATION AND THE PET PROBLEM

As we have seen in our foregoing discussion, the "pet problem" is essentially the result of thoughtless actions on the part of a specific group of people, the irresponsible animal owners. Specifically, the violations of right to life and *telos,* and the abrogation of the social contract with pet animals are a result of ignorance, stupidity, and indifference on the part of those people who cannot respect the responsibilities involved in "owning"—I would prefer to say "adopting"—an animal. Let us present the case for nonrevolutionary legislation, i.e., legislation that would not require the radical (but rationally justified) step of granting legal rights to animals, but that instead protects the animals by controlling, educating, and punishing the people involved. In philosophical terms, the case is obvious. We have seen that all animals enjoy a moral status, and thus have moral rights, including the right to life and the right to *telos*. We have further seen that having moral rights entails (ideally) having legal rights. We have also argued that all this is especially easy to understand in the case of pet animals, who stand in something like a social contract relationship with us. Now since the social system is not yet ready to grant these animals the legal rights to which they are rationally entitled, we must attempt to protect these moral rights as far as possible by other legal means. The most obvious way of doing this is by constraining and punishing the violators of these moral rights. And this leads us to conclude that we need strong legislation dealing with the irresponsible pet owner.

The argument can also be put pragmatically. The pet problem represents a major social problem. The cost of animal control programs are enormous and are borne by all citizens. There is furthermore no sign that these measures are addressing the root of the problem, since the number of unwanted animals remains unacceptably high. The dangers to all members of society are manifest: bites, disease, widespread deposit of excrement, traffic hazards, danger to livestock. These problems are directly attributable to the actions of a body of irresponsible individuals in society, who are apparently unable or unwilling to see the consequences of their actions for others. There is no reason that all of us should pay, economically and in the other mentioned ways, for the actions of those who fail to meet their responsibilities. Therefore, society should protect itself from the actions of these individuals and, at the same time, shift the cost of their irresponsible actions back to them.

Both of these arguments point to the same answer—stronger constraints on ownership and harsh punitive measures for those who violate their responsibilities. Philosophically, it follows from what we have argued throughout this book that one cannot rationally own an animal the way one owns a wheelbarrow, if ownership means that one can do with one's property whatever one sees fit to do. In short, acquiring an animal is morally more like adopting a child than it is like buying a wheelbarrow. If this is the case, society certainly has the right to demand from the person who acquires the animal, as from the person who adopts the child, proof of one's fitness to do so. Furthermore, society has the right to demand that the individual live up to what is required of one who adopts an animal, just as it demands this of those who adopt children, and further, has the right to punish those who fail to do so. Finally, just as society has the right to disallow the person who adopts a child simply to give the child back or kill it if he or she decides they no longer want it, society has the same right *vis-à-vis* animals.

Pragmatically, we can also construct a strong case for such legislation. While automobiles are indeed property, they are property that, if not used properly, can cause enormous danger and expense to other members of society. For this reason, society deems it wise, and indeed obligatory, to set constraints on those who would use an automobile, both constraints on eligibility and on conduct. One must have a license to drive an automobile, one must register the automobile and buy license plates for it, one must drive the automobile in accordance with certain rules; violation of these rules can be punished by forfeiture of the privilege of driving, fine, and imprisonment. A parallel case can be made for animal "ownership." Pet overpopulation and animals running loose represent a danger and expense to society as a whole. For this reason, society should set constraints on eligibility for and conduct of pet ownership. Pet ownership should be seen as a privilege, not a right. The pet owner must be prepared to follow certain rules. Violations of these rules should be punished by meaningful penalties.

What would legislation growing out of these philosophical and pragmatic arguments actually look like? In the first place, it would not allow any individual who feels like it to own as many animals as he or she pleases. Animals are objects of moral concern and are also potentially problematic to society. For both of these reasons, potential owners should be required to demonstrate fitness to have an animal, just as one must show fitness to adopt a child and fitness to drive a car. In response to the moral reasons, potential animal owners should demonstrate that they have both time and space to devote to the animal. In response to both moral and practical reasons, they should be required to demonstrate that they have the knowledge and ability to care for an animal in a responsible fashion. We can thus envision a screening procedure for all potential animal owners, as well as a requirement that they pass an examination testing their comprehension of all aspects of responsible pet ownership. Minimum standards of pet care should figure prominently on the test. Strict constraints should be placed on when an owner can euthanize an animal. Each animal should be licensed and indelibly tattooed with an identification number linking the animal with the owner. This would serve a number of purposes: first, irresponsible owners of stray dogs could be readily found and could no longer simply fail to pick up their dogs; second, responsible owners would find it much easier to locate lost or stolen animals; third, if an animal is killed or injured, owners could be reached quickly. (A tattooing program of this sort has in fact been introduced in Vancouver, British Columbia. The results are gratifying. The number of owners claiming lost dogs has increased. Impoundments have decreased, as have complaints about animals. Far fewer animals have been killed. The incidence of dog bites has been greatly reduced.) Microchip identification makes this even easier.

Owners should be made responsible for any puppies their dog has, exactly as they are responsible for their dog. Incentives in terms of rebates on license fees could be given for sterilizing an animal. And finally, heavy and meaningful penalties should be assessed against irresponsible pet owners. (Again in Vancouver, an aggressive program was instituted to identify such owners, and these individuals were prosecuted vigorously. Unsupervised dogs are now rare in Vancouver.)

This, in outline, is the form that viable legislation could take. There are obviously details to be worked out and problems to be solved, and assumptions made that may be unwarranted. For example, it is assumed that most people are ignorant and apathetic, rather than vicious, and would not mutilate an animal to obliterate the tattoo. It is also assumed that meaningful tests could be devised and that people could be educated in these areas with relative ease. The solutions offered may appear drastic. On the other hand, the problem is a drastic one, both morally and practically. Over sixty percent (60.6 percent) of the mayors polled in *Nation's Cities* magazine rated animal control the number-one problem in U.S. cities. Estimates of the money spent on animal control range from $500 million to over $1 billion. The public health dangers are great. But most important, we must recall that almost 20 million innocent animals are euthanized each year, and countless others die of starvation and neglect. And despite animal control and spay and neuter clinics, the problem is untouched. Major legislation is needed but in itself will not suffice. What is also needed, as our entire discussion has implied, is effective and meaningful education.

THE NEED FOR AN EDUCATIONAL *BLITZKRIEG*

As we indicated in our discussion of laboratory animals, it is not enough to legislate, although legislation is certainly an effective lever for raising public consciousness. People must be made to understand the underlying basis for legislation, so that they do not see it merely as one more attempt to place a straitjacket upon their individual freedom. (Most untutored people would probably resent a leash law more than a law that limits freedom of the press.) The public must be made to *feel* as well as to understand the need for a change in the status quo as it concerns pet animals. To shift people's gestalt, one must strike both at reason and at the passions, as mentioned earlier. People must be made aware of the philosophical principles, the moral theory underlying moral concern for animals. And further, they must be made aware of the factual consequences of the pet problem: the animal suffering, the wasted lives, the dangers to their children. And finally, people must be made more knowledgeable concerning the *telos* of the animals who share their lives and homes.

If it is thought that this seems idealistic, abstract, and utopian, let us recall again the civil rights legislation of the past four decades. In addition to the actual legislation and its implementation, major steps were taken to popularize the philosophical and empirical bases of the civil rights issues: articles appeared in magazines and newspapers, courses were given in universities, the issues were raised in elementary and secondary schools, textbooks were rewritten to include these problems, popular novels and nonfiction works illuminating these questions appeared, black people began to appear in television commercials, television dramas and films began to depict blacks in other than traditional stereotypical roles and later to illuminate the problems experienced by blacks living in a white society. Many intellectuals sneered at this often heavy-handed *blitzkrieg* upon public awareness—but it worked. Black people who had hitherto been invisible, in Ralph Ellison's admirable locution, suddenly were noticed and taken more seriously. Let the reader who is over fifty recall the picture of blacks he or she grew up with. For that generation, blacks were stereotyped as tap-dancing, eye-rolling, Pullman porters who, though often terrified or drunk, loyally followed, served, cooked for, and entertained the *real*, white people. Now compare the picture of blacks that today's children have incorporated in the course of their education. For them there is nothing odd about a black doctor, politician, policeman, or hero. A similar educational assault intended to effect a gestalt shift on women has, of course, also been in progress for a number of years, again designed to teach people to see in a new way.

Such an educational revolution, like the legislative effort, must begin with a nucleus of people for whom the issue in question is of paramount concern, both for moral and for practical reasons. Happily, in the case of animals, and especially pet animals, such interest groups exist. As mentioned earlier, the natural advocates of animal rights, educators of the public, and promulgators of thoughtful legislative innovation in this area are members of humane organizations and veterinarians.

THE ROLE OF ANIMAL ADVOCACY

The humane movement is, of course, the traditional champion of animal welfare and has been the source of most of the progress made in animal welfare in the past hundred years in this country. Humane organizations have been active at the local, state, and federal levels. In the past decade, these organizations have been augmented by animal rights groups, generally more radical than traditional humane societies. The traditional weakness of the movement has been one endemic to many social reform movements whose members feel strongly about a moral issue—an overemphasis on emotion rather than reason. Consequently, the public has formed an image of the animal welfare advocate as a "bleeding heart," a "little old lady in tennis shoes" who speaks with heart, not head. And it is again true that many animal advocates have attempted to change people's gestalts simply by the chronicling of atrocities and by appealing primarily to emotion. Unfortunately, the chronicling of atrocities alone has a tendency to turn people off and sometimes to provoke a reflex denial: "That can't really be happening. What I am being told or seeing is being taken out of context. Scientists wouldn't do that." Furthermore, the real issues often get buried beneath emotional rhetoric. In response to the humane worker who angrily displays a lurid picture of an experimental animal, the scientist who wishes to manipulate contrary emotions has only to display a picture of a dying child and ask, "Would you stop us from curing cancer?" What is forgotten is that there is plenty of room between keeping the status quo and abolishing research altogether.

Emotion is, as I have stressed, a necessary component of morality and moral action; it is also invaluable in motivating changes in gestalt. But reason must be placed in the service of the emotions, or else the emotional response wears off. By all means, the humane movement must graphically demonstrate the horrors resulting from irresponsible pet ownership. As far as I am concerned, I think that every person who brings an animal in to be euthanized for the absurd reasons cited earlier should be forced to witness the killing. In fact, I believe that television advertisements showing the animals killed on a single day in a pound—before and after and even during the killing—would serve to make people graphically aware of the consequences of their actions. But the emotional response engendered should be tied down and secured by rational arguments demonstrating our moral responsibility to animals, their rights, our debt to animals, the cost of irresponsibility, and so forth.

The animal movement has, in recent years, moved significantly in the direction of providing a rational basis for its activities. The Animal Legal Defense Fund has effectively initiated litigation and legislation germane to raising the moral and legal status of animals. Another salient example of this was the creation of The Institute for the Study of Animal Problems by the Humane Society of the United States. This institute, which unfortunately no longer functions, was headed by ethologist-veterinarian Michael Fox, and was invaluable in providing hard scientific and empirical data relevant to animal welfare issues. Its members studied such issues as alternatives to the use of animals in research, ways of improving the lot of farm animals, the abuse of animals in horse racing, and so on. The results of these studies were disseminated widely through journals and publications. In addition, the Institute sponsored symposia dealing with all aspects of animal welfare, in which all sides of an issue are examined. I was privileged to speak at a symposium on stress and pain in animals, where the participants included animal scientists, philosophers, and physiologists. The Institute provided excellent opportunities for genuine interdisciplinary cooperation, and its journal, the *International Journal for the Study of Animal Problems,* published a wide variety of relevant articles ranging from research results to moral philosophy. Most important, perhaps, has been the articulation of a powerful and rational ethic for animals by philosophers like Singer, Regan, Sapontzis, Jamieson, Clark, and others.

Nonetheless, there is much to be done. The animal movement has begun to do a good job in utilizing the mass media to argue its case but has yet to educate the general public on the moral basis for animal concern. In addition, more funding needs to be sought by the movement for scientific research related to animal welfare: research, for example, on stress and suffering in farm animals, alternatives to intensive methods of raising animals, or analgesia for laboratory animals. Also, more public dialogue must be sought with those who use animals without concern for their moral status. In the past, there has been very little public interchange between those who use and abuse animals in research, farming, rodeos, and so forth, and those who champion their welfare. Yet such dialogue is salubrious. As I mentioned, I debated the head of the major U.S. organization that lobbies against animal welfare legislation. His position was, naturally, that everything was fine in biomedical research. Needless to say, such a position was indefensible, and the arguments that can be mustered in its behalf are less than cogent. The result is that the neutral public—and even the partisan public—sees clearly where the truth lies. At the end of my debate, numerous scientists approached me and indicated that while they had come to the debate on his side, they had left on mine. Conversely, I have learned much from arguing with all sorts of adversaries, and this results, I hope, in strengthening my position. Another benefit of open dialogue is, of course, the discovery of common ground where none was suspected.

Historically, the humane movement has been very successful in developing educational programs for children, and some states even legislatively mandate such education in primary schools. On the other hand, virtually nothing has been done at the college, university, and professional school levels. Yet as we have seen in our earlier chapters, this is the most problematic area, and the time of greatest brutalization. It is, after all, fairly easy to influence children, especially about animals. On the other hand, college, graduate, and professional school students are subjected to enormous pressures, not the least of which is the queer combination of macho and "professionalism" we detailed earlier. And it is the medical students, the veterinary students, and the doctoral candidates in the sciences who will be doing the research on animals. It is the law students and liberal arts graduates who will be working in government and setting policies. It is clearly vital that courses of study covering the moral status of animals, the social dimensions of human-animal interactions—the sort of material we have tried to introduce in this book—be introduced into liberal arts and professional curricula. Ideally, for example, a course in the moral and social problems of biomedical research should also be developed, dealing perhaps not only with animals, but also with the ethics of human research and biohazard as well. And it certainly behooves the humane movement to press for such courses, help design them, and offer fellowships or other incentives for teachers interested in developing such courses.

In addition, it is vital that humane societies become involved with adult and community education programs in an innovative, intellectually sound way that will attract and influence the public. The courses that many societies offer in obedience training represent an excellent beginning, but there is much more to be done. Just as some states require that prospective hunters pass a hunter safety course before they can be issued a license, one can envision all prospective animal owners being allowed to pass a course dealing with significant areas relevant to pet ownership in lieu of passing the test mentioned earlier. And the natural place in which such a program would be housed is obviously the local humane organization. But whether or not such a requirement ever becomes a reality, it is clear that the humane movement must take aggressive action toward educating the citizenry about all aspects of the "pet problem." Most important, some basic knowledge of canine and feline anatomy, physiology, behavior, and disease must be imparted. Spaying and neutering programs alone will at best perpetuate the status quo and only attack the symptoms of the disease whose cause is ignorance. In all of these educational activities, the natural ally of the animal welfare group is the veterinarian.

THE ROLE OF VETERINARIANS

It is hard to imagine anyone more suited for active involvement in solving the pet problem than the veterinarian. In the first place, simple self-interest dictates that veterinarians, at least the pet animal veterinarians, ought to be concerned with a social situation that threatens the very basis of their livelihood. After all, there is always the danger, as has happened in parts of Europe, that pet animals will be banned altogether, especially in urban areas. It would really take only one zoonotic epidemic, traceable to the dog, in a place like New York City where the feelings about dog feces already run high, for a strong anti-pet reaction. If pets were banned or if the conditions for keeping pets became too restrictive, the veterinarian would be out of a job. For this reason alone, it would behoove the veterinarian to take the initiative in solving the pet problem.

But the reasons for veterinarians' participating in dealing with this issue run far deeper. The essential *raison d'être* for the veterinarian is the health and welfare of animals. I often pose two models to my veterinary students and to the audiences of veterinarians whom I address and ask them which model is closest to their ideal of their profession. One model compares the veterinarian to an auto mechanic, and the animal to a car. Consider a car owner who brings an automobile into a garage. The mechanic informs him that it will cost X number of dollars to fix the car. The car owner decides it is not worth it, tells the mechanic to junk the car, and the mechanic shrugs. On this view, a veterinarian ought to be simply the agent or tool of the owner, a simple extension of the owner's concern or lack of it. This is, of course, the model that society and the law forces upon the veterinarian: the property model. But we are concerned with what ought to be, and most veterinarians find it abhorrent to destroy or not treat an animal that can be restored to health, simply because the owner doesn't wish to spend the money. On the other model, the veterinarian is like a pediatrician. Though the parents pay the bills, they cannot tell the pediatrician not to cure the child because they don't wish to spend the money or don't have it. (It is their acceptance of this model that leads many veterinarians to do a good deal of unpaid work.)

This, incidentally, illustrates a possible impact of animal rights as far as veterinary medicine is concerned. On the view we have expounded, an animal ought not simply be a piece of property, and no animal should be denied life and health because of the owner's whim or unwillingness to pay. On the other hand, the veterinarian should not be forced to bear the financial burden either. For this reason, the concept of companion animal health insurance, which was successfully pioneered in California, seems to provide an excellent solution. As public moral concern for animals increases and as costs rise, some such program is probably inevitable. In any case, the point is that veterinarians, at least pet animal veterinarians, for the most part do hold a view closer to the one we have developed in this book than to the one codified in our law and practice. Furthermore, veterinarians are (or ought to be) more knowledgeable concerning animal welfare, physical and psychological, than any other group of citizens. Thus they ought to be pioneering in developing rational legislation aimed at solving the pet problem and, even more important, they ought to be educating their clients and the general public regarding animals and responsible pet ownership. (Such educational efforts, if conducted in public forums such as lectures or courses offered through the humane societies, could also provide invaluable public exposure and advertisement for the veterinarian, which in turn would be likely to result in a much enhanced practice.) Given these moral and pragmatic reasons for veterinarian involvement in the pet problem, why has there in fact been, relatively speaking, so little of it? And why, when there has been veterinarian involvement, has it tended to come only as a reaction to some truly oppressive or idiotic ordinance or policy that directly threatens their earning capacity?

There are many reasons for this. In the first place, the animal welfare movement has often tended to see low-cost spay and neuter clinics as the major step in solving the pet problem, and veterinarians are concerned about the effects of such clinics on their income, an income that, on the average, is not terribly high. But this does not seem to be the major reason, for veterinarians have learned to live with and sometimes even support these clinics. The deeper reasons for lack of massive veterinarian involvement in animal welfare work must be sought elsewhere. Perhaps the most important reason can be traced to issues that we discussed earlier pertaining to veterinary and human medical education, and to science education in general. As we saw, the main thrust seems to be the mastery of techniques and facts. Until very recently, virtually no emphasis has been placed in veterinary curricula on the moral and social dimensions of veterinary medicine. The educational process is far too reductionistic and mechanistic. The practice of veterinary medicine is taught as if it were value-neutral, and it is assumed that students will simply pick up the moral and social implications of what they do when they are in practice. Unfortunately, this very often doesn't happen, any more than physicians just pick up expertise in evaluating moral and social problems in human medicine. What in fact happens is that these problems are ignored.

Yet in point of fact, these problems are central to the practice of veterinary medicine, as more and more practitioners and educators are realizing. They are important not only for economic reasons, but for medical reasons as well for, as we saw earlier, all medicine is played out in a social arena.

(One veterinarian I know contends that he doesn't treat animals alone; he treats people and is more a mental health professional than an animal doctor.) A veterinarian cannot merely be technically competent. Even to be a good diagnostician, he or she must be able to communicate on a variety of levels and must understand that the symptoms being described by the owner are being filtered through personal and cultural biases. Technical competence is only a necessary condition for being a good veterinarian. Veterinarians must realize that many malpractice suits arise out of failure on the part of a veterinarian to communicate with a client, not out of incompetence. I recently heard a good example of this. A veterinarian had spayed a bitch and, as is customary, left her in the hospital overnight. During the night, her stitches, as sometimes happens, had torn, and she had compulsively chewed her intestines and died. The veterinarian had done nothing wrong. He could probably have explained the situation to the client, commiserated with him, and avoided hard feelings. What the veterinarian in fact did was greet the client the next morning with a curt, "Yer dog's dead. Ate her guts out." The client hastened to find a lawyer.

As we saw earlier, a major part of the social problems with pet animals stems from ignorance of the animals' *telos*. Veterinarians are usually good sources of information concerning the physical nature, requirements, interests, and needs of the animal. Yet when it comes to the mind of the animal, the psychological and behavioral aspects of the animals' *telos*, the veterinarian too often is as ignorant as the client. It is very unlikely that the veterinarian has had a single course in animal behavior, behavioral pathology, and training, yet the lives of pet animals often depend upon the veterinarian's being able to deal with problems like a dog who urinates on the bed, or who howls at night.

In short, it appears that veterinarians have not taken a more active role in dealing with the enormously complex cluster of issues involved in the "pet problem" primarily because they are not trained to worry about these questions. Organized veterinary medicine must also share the blame. Outside of occasional letters to the editor (for many years by or against Michael Fox), veterinary journals have published very little on the moral and social dimensions of veterinary medicine, though this is beginning to change. For a long time, for example, to most practitioners veterinary medical ethics (like human medical ethics to physicians) meant the sort of issues dealt with in the American Veterinary Medical Association's code of ethics, which is really a code of professional etiquette dealing with such issues as advertising, disseminating medical information to the public, and maintaining a "professional" image. Happily, things are beginning to change. Conferences are being held on the social and moral aspects of veterinary medicine; a few articles have appeared, including some papers of mine, in the AVMA *Journal*. (The *Journal* recently devoted an entire issue to the pet overpopulation problem.) Veterinary colleges are beginning to develop courses such as the one done at my institution. The *Canadian Veterinary Journal* has, in 1991, instituted a monthly column devoted to ethics. And the pressure brought on by public concern with all aspects of the pet problem, be it methods of euthanasia or attempts to limit the number of dogs a person can own, is certain to further stimulate veterinarians to involve themselves with these issues.

This is all to the good. Veterinarians are naturally committed to animal welfare; in my experience concern for animals is the main reason people go into veterinary medicine. They are trained scientists. As a group, they are highly intelligent. Their work puts them in daily and dramatic contact with the tragic consequences of irresponsible pet ownership. If anyone can speak knowledgeably for the rights of pet animals, it is veterinarians. And most important, their work provides them with a natural forum for educating a significant portion of the pet-owning public. Let us hope that we can anticipate and work toward the time when animal advocates and veterinarians have forged a solid bond of cooperation and work effectively together as spokespersons for the moral and legal rights of animals.

Afterword

So much has happened in the past decade regarding the moral status of animals—both socially and in my own thinking and activities—that I actually found it more difficult to prepare the second edition of this book than to write the first! Had I added everything I wanted to say, I would still be writing, and this book would be thousands of pages long. Thus, I have tried hard to restrict myself to updating the original book and not writing a new one.

This activity forced me to take, as it were, an aerial view of the last ten years, to pause and reflect, something I have been far too busy to do otherwise. And I am greatly heartened by the progress I perceive. Meaningful legislation regarding the well-being of research animals has come to pass, something I did not believe could happen before the end of the century. Concern for elevating the moral status of animals and for protecting their rights as determined by their natures has become a major national and international issue. Society is examining and effecting major changes in the treatment of animals in areas long taken for granted, from agriculture to zoos.

Such social ferment regarding a major moral issue can, unfortunately, never proceed without excesses of emotion and stupidity. Nonetheless, I have great faith in common sense and common decency to muddle through and to effect the compromise and resolution and moral progress that is the hallmark of democratic societies. This faith has been buttressed by my own experiences. I have watched such progress occur in my own institution, where faculty members have gone from viewing moral concern for animals with fear and suspicion to viewing it as something self-evident and good. I have seen ranchers and rodeo cowboys respond to the force of moral argument and "recollect," as Plato says, that animals have rights. I have seen sport hunters abandon their recreational passion because they could not escape their own moral conclusions. If rational ethics can indeed work, however haltingly, for beings as powerless and vulnerable and disenfranchised as animals, we are all granted a license to hope, even in the face of the myriad moral atrocities by which we so often feel overwhelmed.

Bibliography

Allen, Robert D., and William H. Westbrook. *Handbook on Animal Welfare: Biomedical, Psychological and Ecological Aspects of Pet Problems and Control.* New York: Garland Press, 1979.

Alumets, J., et al. "Neuronal Vocalisation of Immunoreactive Enkephalin and β-endorphin in the Earthworm." *Nature* 29 (1979): 805.

Aquinas, Thomas. *On the Truth of the Catholic Faith. Summa Contra Gentiles.* 4 books. Providence, N.Y.: Doubleday, 1956.

Aristotle. *Nicomachaean Ethics.* In *The Basic Works of Aristotle,* edited by R. McKeon. New York: Random House, 1941.

Barnett, J. L., et al. "The Welfare of Confined Sows: Psychological, Behavioral, and Production Responses to Contrasting Housing Systems and Handler Attitudes." *Annales de Recherches Veterinaires* 15 (1984): 217–26.

Bayle, Pierre. *Historical and Critical Dictionary.* Translated by R. H. Popkin. Indianapolis: Bobbs-Merrill, 1965.

Beecher, H. K. "Relation of Significance of Wound to Pain Experienced." *Journal of the American Medical Association* 161 (1956): 1609–13.

Bentham, Jeremy. *Anarchical Fallacies: Being an Examination of the Declaration of Rights Issued During the French Revolution.* In *The Works of Jeremy Bentham,* edited by John Bowring. 2 vols. New York: Russell and Russell, 1962.

Clark, Stephen. *The Moral Status of Animals.* Oxford: Oxford University Press, 1977.

243

Committee on Care and Use of Laboratory Animals of the Institute of Laboratory Animal Resources. *Guide for the Care and Use of Laboratory Animals.* Washington, D.C.: U.S. Department of Health, Education and Welfare, 1978.

Cooper, T., and J. Stucki. "Commentary on Rowan and Rollin." *Perspectives in Biology and Medicine* 27 (1983): 18–21.

Darwin, Charles. *The Descent of Man and Selection in Relation to Sex.* (1871). Reprint. New York: Modern Library.

————. *The Expression of Emotions in Man and Animals.* (1872). Reprint. New York: Greenwood Press, 1969.

————. *The Formation of Vegetable Mould Through the Action of Worms, With Observations on Their Habits.* New York: D. Appleton and Co., 1886.

Deichmann, W. B., and T. J. Leblanc. "Determination of the Approximate Lethal Dose with about Six Animals." *Journal of Industrial Hygiene and Toxicology* 25 (1943): 415–17.

Descartes, René. *Philosophical Letters.* Edited and translated by Anthony Kenny. New York: Oxford University Press, 1970.

————. *The Philosophical Works of Descartes.* Translated by E. S. Haldane and G. R. T. Ross. New York: Dover Publications, 1955.

Diner, Jeff. *The Physical and Mental Suffering of Experimental Animals.* Washington, D.C.: Animal Welfare Institute, 1979.

Dworkin, Ronald. *Taking Rights Seriously.* Cambridge, Mass.: Harvard University Press, 1977.

Ettinger, Steven J., ed. *Textbook of Veterinary Internal Medicine.* Philadelphia: W. B. Saunders, 1975.

Evans, M. P. *Criminal Prosecution and Capital Punishment of Animals.* London: William Heinemann, 1904.

Friedmann, Wolfgang. *Legal Theory.* 5th ed. New York: Columbia University Press, 1967.

Gärtner, D., et al. "Stress Response of Rats to Handling and Experimental Procedures." *Laboratory Animals* 14 (1980): 267–74.

Griffin, Donald. *The Question of Animal Awareness.* New York: Rockefeller University Press, 1976.

Hartley, David. *Observations on Man, His Frame, His Duty, & His Expectations.* (1749). 2 vols. Reprint. Delmar, N.Y.: Scholar's Facsimiles & Reprints, 1976.

Hebb, D. O. "Emotion in Man and Animal." *Psychology Review* 53 (1946): 88–106.

Hume, David. *A Treatise on Human Nature.* Edited by L. A. Selby-Bigge. New York: Oxford University Press, 1960.

Ingram, D. L. "Physiology and Behavior of Young Pigs in Relation to the Environment." In *The Welfare of Pigs,* edited by W. Sybesma. The Hague: Martinus Nijhoff, 1981.

Isaac, W. "Causes and Consequences of Stress in the Rat and Mouse." Paper read at the American Association for Laboratory Animal Science Seminar on Stress. Atlanta, Ga.: 1979.

Jeffers, Robinson. *Selected Poems.* New York: Vintage Books, 1965.

Kant, Immanuel. *Critique of Pure Reason.* Translated by Norman Kemp Smith. London: Macmillan and Co., 1963.

―――. *Grundlegung zur Metaphysik der Sitten* [Foundations of the Metaphysics of Morals]. In *Akademie-Textausgabe,* Band IV. Berlin: Walter de Gruyter, 1948.

―――. *Lectures on Ethics.* Translated by Lewis Infield. New York: Harper and Row, 1963.

Keeton, W. T., and J. L. Gould. *Biological Science.* New York: W. W. Norton, 1986.

Kitchener, Richard. "B. F. Skinner—The Butcher, the Baker, the Behavior-shaper." In *Boston Studies in the Philosophy of Science.* Vol. 20. Boston: D. Reidel, 1972.

Kuhn, Thomas S. *The Structure of Scientific Revolutions.* Chicago: University of Chicago Press, 1970.

Leavitt, Emily Stewart, et al. *Animals and Their Legal Rights.* Washington, D.C.: Animal Welfare Institute, 1978.

Loomis, Ted. *Essentials of Toxicology.* 3d ed. Philadelphia: Lea and Febiger, 1978.

Lorenz, Konrad. *Man Meets Dog.* Baltimore: Penguin Books, 1973.

Mader, S. *Biology: Evolution, Diversity, and the Environment.* Dubuque, Ia.: W. M. C. Brown, 1987.

Markowitz, H. *Behavioral Enrichment in the Zoo.* New York: Von Nostrand Reinhold, 1982.

McGiffin, Heather, and Nancy Brownley. *Animals in Education.* Washington, D.C.: Institute for the Study of Animal Problems, 1980.

Melzack, R., and T. H. Scott. "The Effects of Early Experience on the Response to Pain." *Journal of Comparative and Physiological Psychology* 50 (1957): 155–61.

Merillat, A. *Principles of Veterinary Surgery.* Chicago: Alexander Eger, 1906.

Morrison, J. K., R. M. Quinton, and H. Reinert. "The Purpose and Value of LD50 Determinations." In *Modern Trends in Toxicology,* edited by E. Boyland and R. Goulding. New York: Appleton, Century and Crofts, 1968.

Muir, Edwin. *Collected Poems: 1921–1958.* London: Faber and Faber, 1963.

Nerein, R. M., M. J. Levesque, and J. F. Cornhill. "Social Environment as a Factor in Diet-induced Atherosclerosis." *Science* 208 (1980): 1475–76.

Öbrink, K. J. "A Pilot Experiment with Local Ethical Committees for Laboratory Animal Experiments." Address delivered in Lyons, France, September 1978.

Pratt, Dallas. *Painful Experiments on Animals.* New York: Argus Archives, 1976.

Rawls, John. *A Theory of Justice.* Cambridge, Mass.: Harvard University Press, 1971.

Regan, Tom, and Peter Singer. *Animal Rights and Human Obligations.* Englewood Cliffs, N.J.: Prentice-Hall, 1976, 1989.

Regan, Tom. *The Case for Animal Rights.* Berkeley, Calif.: University of California Press, 1983.

Riley, V. "Mouse Mammary Tumors: Alteration of Incidence as Apparent Function of Stress." *Science* 189 (1975): 465–69.

Rollin, B. E. "Animal Consciousness and Scientific Change." *New Ideas in Psychology* 4, no. 2 (1986): 141–52.

———. "Animal Ethics and Toxicology." *Comments on Toxicology* 5 (1987): 289–302.

———. "Animal Pain." In *Advances in Animal Welfare Science 1985–86,* edited by M. W. Fox and L. Mickley. The Hague: Martinus Nijhoff, 1986, pp. 91–106.

———. "Animal Pain, Scientific Ideology, and the Reappropriation of Common Sense." *Journal of the American Veterinary Medical Association* 191 (1987): 1222–26.

———. "Animal Welfare, Animal Rights, and Agriculture." *Journal of Animal Science* 68 (1990): 3456–61.

———. "Beasts and Men: The Scope of Moral Concern." *Modern Schoolman* 55 (1978): 241–55.

———. "The Concept of Illness in Veterinary Medicine." *Journal of the American Veterinary Medical Association* 182 (1983): 122–25.

———. "Definition of the Concept of Humane Treatment in Relation to Food and Laboratory Animals." *International Journal for the Study of Animal Problems* 1 (1980): 234–42.

———. "Environmental Ethics and International Justice." In *Problems of International Justice,* edited by S. Luper-Foy. Boulder, Colo.: Westview Press, 1988, pp. 124–44.

———. "Euthanasia and Moral Stress." In *Loss, Grief and Care,* edited by R. De Bellis. Binghamton, N.Y.: Hawarth Press, 1986, pp. 115–26.

———. "The Frankenstein Thing." In *Genetic Engineering of Animals: An Agricultural Perspective,* edited by J. W. Evans and A. Hollaender. New York: Plenum, 1986, pp. 285–98.

———. "Laws Relevant to Animal Research in the United States." In *Laboratory Animals,* edited by A. Tuffery. London: John Wiley, 1987, pp. 323–33.

———. "Legal and Moral Bases of Animal Rights." In *Ethics and Animals,* H. B. Miller and W. H. Williams. Clifton, N.J.: Humana Press, 1983, pp. 103–121.

———. "Moral, Social, and Scientific Perspectives on the Use of Swine in Biomedical Research." In *Swine in Biomedical Research,* edited by M. E. Tumbleson, New York: Allan R. Liss, 1986, pp. 29–38.

———. "The Moral Status of Research Animals in Psychology." *American Psychologist* 40, no. 8 (1985): 920–26.

———. *Natural and Conventional Meaning: An Examination of the Distinction.* The Hague: Mouton, 1976.

———. "On the Nature of Illness." *Man and Medicine* 4 (1979): 157–72.

———. "The Right to Die." In *Principles of Thanatology,* edited by A. Kutscher and A. Carr. New York: Columbia University Press, 1987, pp. 109–31.

———. "Seven Pillars of Folly: Barriers to Reason in Laboratory Animal Welfare." *Alternatives to Laboratory Animals* 12, no. 4 (1985): 243–47.

———. "The Teaching of Responsibility." The C. W. Hume Lecture. Hertfordshire: Universities Federation for Animal Welfare, 1983.

———. "There Is Only One Categorical Imperative." *Kant-Studien* 67, no. 1 (1976): 60–72.

———. *The Unheeded Cry: Animal Consciousness, Animal Pain and Science.* Oxford: Oxford University Press, 1989.

——— "Updating Veterinary Medical Ethics." *Journal of the American Veterinary Medical Association* 173 (1978): 1015–18.

Romanes, G. *Animal Intelligence.* London: Kegan Paul, Trench, Trubner and Co., 1898.

Rosenfield, Leonora C. *From Beast-Machine to Man-Machine.* New York: Octagon Books, 1968.

Rowan, A. N., and B. E. Rollin. "Animal Research—For and Against: A Philosophical, Social, and Historical Perspective." *Perspectives in Biology and Medicine* 27 (1983): 1–17.

Rowan, Andrew N. *Alternatives to Laboratory Animals.* Washington, D.C.: Institute for the Study of Animal Problems, 1979.

———. *Of Mice, Models, and Men.* Albany, N.Y.: SUNY Press, 1984.

Russell, W. M. S., and R. L. Burch. *Principles of Humane Experimental Technique.* London: Methuen, 1959.

Ryder, Richard. *Victims of Science.* London: David-Poynter, 1975.

Sapontzis, S. *Morals, Reason, and Animals.* Philadelphia: Temple University Press, 1987.

Seabrook, M. F. "The Psychological Relationship Between Dairy Cows and Dairy Cowmen and Its Implications for Animal Welfare." *International Journal for the Study of Animal Problems* 1 (1980): 295–98.

Singer, Peter. *Animal Liberation.* New York: New York Review Press, 1975.

Smyth, D. H. *Alternatives to Animal Experiments.* London: Scolar Press, 1978.

Sperling, Frederick. "Nonlethal Parameters as Indices of Acute Toxicity." In *Advances in Modern Toxicoloxy.* Vol. I, Part I. *New Concepts in Safety Evaluation,* edited by Myron Mehlman, et al. New York: John Wiley, 1976.

Stone, Christopher. *Should Trees Have Standing? Towards Legal Rights for Natural Objects.* Los Altos, Calif.: William Kaufmann, 1974.

Wiggelsworth, V. B. "Do Insects Feel Pain?" *Antenna* 4 (1980): 8–9.

Wittgenstein, Ludwig. *Philosophical Investigations.* Translated by G. E. M. Anscombe. Oxford: Basil Blackwell, 1963.